D1548015

Color Stories

Recent Titles in
Intersections of Race, Ethnicity, and Culture

Revolvers and Pistolas, Vaqueros and Caballeros: Debunking the Old West
D.H. Figueredo

Finding Baseball's Next Clemente: Combating Scandal in Latino Recruiting
Roger Bruns

Color Stories

Black Women and Colorism in the 21st Century

JeffriAnne Wilder

Intersections of Race, Ethnicity, and Culture
Gary Y. Okihiro, Series Editor

An Imprint of ABC-CLIO, LLC
Santa Barbara, California • Denver, Colorado

Library of Congress Cataloging-in-Publication Data

Wilder, JeffriAnne, author.
  Color stories : black women and colorism in the 21st century / JeffriAnne Wilder.
      pages cm. — (Intersections of race, ethnicity, and culture)
  Includes bibliographical references and index.
  ISBN 978-1-4408-3109-6 (alk. paper) — ISBN 978-1-4408-3110-2 (ebook)
  1. African Americans—Color. 2. African American women. 3. Black race—Color. I. Title.
   E185.625.W5195 2015
   305.48'896073–dc23   2015024393

ISBN: 978-1-4408-3109-6
EISBN: 978-1-4408-3110-2

19 18 17 16 15   1 2 3 4 5

This book is also available on the World Wide Web as an eBook.
Visit www.abc-clio.com for details.

Praeger
An Imprint of ABC-CLIO, LLC

ABC-CLIO, LLC
130 Cremona Drive, P.O. Box 1911
Santa Barbara, California 93116-1911

This book is printed on acid-free paper ∞
Manufactured in the United States of America

Contents

Series Foreword

Intersectionality, named by critical race scholar Kimberlé Crenshaw in 1989, refers to the multiple and conjoining forces that constrain and oppress all peoples. Two decades before Crenshaw's articulation, activist Frances Beale organized the Black Women's Alliance and then the Third World Women's Alliance to mobilize against the racism, sexism, heterosexism, and classism faced by women of color in the U.S. Critically important was Beale's recognition that African Americans, American Indians, Asian Americans, and Latinas comprised a collective group, across racialized divides, as women of color or, in the parlance of the 1960s and 1970s, Third World women. The wider term linked the condition of women of color in the U.S. with women in Africa, Asia, and the Caribbean and Latin America.

African American women of the Combahee River Collective, a black feminist group formed in Boston in 1974, best described what Crenshaw later called intersectionality. We are committed, the Combahee River Statement declared in April 1977, "to struggling against racial, sexual, heterosexual, and class oppression, and see as our particular task the development of integrated analysis and practice based upon the fact that the major systems of oppression are interlocking. The synthesis of those oppressions creates the conditions of our lives." Significantly, the theorists of the Collective observed from their everyday life experiences that the forces that oppressed them were systematic and intersecting. They were not random but organized, and not additive, as in racism plus sexism plus heterosexism, but relational and overlapping, as in gendered races, sexualized genders, and so forth.

The power of those analyses and practices must not escape us in the 21st century. They are as fresh and vital as when they were first experienced and theorized. This series, "Intersections of Race, Ethnicity, and Culture," aspires to continue and extend the struggles against all forms of oppression. Our authors understand the past as prologue, and they offer fresh perspectives to contemporary social issues in highly accessible language. Moreover, our authors present engagements beyond the white–nonwhite binary to relations among peoples of color and enlarge upon the U.S. social formation as race, but also and simultaneously, gender, sexuality, class, and nation. Finally, their studies show how peoples of color cast a different light on the United States, revealing the nation in its fullness and verity.

Peoples of color have reshaped America fundamentally, and we establish that claim in this series.

Gary Y. Okihiro

Acknowledgments

I did not anticipate that it would take me so long to publish this book. While I have always been passionate about the issue of colorism, there was a point during the past few years that I was not sure if I was still enthusiastic enough about this work. If what I had to say—or these women's stories—even mattered anymore. Thankfully, I have a renewed sense of energy and excitement that I can barely contain.

A large part of my renewal and regeneration is due to the birth of my daughter, Lela. When she came into the world, my entire life changed. Being her mother reminded me of my goals, dreams, and aspirations. Her life truly reaffirmed my life's ambition. Without her, I am convinced, this work would still be in the form of a dissertation lying on a dusty bookshelf in my office.

I would like to thank Series Editor Gary Okihiro and ABC-Clio Senior Editor Kim Kennedy White for believing in this project. More importantly, I thank them for giving me the space and the time to make this book a reality.

I also owe a significant amount of gratitude to my family, who has always loved and encouraged me. To my mother, Gloria Woullard Wilder, I say thank you for being a living, breathing example of strength, fortitude, and pride. Your love for God, family, and education continue to inspire me. It is truly an honor to be your daughter. To both of my fathers, Jeff Wilder and Joe Wilder, thank you for all your quiet support and love. I also want to thank all of my siblings, but especially Michelle, Junior, and Michael, for being my biggest cheerleaders from near and far. I additionally wish to thank my aunt Linda Wilson-Jones and my cousin Joyce Ladner for providing me with examples of fierce (and real) black women in academia. I must also thank my grandmother, the late Mary Lou Wilson, who was a true lady and quintessential black female scholar.

I would also like to thank my friends and colleagues at the University of Florida and the University of North Florida. I am especially indebted to my dissertation chair and mentor, Milagros Peña, and to Connie Shehan, Stephanie Evans Byrd, Edythe Abdullah, and Kareem Jordan. Thank you for always challenging me and providing me with guidance, encouragement, and undying support.

To my sociology sisters, Dana Berkowitz, Namita Manohar, and Colleen Cain West, thank you for more than a decade of friendship, support, and love. To Dana, thank you for all of your motivation, encouragement, and thoughtful feedback on my work throughout the various stages of this process. To Namita, I say thank you for all the prayers, feedback, and faith sharing up to the very end, when times became difficult and disappointing. To Colleen, I am so thankful for your role in this research journey, and I am even more thankful that we were able to share our color stories together throughout this process. You have been one of my biggest supporters, and you are the premiere example of solidarity, sisterhood, and coalition building in this struggle against colorism. Your passion for this work inspires me. I send a special thank you to Billy Jeffries, who was my first friend at my doctoral program at the University of Florida, and who has been like a brother ever since.

I am especially grateful to my real-life "sisters in the academy," La'Tara Osborne-Lampkin and Tamara Bertrand Jones. I am so thankful for our partnership and your prayers. To La'Tara, thank you for all of our "5-minute" turned 2-hour chats and breakthroughs. Your wisdom and honesty have truly propelled my thinking and faith forward. I have learned so much from both of you, and I am undoubtedly a better scholar because of you.

To Alicia Emanuel Wade, I cannot express to you how much your friendship has encouraged and motivated me. Thank you for being my number-one sister-friend, cheerleader, and coach since the very beginning. We've experienced a lot of personal, professional, and spiritual growth together. Love you, girl!

To my beloved sister friends, Kutura Watson, Sheila Lamarre, Melanie Ling, Jerri Richardson, Telisha Martin, Desiree Schnoor, Selena Brown, Erica Wilson, and the 11 "Irreplaceable Ivies," my line-sisters from the Mu Upsilon Omega chapter of Alpha Kappa Alpha Sorority, Incorporated: I treasure your support, sisterhood, and love throughout the years.

I send a special thanks to my research assistants at various points over the past decade, Joanna Braganza, Kristin Staggs, Taylor Tregmann, Sarah Wining, Vanesa Allen, and Britanny Armalin. This book would not have been possible without your hard work.

Whenever I was doubtful about the future of this project, my students always reminded me at just the right time how important colorism is and that I needed to keep pushing. I want to send a huge shout-out to the students in my fall 2009 *Colorism in the United States* course—especially Terri Scott, James Edmonds, Mario Brewer, Watt Young, Lina Francis, Ashley Trotter, Tia Byrd, Ashley Miller, Hope Davis, Alissa Adkins, and Regina Fishburne. To all of the students in the fall 2014 colorism course—Keshia Scott, LaToshia Chaney, Judy Lewis, Sh'Terra Barber, Melisa Paige-Baille, Cari Whitmire, Deongelo Niblack, Kay'Trina Dunbar, Victor Eaves, and Casey Roth—thank you for providing me with one of the best teaching and learning environments I have ever experienced in my career as a professor. Your class single-handedly made me become obsessed with colorism all over again.

To Renee Young, thank you giving me your prayers of grace to complete this project.

To Valerie Marie Moore, thank you for being a friend, agent, publicist, babysitter, shoulder to cry on, and crazy person to laugh at. You saw it all, good and bad. Thank you for being my "ride or die" family away from family. Lela and I truly love and appreciate you.

This research project would be impossible without the courageous women and men who participated in the focus groups and interviews. Finally, and most importantly, I thank each one of you for your strength and honesty, for speaking out and sharing your color stories. Keep fighting, and keep embracing your own unique beauty.

I give my final thanks to my almighty God, who has given me peace, grace, and now, restoration.

Preface

WHY ARE WE STILL TALKING ABOUT COLORISM?

When I share my research on colorism with others, many people are immediately engaged in the topic, and some even offer a personal story. In general, many folks are excited to talk about this issue and want to hear more about my work. There are, however, some individuals who offer the proverbial "eye-roll" and question what new knowledge can be gained or learned *now*. "Why are we *still* talking about colorism?" some ask. After all, colorism has been a mainstay in black American communities for generations, and talk of complexion bias is nothing new. Even within the early stages of the academic peer-review process of my project, scholars rightfully questioned, "Who cares about this, and why?" One person even noted that while colorism was interesting to them personally, within the academic context of manuscript "appeal," there was nothing cutting-edge or fresh about the topic.

In actuality, the scholarly work—specifically, books devoted solely to colorism in the black community—is still in its infancy. In 1993, Kathy Russell, Midge Wilson, and Ronald Hall published *The Color Complex*—a groundbreaking work that squarely addressed the contemporary nature of colorism and skin color politics in the African American community.[1] Their book was monumental because it was the first manuscript to shed light on the controversial issue of color bias in the post–Civil Rights era. They have since revised this work in a second edition published in 2013. In the twenty-year period since the original publication of *The Color*

Complex, there have been fewer than a dozen nonfiction books dedicated to exploring skin color politics in black America. All of these works—from Marita Golden's riveting autobiography *Don't Play in the Sun*[2] to sociologist Margaret Hunter's *Race, Gender, and the Politics of Skin Tone*[3] to Yaba Blay's *(1)ne Drop*[4]—are important texts that expand our knowledge and understandings of race, racism, and their inexorable connections to colorism. More importantly, these works help us to understand the complexities and implications of denying blackness and seeking whiteness. Although racism remains an important matter of social, political, and scholarly focus, I contend throughout this work that studying colorism simply yields a deeper understanding of this complex issue.

My goal in this book is to add to the modest yet brilliant collection of work in the academic storehouse on colorism in the black American community. *Color Stories* offers an in-depth, sociological exploration of colorism in the everyday lives of black women, investigating the lived experiences of a phenomenon that continues to impact women of African descent in a new generation and century. This research provides an important perspective of black women who are still struggling with colorism today.

Colorism is currently trending as one of the hottest topics in popular culture. It only takes a cursory glance at current events to validate the need for further empirical research on colorism. Take for instance the worldwide obsession with one of today's "It" girls, Oscar winner Lupita Nyong'o. The Mexican Kenyan actress who studied at Yale pushed discussions of dark skin and beauty from the margins of the black community into the center of mainstream discourse during her acceptance speech at a 2014 *Essence Magazine* awards luncheon.[5] Lupita's candid views on colorism have been hotly discussed by bloggers, scholars, and tweeters alike. Or consider even the media buzz over convicted felon Jeremy Meeks's mug shot. His arrest—and subsequent posting of his photo on the Stockton, California, police department's Facebook page—created a viral explosion of tweets and "likes" as Meeks was heralded as the world's "sexiest criminal," partially due to his light skin and blue eyes.[6] Thanks to newer forms of knowledge sharing and dissemination (Facebook, Twitter, etc.), the renewed conversations on colorism are now more public, and perhaps more honest, than ever before. The color stories I bring to you in this book aim to add a clearer voice to this important discussion.

Color Stories is part autobiography, part social commentary, and part academic examination. I offer a theoretical and empirical analysis of *everyday colorism* that is meant to be accessible and easily understood by all types of audiences. As a feminist researcher, I employ a reflexive stance to the work that I do. Unlike some academic studies infused with distance, objectivity, and neutrality, a reflexive approach to research requires scholars to consider their personal stories and experiences throughout the process of gathering data. I became deeply embedded and invested in this research. So, as I share with you the stories of the women who participated in my study, I will also be sharing glimpses of my story and the development of my own color consciousness throughout the process. For me, this work is both personal and political. It is what I call my black academic "divalicious" approach to discussing colorism in the academic and everyday (or nonacademic) contexts. All too often, these two realms operate in two separate, incongruent spheres. Quite often, the academic world does not "talk out" enough to the public arena and communicate the many fresh, exciting ideas being generated from within the ivory tower.

Why continue to study colorism in the 21st century? The answer is simply because colorism will always be a timely and interesting topic of discussion for many black women. While many of my research findings resonate with the work of previous scholars and generations, colorism never gets old. In the same way that we look back to the work of race scholar W.E.B. Du Bois (I am always making contemporary connections to Du Bois's prophetic 1900 statement, "The problem of the 20th Century is the problem of the color line"[7]) to understand modern-day notions of racism, we should never grow tired of interrogating, and complicating, colorism. The color stories presented here are credible and legitimate and warrant further examination by scholars and laypeople alike. Colorism remains a pressing concern in today's society, and sharing these stories with you is an important step in furthering the public dialogue. It is my hope that the knowledge produced from this research will inform recommendations for action and social change and broaden our understandings of colorism on a global level.

Introduction

The Continuing Significance of Colorism in the 21st Century

As a child growing up, I always had situations where the **other girls had the perception that I had unlimited access because of my lighter skin color.** I had people who wanted to fight me that I had never even exchanged words with, who perceived that I was stuck up, who perceived that I thought I was better, or you know, just come to all kind of conclusions of who I was based on that, without even getting to know me, so **I always had this need to prove my ability to be down to earth, to know who I was, instead of what I was.**

—*Keleechi, 18, Ft. Washington, Maryland*

I had an Aunt who always equated dark skin with unattractive, so I always heard, "Black and ugly." **It was like there was one word: "Blackandugly."**

—*Nicole, 41, Washington, D.C.*

It's difficult to talk about this colorism issue only in terms of race. I think gender is very important because being black women, all this crap about beauty, looks and all . . . that's why it's important, is **because it's about women.**

—*Patricia, 35, Dominican Republic*

Colorism is obviously about the disadvantages or advantages you get from being a certain complexion. But I think more importantly, it's something that plagues black women rather than men. . . . I was drawn here because **it's something you could never really get tired of talking about because it always seems to be an issue.**

—*Becky, 21, Ft. Lauderdale, Florida*

Screw black, screw light. I'm moving to another country. I'm moving to a country where there's something else, because **I'm tired of being totally ignored by White guys and competing for Black men.** I'm tired of doing that. I need to go somewhere else where there is more to be seen, you know what I mean? I could be different

—*Trina, 22, Miami, FL*

Almost every black woman I know has a color story.[1] Good, bad, or indifferent—skin tone (in conjunction, of course, with our race, class, and gender) shapes our attitudes, beliefs, experiences, and, at times, choices.

Since I was a young adult, I have been acutely aware of skin tone differences in the black community; my skin tone has been just as much a part of identity as my race, class, and gender. The issue of color in my personal relationships and day-to-day life is incredibly significant. I have been called many names—from "caramel" to "dirty red" to "fried-chicken brown"—and have felt judged and discriminated against because of my skin tone, hair texture, and facial features.[2] Admittedly, I have even judged, discriminated, and, at times, thrown a bit of "shade" to other black women based upon their color. And as a black feminist scholar, I know better. Yet, much like racism, colorism intrudes upon my daily life in many clever and unexpected ways.

My color story—in the beginning, at least—started as one of indifference. As a young girl, I never gave much thought to my skin color. I remember loving my light-brown skin and feeling that I had the perfect complexion. I saw people in my family with different complexions—from my older sister, who is very light-skinned, to my mother, who is slightly browner than me, to my grandmother, who was dark-skinned—and never wished for their skin tone. I was always content with the skin I was in. Growing up, I never felt "bad" about my skin tone, but I do remember learning in elementary school that there was something different about the lighter-skinned girls. Kiyoko Charles—one of my close friends in grade school—was half black and half Japanese.[3] We became best friends in the fifth grade because of her sweet nature. Everyone else in our class—both the girls and the boys—coveted Kiyoko's porcelain-toned skin and wavy, black pigtails that cascaded down her back. Another classmate, Alexis Taylor, whose parents were both black, garnered even more attention from our peers for her light skin and wavy hair.[4] Although these two girls had lighter skin and longer hair than mine, I was always happy with who I was and what I brought to the table.

As a self-professed nerd, I concentrated more on studying, practicing the violin, and going to college than ideals of beauty. From the start of elementary school and on into high school, I easily made friends with girls of different skin tones and races and can't recall one negative comment, joke, or remark about my skin tone. While I do remember a few comments about my "pretty" hair, I cannot recall a time in which I was made to feel different about my skin tone. There was one occasion when I was visiting family in Mississippi that one of my cousins called me "bright." I took this as a compliment, thinking that she was referring to my good grades. I later discovered that my cousin was actually talking about my skin tone, and I asked my mother to explain this difference. She quickly dismissed my question and told me not to pay attention to silly comments about skin color—that no matter what color, we (black people) were all the same.

Over time, I learned that was just not true. Despite my mother's teaching, I was aware of the differences placed on light and dark skin. However, I did not think much about what those differences meant. In my mind, color differences—like socially constructed race or gender differences—were just *there*. They existed, but in my own personal experience, I had not seen how color mattered.

My color story abruptly shifted from one of indifference to one of preoccupation while in college. As an undergraduate student at Allegheny College, a small liberal arts school in Meadville, Pennsylvania, I quickly learned about the complexities of skin tone among my black female peers. At a predominately white school, competition for black men (and black women, for that matter) was rather fierce, and it became evident that light-skinned women were seen as the ideal. I did not consider myself among the lightest of the African American female students, nor was I was placed in the same category as the dark-skinned women. Making friends on both sides of the color spectrum, I began to hear the color stories of my peers. My light-skinned and dark-skinned friends spoke of the same pain, frustration, and sadness connected to their skin tone. Theirs were stories of rejection, exclusion, and marginalization. I could not understand why my friends were so deeply impacted by their color. Furthermore, I could not understand why I was not.

Compelled by their stories, I began to do more research on skin-tone differences in the African American community, and that is when I learned about the history of colorism and the academic field of *colorism studies*. I became so enthralled with this hidden world of bias and discrimination within the black community that I explored the topic for my undergraduate senior thesis. I conducted interviews and centered my independent research project on the question *Is Black Beautiful in America?* In hearing more about the experiences of the 15 black women that I interviewed for my thesis, I developed my own personal and academic color complex—forever fascinated, intrigued, and ultimately changed by the nature of skin tone in the lives of many black women.

My preoccupation with other folks' preoccupation with color only intensified into my adulthood. In fact, my color story became much more complex when I became a parent. I am the proud mother of a very active preschooler, Lela Faith. From the moment that she was born, I have been overjoyed at this precious little being that has forever changed my life. In my eyes, Lela is perfect. Everything about who she is is simply wonderful. There is not one thing that I would change about her. But before she was born, there were lots of people—mostly black folk—who had begun to craft (in both subtle and direct ways) my daughter's color story. This is actually quite common in black culture. Feminist scholar Margo Okazawa-Rey and her colleagues share,

> In the presence of a newborn, one can still hear passed down folklore which predicts the baby's future skin color and hair texture. Though oblivious to these concerns, the young black infant must learn to function in a society in which the shade of one's skin functions as a status-determining characteristic.[5]

My former husband is biracial (black father, white mother) with very light skin and green eyes. In fact, when I married him, many people made comments about how pretty our children would be, given his half-white ancestry and my decidedly "good" features. (Throughout my life, extended family and others have remarked about my eye shape and nose shape.) When I was pregnant with Lela, I heard many predictions about Lela's skin tone, hair, and facial features. The vast majority of folk had decided that Lela would have a "nice" skin tone—a color not as light as her father's, but not as brown as mine. Whenever I would hear these kinds of forecasts about my unborn child's color, I would get very annoyed. Inherent in these color projections was an implicit bias against my brown color—one that I had always loved and never wanted to trade. On one occasion, I remarked to a close friend that it *was* plausible for Lela to have brown skin. But she, and many others, did not buy into my theory.

I gave birth to Lela on November 9, 2011. Like many proud new parents in this digital age, I sent a picture text message to friends and family showing off my baby girl. Many of the responses were congratulatory, but within hours of her entrance into this world, I received a few messages about how brown my daughter's ears were compared to the rest of her newborn color. This was a dead giveaway. Lela's ears were a faint brown color—not yellow or red, but *brown*. It is commonplace for many black children to be born with a lighter skin tone, which darkens shortly after birth. As the hours turned into days and into weeks, Lela's color gradually changed from a faint shade of brown to a more distinctive caramel shade. In fact, Lela is the same complexion as I am—which to some is a medical mystery! In fact, some people marvel at the fact that Lela is unambiguously black, puzzled that her white ancestry is not more prominent in her physical make-up. Even Lela's white grandmother made a comment about my daughter's complexion. Upon first meeting her at four days old, she remarked that she looked "much different" than she did in her newborn photos. Although she did not explain what she meant by "different," it was obvious that she was referring to the change in her granddaughter's skin tone since she was born. Lela's grandmother loves my daughter very much, and I am certain that my former mother-in-law meant no harm in this statement. Yet, her reaction shows how white folks, too, unknowingly participate in and reproduce colorist ideology.

What happened during the birth of my daughter will always stay with me, as it speaks volumes to the prominence of colorism in the black community and, specifically, the cultural currency attached to being a light-skinned girl. Representative of countless similar exchanges and interactions occurring over my lifetime, this story served as a *magnified moment* of colorism. As sociologist Arlie Hochschild explains, a magnified moment is an ordinary event that provides *extra*ordinary insight and awareness.[6] Some individuals' reactions to my daughter's skin tone imply that in some way she was shortchanged or unlucky to have brown skin like me and to not bear more of a resemblance to her father's "white side." Because my daughter "turned" from light to brown, her value and potential had in many ways decreased in the minds of individuals who buy into colorist ideologies. However, I frequently hear comments about her beautiful curls (or "good hair"), which appears to hold a redemptive quality and value on its own.

In this age of a theoretically color-blind, "post-racial" society (a world in which folks can't see race and/or color, therefore race does *not* matter), my daughter—and countless other black women and girls like her—will inevitably deal with the subtle and at times blatant challenges attached to her race, class, gender, *and* skin tone. This magnified moment demonstrates the reality of racism *and* colorism in the 21st century, affecting black women in more distinctive ways than black men. Like racism, colorism remains a part of everyday life for many black people, particularly women. Since my senior year at Allegheny College, I have spent nearly two decades deeply entrenched in the diverse array of black women's color stories, exploring the phenomenon of colorism throughout the course of my graduate education and now career as a sociologist, seeking to make meaningful contributions to the body of knowledge of this bourgeoning area of scholarly inquiry.

SO, WHAT EXACTLY IS COLORISM?

In 1712, British slave owner Willie Lynch purportedly delivered a speech to a crowd of Virginia slave owners on the banks of the James River.[7] His address, entitled *The Making of a Slave*, provided white Americans step-by-step guidelines for controlling African Americans. Lynch suggested that the key to keeping black people subjugated and oppressed was through the creation of differences, namely by separating them on the basis of their skin tone. According to Lynch, pitting the light-skinned slaves against the dark-skinned slaves (and vice versa) would generate envy and resentment for generations. Although there has been much debate over the existence of Willie Lynch and the authenticity of this speech (some believe that Willie Lynch and his infamous oration are ficticious), what cannot be disputed is the long-standing history of difference and discrimination among African Americans on the basis of color that many scholars refer to as colorism.

Colorism (also referred to as the "color complex" or even "shadeism") is defined as the unequal treatment and discrimination of individuals *belonging to the same racial or ethnic minority group* (e.g., African Americans) based upon differences in physical features—most notably skin complexion (color), but also facial features and hair texture. Although racism and colorism have been used interchangeably, each form of bias is different, despite sharing similar qualities, manifestations, and consequences. Colorism is not unique to black Americans; people of color around the world— from Africa, Latin America, Asia, and the Caribbean, etc.—are impacted by *global colorism,* or the widespread elevation of light skin tones over darker skin across all communities of color. Among black folk in the United States, colorism is a form of internalized racism that promotes bias and favor for light skin, European features and "good (i.e. straight) hair." Like the history of slavery and racism, colorism is part of black America's cultural DNA.

Spoken of as a "colortocracy" by W.E.B. Du Bois in 1903,[8] "color-struck" or "partial to color" by St. Clair Drake and Horace Cayton in 1945,[9] and later coined *colorism* by Alice Walker in 1983,[10] skin-tone bias is perhaps the most permanent feature of slavery, dividing the black community for almost as long as racism has divided America. Often referred to as the "last taboo among African Americans,"[11] the term *colorism*—formally named by many in academic circles—has yet to be fully incorporated into daily, informal African American language and culture. It has instead found its way into the everyday names and practices used among family, friends, and in social situations that perpetuate and reinforce the discourse of discrimination attached to skin tone. From "high yella" to "blue-black," various skin tones are placed on a continuum from light to dark. Lighter skin has typically translated into the perception of better opportunity, more resources, and overall privilege as a black person in society. Recent research, including the cutting-edge scholarship of sociologist Ellis Monk,[12] political scientist Vesla Weaver,[13] and scholars Lance Hannon, Robert DeFina, and Sarah Bruch,[14] show that skin tone has the potential to shape educational attainment, household income, electoral politics, and school disciplinary practices for many African Americans today. Like race, skin color differences persist in the 21st century.

THE ORIGINS OF COLORISM IN BLACK AMERICA

While anthropologists note that skin color difference can be traced back to biblical times, the history of colorism in black America starts with the history of race in America. As race scholar Joe Feagin explains, "racist thought did not come accidentally to the United States. It was, and still is, actively developed and propagated."[15] Since the onset of colonial expansion into the United States, the history of this nation has rested upon a clear binary divide—black and white.[16] The institution of colonialism brought more than slavery into this country; a racist ideology followed, which cultivated a system of language, classification, and domination privileging whiteness over blackness. Using the biological differences of skin color as a justification for the oppression and enslavement of Africans, European colonizers developed a social hierarchy that aligned whites at the top and blacks at the bottom. The inferiority associated with blackness translated into socially constructed ideas about skin tone and phenotype that continue to shape identity, status, and opportunity.

In addition to defining a color line that separated blacks and whites, racist ideology subsequently caused internalized divisions among African Americans. The frequent "mixing" of the races (commonly through the sexual exploitation of black female slaves by white male slave owners) resulted in biracial offspring. In order to prevent any ambiguity in regard to racial classification, *and* to preclude blacks with white ancestry from gaining the same legal status as full-blooded whites, lawmakers mandated the rule of the hypo-descent, or the *"one-drop"* rule: even the smallest amount (or drop) of African ancestry legally defined a person as black.[17] This statute set the United States apart from many other societies who operated under more fluid, multi-racial categories of personal and group identification.

Although the enforcement of the "one-drop" rule equalized all blacks in the eyes of the law, in everyday practice, significant differences developed between blacks of varying skin tones, hair textures, and facial features. Consequently, colorism became an undeniable social force in the black community that caused division and separation within the race based upon one's proximity to whiteness. While blackness emerged as an inferior social, cultural, and political category in opposition to whiteness, lightness and darkness ensued as secondary categories that carried their own sub-system of social, cultural, and political significance within the black community.

Sociologists Verna Keith and Cedric Herring explain, "Whites placed greater economic value on slaves of mixed parentage and used skin tone or degree of visible white ancestry as a basis for the differential treatment of bondsmen."[18] It has been regularly documented that during slavery, lighter-skinned slaves were afforded more resources and assigned duties that placed them indoors and in direct contact with white slave masters.[19] Darker-skinned slaves, in comparison, were relegated to labor-intensive tasks outdoors in the open field and sun. Further, whites developed a terminology for distinguishing varying levels of African ancestry. The terms *mulatto*, *quadroon*, and *octoroon* were adapted to designate a black person with three-eighths, one-fourth, or one-eighth of African ancestry, respectively.[20] Because of their partial white heritage, light-skinned blacks were considered smarter and superior to dark-skinned blacks. As a consequence, many light-skinned multiracials began to internalize the same principles of racism within the black community, actually believing that they were better than their darker counterparts and acting accordingly.[21] Light-skinned blacks and mulattos formed their own social class apart from darker-skinned blacks and saw more opportunity and advantage in the white-dominated society. This included broadened opportunities in education, manumission from slavery, and the acquisition of land and property. With the eventual abolition of slavery, the members of this newly formed group continued to set themselves apart from darker blacks by socializing, marrying, and procreating with one another.

Wealthy light-skinned blacks emerged after Reconstruction to form what came to be known as the Black Elite and were responsible for reinforcing classist and racist attitudes in the African American community. As sociologist and filmmaker Tukufu Zuberi explains, some middle-class African Americans held the same type of hatred toward lower-income blacks as whites expressed for all blacks.[22] By the turn of the 20th century, many black institutions—including colleges and churches—continued to reinforce this distinction by distancing themselves from darker-skinned blacks and implementing separatist standards such as the *brown paper bag, pencil, ruler,* and *door* tests.[23] These informal but well-known "tests" kept those who had shorter, coarse hair, and skin tones that were darker than a paper bag or door out of these institutions. Organizational colorism thrived through exclusionary social clubs and societies—namely Blue Vein societies, Brown Fellowship, The Links, and Jack & Jill—that were originally founded to perpetuate this separation based on skin tone. Admission to such organizations *required* light skin, "good" hair, and European features. Throughout the years, these stereotypical beliefs made their way from one generation to the next, and some African Americans today continue to place a premium on lighter skin tone, seeing the different shades of brown as varying degrees of status, acceptance, and achievement.

THE CONTINUING SIGNIFICANCE OF COLORISM: 2000–2015

Colorism remains an issue of great social, political, and cultural influence for many black Americans in the 21st century. Without a doubt (and for good reason), racism has garnered more public attention and concern in broader American discourse. Skin color bias and discrimination is not as relentless in American society compared to racial bias and discrimination. Yet, the competing narratives of post-racialism (*"racism is over—especially now that America has elected its first black president"*) and the continuing significance of race (*"racism is alive and well"*) tend to hide and overshadow the equally compelling reality of colorism for many individuals *in addition to* racism. As a social problem related to, but separate from, racism, colorism is gaining more attention, dialogue, and awareness. In reflecting on this evolution, I developed a timeline of events occurring since the year 2000 (see Figure 1) that have shaped the contours of knowledge and consciousness related to skin color prejudice and discrimination.

At first glance, many of the pivotal "color moments" seem to be rather obvious and have a clear relation to the continuing significance of colorism. For instance, the publication of Lawrence Otis Graham's *Our Kind of People* in 2000 unearths the inside world of the black elite and exposes the powerful nature of colorism from within many historically black clubs and organizations.[24] Similarly, the 2001 release of songstress India Arie's "Brown Skin" offers a celebratory anthem to darker skin tones. Other entries on the timeline, such as the backlash over a Detroit party promoter's "Light-skin Bash"[25] (and other subsequent paper bag parties) are representative of

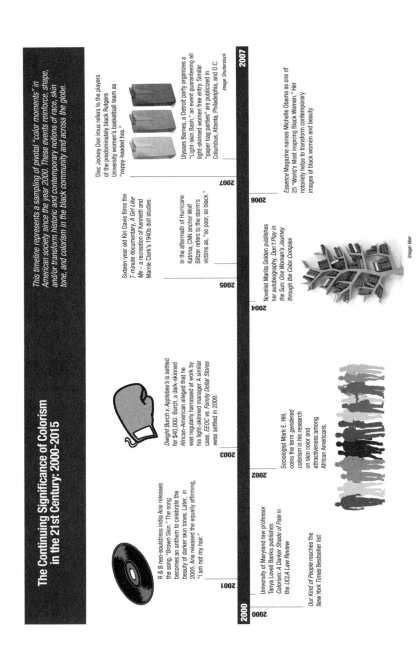

The Continuing Significance of Colorism in the 21st Century: 2000–2015

This timeline represents a sampling of pivotal "color moments" in American society since the year 2000. These events reinforce, shape, and/or transform historic and contemporary notions of race, skin tone, and colorism in the black community and across the globe.

2000

2001

R & B neo-soulstress India Arie releases the song, "Brown Skin." The song becomes an anthem to celebrate the beauty of darker skin tones. Later, in 2005, Arie released the equally affirming, "I am not my hair."

University of Maryland law professor Tanya Lovell Banks publishes *Colorism: A Darker Shade of Pale* in the *UCLA Law Review*

Our Kind of People reaches the *New York Times* Bestseller list

2002

Sociologist Mark E. Hill, coins the term *gendered colorism* in his research on skin color and attractiveness among African Americans.

2003

Dwight Burch v. Applebee's is settled for $40,000. Burch, a dark-skinned African-American alleged that he was regularly harrassed at work by his light-skinned manager. A similar case, *EEOC vs. Family Dollar Stores* was settled in 2009.

2004

Novelist Marita Golden publishes her autobiography, *Don't Play in the Sun: One Woman's Journey through the Color Complex*

2005

Sixteen-year old Kiri Davis films the 7-minute documentary, *A Girl Like Me* – a recreation of Kenneth and Mamie Clark's 1940s doll studies.

In the aftermath of Hurricane Katrina, CNN anchor Wolf Blitzer refers to the storm's victims as, "so poor, so black."

Image: Veer

2006

Essence Magazine names Michelle Obama as one of 25 "World's Most Inspiring Black Women." Her notoriety helps to transform contemporary images of black women and beauty.

2007

Disc Jockey Don Imus refers to the players of the predominately black Rutgers University women's basketball team as "nappy-headed hos."

Ulysses Barnes, a Detroit party organizes a "Light-skin Bash," an event guaranteeing all light-skinned women free entry. Similar "paper bag parties" are publicized in Columbus, Atlanta, Philadelphia, and D.C.

Image: Shutterstock

Figure 1: The Continuing Significance of Colorism, 2000–2015

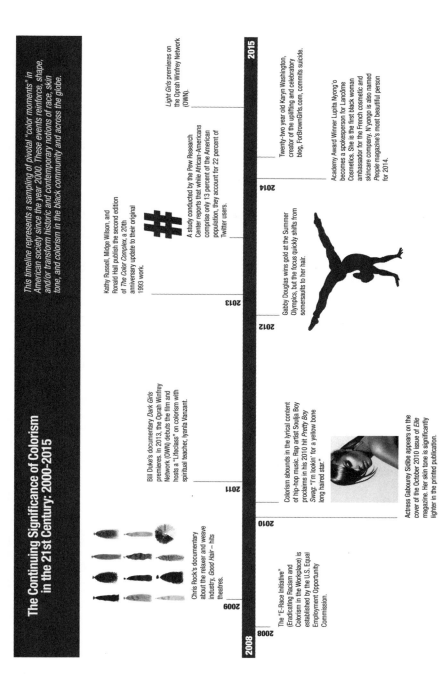

The Continuing Significance of Colorism in the 21st Century: 2000-2015

This timeline represents a sampling of pivotal "color moments" in American society since the year 2000. These events reinforce, shape, and/or transform historic and contemporary notions of race, skin tone, and colorism in the black community and across the globe.

2008

The "E-Race Initiative" (Eradicating Racism and Colorism in the Workplace) is established by the U.S. Equal Employment Opportunity Commission.

2009

Chris Rock's documentary about the relaxer and weave industry, *Good Hair* – hits theatres.

2010

Actress Gabourey Sidibe appears on the cover of the October 2010 issue of *Elle* magazine. Her skin tone is significantly lighter in the printed publication.

2011

Bill Duke's documentary *Dark Girls* premieres. In 2013, the Oprah Winfrey Network (OWN) debuts the film and hosts a "Lifeclass" on colorism with spiritual teacher, Iyanla Vanzant.

Colorism abounds in the lyrical content of hip-hop music. Rap artist Soulja Boy proclaims in his 2010 hit *Pretty Boy Swag*: "I'm lookin' for a yellow bone long haired star."

2012

Gabby Douglas wins gold at the Summer Olympics, but the focus quickly shifts from somersaults to her hair.

2013

Kathy Russell, Midge Wilson, and Ronald Hall publish the second edition of *The Color Complex*, a 20th anniversary update to their original 1993 work.

A study conducted by the Pew Research Center reports that while African-Americans comprise only 13 percent of the American population, they account for 22 percent of Twitter users.

2014

Twenty-two year old Karyn Washington, creator of the uplifting and celebratory blog, ForBrownGirls.com, commits suicide.

Academy Award Winner Lupita Nyong'o becomes a spokesperson for Lancôme Cosmetics. She is the first black woman ambassador for the French cosmetic and skincare company. N'yongo is also named *People* magazine's most beautiful person for 2014.

2015

Light Girls premieres on the Oprah Winfrey Network (OWN).

past-in-present or "throwback" events reminiscent of colorist ideals and phenomena commonplace in the black community in the early half of the 20th century. Another example is the 2005 documentary produced by (then) teen Kiri Davis that was a symbolic re-formation of the classic doll tests of the 1940s.[26]

There are other events on the timeline that are more ambiguous, yet underscore the complexities of colorism. In 2005, in his live coverage of the devastation of Hurricane Katrina in New Orleans, CNN anchor Wolf Blitzer reported, "so many of these people, almost all of them that we see, are so poor and they are so black."[27] Many viewers were outraged at the journalist's commentary, labeling his remarks as insensitive and racist. Mr. Blitzer's word choice also reflects colorism, as his description of the storm's victims as "so poor and so black" highlights the conflation of racism and colorism. Oftentimes, many of the same issues that are race-related are similarly matters of color, too. Furthermore—consciously or not—Blitzer makes an undeniable association between dark skin and poverty, a link that is commonly made (albeit in a more blatant manner) within the African American community. This reflects, of course, the *intersectional* nature of colorism. That is, skin tone is inexorably linked to, and intersects with, race, class, and gender.

Collectively, the occurrences on this timeline represent a variety of "flash-points" that reinforce, shape, and/or transform both historic and contemporary notions of colorism in the early 21st century. This list is not exhaustive, but rather a sampling of events that point to the building momentum of colorism in academic and public discourse. For instance, the release of Chris Rock's documentary *Good Hair* in 2009, and the premiere of Bill Duke's critically acclaimed films *Dark Girls* and *Light Girls* on the Oprah Winfrey Network (OWN)—in 2013 and 2015 respectively—are emblematic of the reality that this "good hair/bad hair, light-skin/dark-skin" thing has transcended far beyond the black community. As this book heads to press, there are even more noteworthy moments that could be added to this timeline—ranging from Viola Davis's awe-inspiring "wig-reveal" on a recent episode of the ABC drama *How to Get Away With Murder,*[28] the "scandal" over actress Kerry Washington's seemingly white-washed skin on the cover of the February 2015 *InStyle* Magazine, or to the backlash and criticism megastar Beyoncé received for "stealing" the 2015 Grammy performance of the gospel song *Precious Lord* away from the less popular (and dark-skinned) R & B songstress Ledisi. Many folks in the black community asserted that colorism—more specifically, Beyoncé's light-skin privilege—was at the center of the controversy. Regrettably, very few people recognized colorism to be at the center of the widespread disapproval of Bey's performance. Beyoncé was accused of singing too "pretty" and that she did not possess enough gospel-singing "grit" to move anyone to tears. Apparently, that is a skill reserved only for dark-skinned, "big-boned" women like Mahalia Jackson and Ledisi. Regardless of how big, small, commonplace or extraordinary this collection of color moments is, each event points to the continuing and increasing significance of colorism in modern-day society. Perhaps, more importantly, what is depicted in this timeline represents the broad and complex contours of colorism, particularly now and against the backdrop of the larger landscape of race, class, and gender in the post–Civil Rights era.

ADDRESSING THE COMPLEX INTERSECTIONS OF RACE, GENDER, AND COLOR IN THE BLACK COMMUNITY

By 2050, it is estimated that people of color will comprise half of the American population.[29] As the demographics of our society change and the overall skin tone of Americans deepen in the new millennium, many scholars are calling for continued dialogue and increased awareness on colorism, as some predict that in 50 years, colorism will replace racism in significance. For instance, sociologist Eduardo Bonilla-Silva proposes, "colour gradations, which have always been important matters of within-group differentiation, will become more salient factors of stratification."[30] That is, our society could begin to place more emphasis on complexion and less importance on racial category. Simply stated, colorism could be the "new" racism. Anthropologist Nina G. Jablonski highlights in her 2012 book, *Living Color: The Biological and Social Meaning of Skin Color*, that there is a recent trend toward colorism in the 21st century and refers to the issue as a "major social force and challenge to human equality."[31] It remains critical to examine the implications of this new racial trajectory and the specific consequences for black Americans, particularly black women and girls.

In March of 2014, the Black Women's Roundtable (an affiliate program of the National Coalition on Black Civic Participation) published *Black Women in the United States, 2014*, a special report outlining the status of black women in the 21st century.[32] The report highlights key facts and statistics related to varied aspects of black women's lives—from education to health, and from politics to entrepreneurship. While black women have seen exceptional progression in some areas, they lag far behind their black male and female counterparts in many others. On the importance of developing a special issue focusing specifically on black women, co-authors Melanie Campbell and Avis Jones-DeWeever write:

In the White House now sits the nation's first Black President and First Lady. And while the overt implementation of Jim Crow has been relegated to history books, its vestiges still remain. Stubborn differences persist across both race and gender in America. Black women in particular, live lives at the intersection of these points of difference. Yet their struggles and triumphs are rarely examined specifically, especially in a way that provides not only raw facts, but also depth, context, and an eye towards a path forward.[33]

In the opening pages of their groundbreaking text *Gender Talk: The Struggle for Women's Equality in African American Communities*, black feminist scholars Johnnetta Betsch Cole and Beverly Guy-Sheftall declare the need for an open dialogue and public acknowledgement of the issues of gender and sexual politics in the black community:

> Rarely, except among a small group of feminists and other gender-progressives, is there a consideration of moving beyond a race-only analysis in understanding the complexities of African American communities and the challenges we face. While we are certain that institutionalized racism and the persistence of economic injustices are responsible for our contemporary plight as second-hand citizens, we boldly assert that gender matters too.

They go on to say,

> There is perhaps no intracommunity topic about which there has been more contentious debate than the issue of gender relations in Black America.[34]

My objective in *Color Stories* is akin to the work of the Black Women's Roundtable and to the declaration of Drs. Cole and Guy-Sheftall. I make the bold assertion in this book that colorism is a similarly antagonistic intracommunity concern in contemporary black society. Color matters among black women deserve pressing attention, dialogue and, most importantly, solutions. The broad body of literature on colorism in the African American community spans decades, but more studies need to direct their focus on women, particularly the everyday experiences of black women. The status of black women in the 21st century is unique and distinctive from black men, white women, and other women of color (see Sidebar). This work gives an important voice to the intersectional nature of race, gender, class, and color for black women in the 21st century. Exploring colorism with "an eye toward" black women is essential.

THE RESEARCH PROJECT: BRINGING BLACK WOMEN TOGETHER TO DISCUSS COLORISM

When black women come together, it can be very powerful. Growing up, some of my fondest memories as a child were ones that involved my mother, sister, grandmother, aunts, and other female relatives sitting down together and just talking. Although I did not realize it at the time, it was in these "circles of sisterhood" that I learned about life—the triumphs and struggles—as a black woman.

Black women have historically gathered informally in family groups, churches, salons, and other places to socialize, share stories, and to uplift one another. More formally, black women have come together to advocate for social justice and protest against oppression and inequality (such as the 1970s *National Black Feminist Organization*) or to embrace and empower black women and girls, like today's *Black Girls Rock!* campaign. Large or small, these spaces serve as domains to give space and voice to the complex stories of black womanhood. These stories shape the collective memory of black women's experience.

Many black female scholars in the academy situate the unique identity, experience, and standpoint of black women within the context of *black feminist thought*—a critical social theory emerging from the historical invisibility and marginalization of black women. Black feminist thought aims to bring the silenced voices of black women from the margins to the center and insists that every black woman is an agent of knowledge and intellect. A black feminist perspective also recognizes that there is no singular voice of all black women; rather, our lives represent a multiplicity of voices that is shaped by both our collective journeys *and* individual biographies.

Based upon my personal and academic experience—and equally grounded in the core principles of black feminist theory—I embarked upon a dissertation study to understand the extent to which black women are affected by colorism.[35] At the onset of the project, I set out to examine how black women talk about and understand colorism in their everyday lives. I wanted to know: *What are black women saying about the presence of colorism in their everyday lives? How (if at all) does skin tone play a role in their day-to-day experiences?* Over a period of more than two years—from April 2005 to October 2007—I brought small groups of black women together for more than a dozen circles of sisterhood. It was in these focus-group discussions that 66 women between the ages of 18 and 45 (and even a group of six black men) shared their color stories.[36]

Central to this study is an exploration of how black women talk about how colorism reflects a shift in color consciousness, or if there has been any change in the discourse compared to previous research and documented accounts of skin-tone bias within African American culture. Because knowledge, truth, self-definition, lived experienced, and storytelling are key features of the black feminist tradition, electing to ground this research on colorism within this approach seemed like a natural choice. This work utilizes black women's experiences as a starting point to address and understand colorism and to produce strategies for social transformation and change. As sociologist Patricia Hill Collins discusses in her scholarship, more and more black women researchers are using what she terms a *black feminist epistemology* to frame their work on black women's experiences. This methodological orientation, as she explains, "enrich[es] our understanding of how subordinate groups create knowledge that fosters their empowerment and social justice."[37] As one such black feminist researcher studying black women, I wanted the participants in my project to feel empowered. I wanted their lived experiences with colorism to be the foundation for the creation of knowledge and solutions. I wanted the voices of the women in my project to be heard and validated.

Using this focus group data, I extend race and gender scholar Philomena Essed's theoretical framework of *everyday racism*.[38] I posit that similar to the characteristics of racism, *everyday colorism* is a system of language, beliefs, and practices that govern the everyday interactions and experiences of black women as it relates to skin tone. The findings from my work offer a compelling empirical and theoretical analysis of colorism in key areas including family, schools, peer friendships, and intimate relationships. The central argument of my research is that (skin) color matters for black women *in the same way* that race, class, and gender matters. Further, this project illustrates the pressing need for continued research on colorism studies, a growing inter-disciplinary, academic sub-field in the broader area of race and racism studies.

This book pays specific attention to the ways in which black women are impacted by colorism. Comparative discussions of colorism are quite useful in understanding this nationwide issue. For instance, some scholars have examined how black women and Mexican American women experience skin-tone discrimination in similar and disparate ways;[39] others have explored how all U.S. communities of color navigate the terrains of colorism in their respective racial and ethnic groups.[40] Further, illuminating the issue of colorism among black men is also of key importance to our broader knowledge of colorism. My work in this text does not attempt to cover the broad spectrum of colorism but, rather, to hone in on the unique perspectives and experiences of black women. In the same vein, many people understand colorism to be more than a matter of skin tone; the context of colorism also extends to the important discussion of hair. As increasing numbers of black women are opting out of chemically "relaxing" their hair and choosing instead to wear their hair in its natural state, inserting hair into this discourse is also important. What I present in this book does not fully explore this important matter, but it is my hope that future scholars use my work as a platform for discussion on this and other avenues for continued research.

Chapter 1 explores how colorism has shifted from a private matter—one often discussed as "dirty laundry" in the black community—to a widely debated issue in mainstream culture. I introduce this section with a discussion of the personal dilemmas I have faced as a black woman studying black women and colorism. This includes a difficult dialogue surrounding the consequences of breaking the silence of colorism in the pursuit of my research endeavors. I then move my analysis of three critical developments in the early part of the millennium contributing to this shift in the public discourse of colorism.

Chapter 2 focuses on the theoretical foundations of colorism influencing my model of *everyday colorism*. I begin with a discussion of the distinguishing features of color and provide an overview of the traditions of colorism theory. Lastly, I introduce my theoretical model of everyday colorism and provide directions for future theorizing on colorism.

Chapters 3–5 represent the results of my analysis. Chapter 3, "The Language, Scripts, and Practices of Everyday Colorism,"[41] is an investigation of the contemporary names and attitudes surrounding skin color and also examines how the language and internalized ideas of skin color translate into everyday behavior and practice. I also report on the detailed color practices that black women engage in on a regular basis. Chapter 4, "Getting to the Roots of Colorism," deals with how the research participants understand the roles of family, school, and relationships (both peer relationships and intimate dating relationships) in mediating colorism in their lives and within the black community. Chapter 5, "Place Matters," addresses three important counter-narratives, or alternative color stories, emerging throughout the focus groups. Participants noted a perceived absence of colorism in the northern region of the United States, a higher prevalence of colorism in Caribbean nations (Haiti and Jamaica especially), and the declining importance of skin tone for the millennial generation.

The concluding chapter, "If the Present Looks Like the Past, What Does the Future Look Like?" offers my commentary on the status of colorism today and whether, in fact, the present mirrors the past. Considering this, a discussion about the future of colorism appears in this section, in addition to proposed solutions and recommendations for black women's empowerment toward change.

This book will be essential reading for anyone interested in learning more about the historical and contemporary significance of colorism in black America. While much of what is written in this book focuses primarily on the voices, lives, thoughts, and stories of black women, it is important for all of us to remember that colorism is a global issue for men and women around the world. And even white folks participate in colorism, too. The recent work of sociologist Lance Hannon uses empirical data to support the notion of "white colorism."[42] Recall the ever-so-subtle comment made by my daughter's grandmother about her change in skin tone.

On the position of improving the lives of women in the corporate workplace, Facebook COO and business extraordinaire, Sheryl Sandberg, notes in the opening of her monumental work, *Lean In*: "we can reignite the revolution by internalizing the revolution. The shift to a more equal world will happen person by person. We move closer to the true equality with each woman who leans in."[43] While Sandberg does not address explicitly how leaning in looks markedly different for women of color (because it certainly does), the urging in her message is appropriate here. In order to effectively challenge colorism in the black community and beyond, we must all own—and be accountable to—the fight. This means openly acknowledging the presence and power of color prejudice and discrimination in our society. We are *all* connected to colorism. And we are *all* responsible for eradicating colorism. It is time for a color revolution.

Sidebar 1. The Struggle of Black Women and Girls in the 21st Century: Balancing the Wimpy White Boy Syndrome in a Crooked Room

This past fall, I decided to volunteer at my daughter's preschool and assist with passing out candy during their Halloween festivities. I was paired up with another mom, and as we waited for the young children to fill the hallways searching for candy, we began to chat and get to know one another. Initially, our conversation began as small talk about our children. I don't remember the woman's name, but I do recall her beaming with pride as she spoke about her four-year-old daughter who was enrolled in Pre-K. Our discussion shifted quickly when I casually asked the young white woman if she had any other children. Almost instantly, her face turned sad. She began to tell me about her precious son—born two years *before* her daughter—who passed away as an infant. Born at just 26 weeks old, this little baby spent several weeks in the NICU fighting for his life, but as his mom explained, he was just too weak to pull through. Immediately, the woman looked at me and said, "Your daughter would have made it. My son didn't pull through because he was just a wimpy little white boy."

Puzzled, I could not understand what she was saying. The mother went on to describe the trend some people in the medical community are calling "wimpy white boy syndrome," or WWBS.[44] Apparently, for little white boys who are born prematurely, the odds of survival are the worst compared to infants of other races. Black males tend to fare better than white males but have a lower rate of survival compared to white preemie girls. Little black girls who are born premature have the highest rates of survival; for some reason, they tend to fight harder than other babies.

Our discussion ended abruptly as the school's Halloween parade began. Throughout the entire day, I kept thinking about this wimpy white boy syndrome and the sheer irony of this phenomenon. Even as preemies, black girls are cast as strong and resilient. But once these baby girls make it into the real world, the tables turn. White males have the most access to privilege and power, while black girls have to contend with a lifetime of oppression and inequality due to their race, gender, and other social identities. Melissa Harris-Perry, political scientist, TV host, and black feminist scholar, refers to the lives of black women in the United States as a "crooked room." She writes in her seminal work, *Sister Citizen: Shame, Stereotypes, and Black Women in America*: "When they confront race and gender stereotypes, black women are standing in a crooked room, and they have to figure out which way is up. Bombarded with warped images of their humanity, some black women have to tilt and bend themselves to fit the distortion."[45]

How does Harris-Perry's crooked room metaphor connect to the color stories presented in this work and to the broader discussion of colorism in the lives of black women? On the opposite spectrum of the wimpy white boy syndrome lies the ailment of the "struggle disorder" for little black baby girls. Black women and girls struggle harder to survive, exist, and ultimately remain visible in a crooked room. As Dr. Harris-Perry suggests, this room is rife with the struggle against racism and sexism. In the 21st century, the struggle against colorism lives in this room, too. On the most basic level, fighting colorism is about connecting to the citizenship, agency, and sisterhood of all black women (even if some black women do not have a color story to share) in the United States and, ultimately, women of color around the world. While some may be tempted to construct the fight against colorism as a personal, internal battle for individual black women to sort through, colorism reflects the broader complexities of the social condition of black womanhood. As a black woman who is the mother to a little black girl, I will spend my lifetime encouraging her, myself, and many other black women to stand up straight and fight.

CHAPTER 1

Breaking Silence and Going Public: Shaming, Naming, and Circulating Truth

Moving from silence into speech is for the oppressed, the colonized, the exploited, and those who stand and struggle side by side a gesture of defiance that heals, that makes new life and new growth possible. It is that act of speech, of "talking back," that is no mere gesture of empty words, that is the expression of our movement from object to subject—the liberated voice.

—bell hooks, *Talking Back: Thinking Feminist, Thinking Black*[1]

Although important, private naming is not enough—truth must be publicly proclaimed.

—Patricia Hill Collins, *Fighting Words: Black Women and the Search for Justice*[2]

In the black community, colorism is a sensitive topic that stirs up such emotions as anger, fear, and pain. Many people within the African American community would rather not talk about, focus on, or draw attention to an issue that shames and embarrasses blacks in the face of larger (white) American society. After all, the black story in the United States centers on the struggle for racial justice. The African American legacy is, in many ways, shaped by racism, slavery, and the period of institutionalized segregation in the century following the end of formalized bondage of black Americans. Accordingly, colorism was a secret to the American "public" for many years. Many African Americans describe open talks of color prejudice as "airing the dirty laundry" of black America. However, in this new millennium, discussions (and even public debate) of the bias, prejudice, and discrimination attached to colorism are becoming more frequent, open, and commonplace. For instance, in April of 2015, award-winning journalist Kim Lute penned a provocative commentary on what she deemed the persistently competitive nature of African American "sisterhood" in a *Huffington Post* blog entitled, "The Problem with Black Women."[3] Ms. Lute asserted that her light skin, green eyes, and French Creole ancestry regularly prevented her from building and solidifying lasting friendships with darker-skinned black women. The writer went on to proclaim that she finds it easier to socialize and forge meaningful relationships with white women so as to avoid the "drama" that has typically plagued her interactions with black women. Lute's personal story of pain and rejection is just one example of many black women who are now opening up, breaking silence, and giving voice to the difficult dialogues and stories of colorism in such a free and seemingly unrestricted manner.

While I found Kim Lute's public attack on black womanhood both divisive and reprehensible (there are more constructive ways to share your color story without simultaneously maligning all dark-skinned black women), the manner in which she "called out" colorism is indeed a sign of our times. In many ways, the early part of the 21st century has been about the "outing" and public shaming of this secret. I've had conversations with individuals about this recent trend, and many of them are curious about why and how colorism (or discussions of the topic, at least) appears to be escalating. The move to an open and public discourse did not happen overnight, nor can it be attributed to one event. Rather, I believe that the ubiquity of colorism lately has occurred alongside a combination of several important societal shifts. In what follows, I discuss this critical shift in the discourse from that of "family business" to widely debated topic among people of all races. I begin with my own dilemmas I have faced in conducting research on the contentious topic of colorism. Breaking the silence on colorism in the pursuit of my scholarly endeavors came with some very personal (and, ultimately, political) consequences. Next, I discuss three key developments central to the "going public" nature of colorism in modern society. In searching for the truth, as black feminist scholar Patricia Hill Collins explains, the open proclamation of an issue must take place in order for change, and ultimately transformation, (i.e., justice) to occur. The secret of colorism is out, and the search for truth has been publicly declared.

BREAKING SILENCE: BEING A BLACK WOMAN STUDYING BLACK WOMEN AND COLORISM

> I decided whose side I was on and resolved within myself that as a black social scientist, I must take a stand and there could be no value-free sanctuary for me.
>
> —Joyce Ladner, *Tomorrow's Tomorrow*[4]

In 1971, civil rights activist and sociologist Joyce Ladner published *Tomorrow's Tomorrow*, one of the first sociological studies on black women (conducted by a black woman) that refused to represent black adolescence and womanhood as stereotypical, deviant, and pathological. Ladner's ethnographic account of young black girls living in the projects of St. Louis took courage because, at that time, the traditions of sociological research were grounded in "hard science" that was objective, abstract, and unemotional. Yet Dr. Ladner—herself a young black woman from rural Mississippi—was keenly aware of her dual identities as a black woman and an academic. As the excerpt above suggests, Ladner determined that the only way to stay true to herself and to the young black women she studied was to acknowledge this duality, embrace her blackness, and to approach her research from a standpoint of subjectivity, reflection, and emotion. She lays the foundation on how to conduct valuable and credible research that is sociological yet distinct from the traditional and, at times, constraining world of social science. Dr. Ladner's groundbreaking work is such because she offers an honest treatment of black women's lives *and* because her research journey as a black woman is self-liberating. An important lesson we learn from Ladner is that if you are a black woman studying black women, it is neither possible nor recommended to place large amounts of distance between yourself and your research participants. Further, as a black woman, you *can* conduct research on black women that is simultaneously empowering and scientifically credible.

For me, this lesson has been a tough one. As a black woman, fellow sociologist, and Ladner's cousin (she and my mother are first cousins), I inherit her rich legacy of embracing work that is deeply personal and even more political. Undoubtedly, there have been significant benefits to being a black woman studying black women and colorism. My own life experiences have enabled me to recognize the value of this research project in the black community and in the academic world. Due to the sensitive and protected nature of this topic, it would be very difficult (though not impossible) for a non-black woman to gain access to and build rapport with the women in this study.[5] I do not consider myself an expert but, rather, a curious insider, and this has allowed me to reach many women who want to share their stories and experiences with colorism.

Despite the advantages of being a black woman, I have encountered significant moral and ethical challenges throughout my research journey. For all researchers, ethics are of chief concern from the conception of a research idea to the publication of the final product. For example, many scholars are concerned with ensuring that their participants are not harmed or exploited and remain appropriately informed in the course of data collection and analysis. My objectives in this research were simple: 1) to place black women's voices and stories at the center of analysis and discussion; and 2) to produce culturally relevant knowledge that would inform recommendations for personal empowerment and social change. As I developed my research plan and designed a project that would be methodologically sound and academically rigorous, I gave careful consideration to suitable research protocol and procedures. Notwithstanding, I was blindsided by the "cultural dilemmas" I faced from members of the African American community as I carried out this project and broke the silences of colorism. On achieving validation and legitimacy in their work, scholar Patricia Hill Collins cautions that black women who are engaging in black feminist work within their own communities do have added layers of accountability compared to others. She writes:

> [Black women who are] scholars must be personal advocates for their material, be accountable for the consequences of their work, have lived or experienced their material in some fashion, and be willing to engage in dialogues about their findings with ordinary, everyday people.[6]

Some of the consequences I had counted on, while others I had not carefully weighed. My blackness, allegiance, and motives were called into question far more times than I was prepared for. My personal platform to open up and spread the truth about modern-day colorism turned into a very political and vulnerable act: I became just as vulnerable as the women sharing their stories with me. I simply had not anticipated this particular dynamic of doing this work. In this same spirit of reflexivity and emotion observed by Joyce Ladner and articulated by Patricia Hill Collins, I devote this section to an important discussion of the dilemmas of my broken silence.

Dilemma #1: Whose Side Are You On?

The term *colorism*—although it has persevered within the black community for centuries—has yet to be formally named and acknowledged in mainstream society in the same way as racism. Although the issue has found its way into mainstream discourse, talking about colorism openly is still off limits for some African Americans. On the writing of his controversial book inside the life of the black elite, *Our Kind of People*, author Lawrence Otis Graham states:

> For many people, this book is a political or social hot potato in the sense that even though most blacks talk about issues of elitism, racial passing, class structure, and skin color, they don't want to see it broadcast in a book. For a few black members of the media, the topic struck too close to their own past experiences of being excluded by snobbish members of the black elite. Some of them quietly told me that they were glad that I wrote the book . . . but that they could not publicly support the book . . . because their black audiences would find the subject too painful.[7]

Likewise, Kathy Russell, a light-skinned black woman and co-author of *The Color Complex*, writes that she was scorned and berated by her black peers for even considering publishing a book with such sensitive subject matter. She often heard comments like, "Just one more thing for White people to use against us."[8]

Whenever I talk openly about my research on colorism, I hear the same criticisms that were aimed at Graham and Russell. Although there are people who are excited that I am exploring an issue that is so private and personal, there are some members of the black community who are less than enthusiastic about my research. I often hear concerns that I will be placing unnecessary focus on colorism when the real focus in the 21st century should be on eradicating racism. Rather than divide the black community on issues of colorism, some suggest that I use my position as a black sociologist to bolster and unify the black community in our struggles against racism. In the wake of recent events such as the crises in Ferguson, Missouri, and Baltimore, Maryland, this struggle is great. I am sometimes made to feel guilty about airing the dirty laundry of African Americans so publicly and in the face of whites. On two separate occasions, I have had two black female students confront me about my decision to discuss colorism in my classes. One woman told me that as a fellow black woman, I was complicating and furthering negative images of black womanhood, and she was of the opinion that my research did not embrace the true ideals of black feminism. Although I was initially offended, I concede that this student raises a very interesting ethical concern. *How can I as a black woman conduct research on black women that portrays black womanhood in a negative light?* Traditional social science has oftentimes pathologized black women by constructing negative, yet power-controlling images. Black feminists have always worked to deconstruct distorted images of blackness, particularly black femininity. Yet my work on colorism specifically identifies the ways in which black women discriminate against each other based upon skin tone. I have resolved this issue of allegiance by formulating a research project that aims to bring a much needed (and loud) voice to colorism by empowering black women and finding strategies that will, in fact, effect personal and social change. Contrary to what my former student suggested, this research on colorism is carefully aligned with the core principles of *black feminist thought*, a conceptual framework which aims to: 1) critically engage how colorism is a by-product of racism; and 2) explore, as sociologist Patricia Hill Collins describes, "how institutionalized racism produces color hierarchies among U.S. women."[9] Providing a platform for black women to discuss colorism enables them to speak up and talk back about an often subtle yet powerful form of oppression.

This question of allegiance expands beyond my membership in the black community. As a black woman and a sociologist, there is a conflict of interest between my academic identity and my personal identity. Feminist scholar Daphne Patai refers to this dilemma as a confrontation of dual allegiances.[10] She points out that feminist researchers are concerned with fulfilling their academic obligations yet are equally committed to the "transformative politics" of feminism. Other women of color have also documented their experiences with the same dilemma.[11] In thinking about my own research, I am faced with some of the same questions: *Whose research is this, and for whom do I intend the knowledge that I produce? Do I have a responsibility to the black community? Do I allow my intuitions as a black woman to situate my work, or my knowledge as a sociologist to guide my research?* In order to answer these questions, sociologist Miriam Glucksmann recommends that feminist researchers go into their research projects openly aware that inequities and divisions of knowledge will always exist and that, despite the goals of producing "feminist" research, it is unlikely that researchers will ever achieve a balance of knowledge and power.[12] As she explains, "No amount of sensitivity or reciprocity . . . can alter the fact that while the task of the researcher is to produce knowledge, those being researched have a quite different interest in and relation to their situation."[13] Without a doubt, my objective in this research is to get black women talking about the impact of colorism in the black community. Moreover, I am hopeful about developing concrete strategies for social change; I am constantly reminded that my research must address the "So what, who cares?" question. This important line of inquiry challenges me as a researcher to find relevance, significance, and meaning in the work that I do for the women involved in this research project and for those of you who are reading this book, looking for concrete and accessible answers to this pressing social problem. To address this dilemma of personal and academic conflict, it is important for me to maintain a reflective practice throughout the research process.

Dilemma #2: If You Study Colorism, Why Aren't You *Living* It?

I vividly recall one afternoon in the last year of my doctoral program at the University of Florida. I was discussing my work on colorism with a fellow doctoral student—also a black woman and sociologist—and we were talking about my findings, analysis, and the dissertation writing process. As we were talking, my friend asked me a question that I was not prepared for: How can you conduct research on colorism and wear a relaxer? A bit stunned, it took me a moment to "process" the depths of her inquiry. She went on to explain that it seemed a bit hypocritical; how could I produce such empowering work while simultaneously reinforcing the very hegemonic, white racial ideals of female beauty that I strive to challenge? Wouldn't I be better positioned for "true" colorism work if I wore my hair natural? In some way, I believe my friend (who was herself a proud naturalista) was trying to stage a hair intervention with me that day.

Two years later, I was giving a lecture in my Colorism in the U.S. course (made up of approximately 25 black students and 6 white students) when the conversation of skin tone bias and discrimination shifted to my personal life. Several of my black male students expressed their disappointment with me after meeting my then fiancé the previous week. (Our class hosted a university-wide symposium on colorism, and the students had met him there.)

"Dr. Wilder," one student asked, "how can you be so passionate about colorism and decide to marry a light-skinned, biracial man? We expected more from you." The students went on to explain that they envisioned that I would (and even should) marry a dark-skinned man because I was so "pro-black." In their minds, my decision to marry someone with light skin was a violation of some unwritten code of anticolorism activism and advocacy.

My friend and my students believed that my private life and my public work on colorism were not congruent because my hair was chemically relaxed and my partner at the time was biracial. There have been similar concerns leveled at me from other members of the black community, and to be quite honest, I have reflected deeply (and perhaps a bit too long) on these issues. Does my decision (and more importantly, my struggle over the years to completely "transition" back to my natural hair) to straighten my hair every other month make me a less competent—or even less authentic—ambassador of colorism studies? Might my message receive more validation from the black community if I made a conscious choice to date only dark-skinned black men? Why should I even care?

Truth is, my dilemma speaks to the paradoxical nature of colorism. While black folks who are knowledgeable about the havoc that colorism wreaks in the lives of black women, those same people (intentionally and unintentionally) reinforce colorism. Further, as someone who regularly teaches and researches colorism, I am still bothered and impacted when I am confronted with it. The notion that the ideal colorism "scholar" must be an all-natural sista with a dark-skinned partner (nothing wrong with either one of these, by the way) only reinforces the normative views of light skin and dark skin (and sexism) in black culture. (Would anyone openly challenge a black male scholar of African American culture for sportin' waves over dreads and choosing a light-skinned partner?) This struggle is all too real; a colorist mindset is very difficult to break for even some of the most socially and politically conscious people of color.

Dilemma #3: How Can Black People Be Racist?

In the spring of 2013, I gave a talk for an organization hosting an event aimed at combating racism within their local community. In that speech, I encouraged the audience to tackle the difficult dialogues attached to race, including how people of color—just like white folks—are capable of being racist. At the end of my talk, I fielded a few questions from the audience. A white woman, who was clearly agitated, stood up and admonished me in front of the group of 50 about my comment. She pointed out to me that it was impossible for black people and other minorities to be racist because they did not have (white) privilege or power. The sassy sista in me wanted to "check" this lady for her "all-wise, all-knowing position," given that she was not black nor a race scholar. I respectfully disagreed with her, first pointing out that while people of color do not have the power or privilege to be racist on a structural level, black folks can be racist on an individual level.[14] Secondly, I asked this woman if she had ever heard of colorism. She replied no. Colorism, I explained, was a form of racism that enabled black people to exert power and privilege (albeit on a much smaller scale than white racist structures) over each other from within the black community. As this woman took her seat, I was reminded of just how complicated colorism work can be.

This particular dilemma is a very controversial one in the black community, and I recognize that there are plenty of black Americans and black sociologists—especially earlier generations of African Americans who grew up in the Civil Rights movements of the 1960s and before—who may vehemently disagree with my position. However, the existence of colorism, from the wide range of exclusionary color practices that flourished in the early half of the 20th century to the more contemporary expressions of color bias, underscores the presence of racism and, more importantly, the capacity for black people to practice interpersonal racism.

I understand that colorism is not an easy topic to address. Further, I acknowledge that in researching this subject as a black woman and a sociologist, I walk a fine line between community responsibility and professional duty. I am aware that my research must begin with my own self-reflection. Like many other black feminist researchers, I know that there is no easy solution to these dilemmas, and it remains difficult to produce emancipatory research that is neither disempowering nor oppressive in any way.

GOING PUBLIC: COLORISM ON THE RISE

The Public Presence of Black Women

In 1851, when African American abolitionist and women's rights activist Sojourner Truth spoke at the Women's Convention in Akron, Ohio, she asked a simple question: *Ain't I a Woman?*[15] Over time, this dialectic of recognition, humanity, and equality has become an enduring question for black women in American society. As many black women scholars have illustrated, black women are still searching for agency, dignity, and visibility in a white, male-dominated world.

On a regular basis, black women have to contend with *separation anxiety*: separating who we are as distinct individuals from the negative, one-dimensional stereotypes and distorted images (including Mammy, the Welfare Mother, and the newly pervasive "side-chick")[16] that have constrained black womanhood since slavery. As a black female professor at a predominately white institution, I often find myself in a position of invalidating these injurious stereotypes in defense of my real self. In many aspects of life for black women and girls, there is room for growth and improvement. However, there are two stories to be told about black womanhood today. In the 21st century, black women and girls are accomplishing things we have never accomplished before. We are trailblazers in education, politics, sports, music, business, and many other arenas. Every day, black women and girls are breaking barriers, defying stereotypes, and challenging the odds. From the three generations of black women currently residing in the White House (Marian Robinson and Michelle, Sasha, and Malia Obama) to Xerox CEO Ursula Burns (the first African American woman to head a Fortune 500 company) to screenwriter and producer Shonda Rhimes (and the black female actresses Chandra Wilson, Kerry Washington, Aja Nicole Naomi King, and Viola Davis, who are a part of ShondaLand) to the wildly popular Disney character "Doc McStuffins," images of black women and girls today are broad and diverse. While these larger-than-life ladies are broadening the imagery of black womanhood, the successes of everyday black women have similarly worked to reshape and redefine the societal definitions of the black female experience in the 21st century.

As the presence of black women in more mainstream audiences has increased, the lives, experiences, and unique perspectives of black women has reached a level of mainstream familiarity and understanding. Before, the lens of black womanhood was tilted inward, and our issues and concerns were voiced (and resolved) from within our communities. Now, as the individual and collective stories of black women have more reach and legitimacy, matters pertaining to black women are more public. Purposefully or not, everyday black women and celebrities alike have become public griots, sharing their personal stories of resilience and liberation to reflect a collective reclamation, empowerment, and self-definition of black womanhood. On the matters of black women and colorism, black women themselves have used their mainstream platforms and spheres of influence to give voice, truth, and power to their personal and community struggles with colorism. As visual artist and writer Tania Balan-Gaubert explains in an essay she penned on black women and colorism,

> Many black women aim to deconstruct the light skin versus dark skin dichotomy that prevails over most experiences with colorism. Several aim to decolonize beauty standards as a means to dismantle understandings on skin color discrimination. As a result, some women have integrated color complex and racial identity discourse into their public campaigns for black female empowerment. By providing spaces

for black women to air their struggles with self-acceptance, many are making strides to tackle colorism head on. With the popularity of social media platforms, blogging, and other online media outlets, women are discussing colorism and promoting healthy skin acceptance at an unprecedented rate.[17]

There are many examples of this:

In June of 2014, *Today Show* anchor Tamron Hall debuted her natural hair—as she described on Twitter, sans flat iron or chemicals—on the air of the popular NBC morning show, which averages 3.5 million viewers each day. That day, the popular journalist received overwhelmingly positive praise via social media for the curly version of her trademark pixie cut.[18]

Actress Lupita Nyong'o's meteoric rise to stardom provided her with a series of high-profile opportunities to shed light on her struggles with colorism. At the 2014 Essence Awards Black Women in Hollywood Luncheon, the starlet shared:

I remember a time when I too felt unbeautiful. I put on the TV and only saw pale skin. I got teased and taunted about my night-shaded skin. And my one prayer to God, the miracle worker, was that I would wake up lighter skinned. The morning would come and I would be so excited about seeing my new skin that I would refuse to look down at myself until I was in front of a mirror because I wanted to see my fair face first. And every day I experienced the same disappointment of being just as dark as I was the day before. I tried to negotiate with God; I told him I would stop stealing sugar cubes at night if he gave me what I wanted, I would listen to my mother's every word and never lose my school sweater again if he just made me a little lighter. But I guess God was unimpressed with my bargaining chips because He never listened.[19]

Oprah Winfrey and Iyanla Vanzant brought the topic of colorism to Oprah's *Lifeclass*. The January 10, 2014 episode brought the secret shame of colorism to both a live audience and social media community in a discussion centered on "how colorism affects people around the world."[20]

These public declarations—and many other stories—are oftentimes shared and exchanged through black women's blogging spaces and online media outlets. In addition to *Essence Magazine*, the oldest magazine for black women, there are numerous other sites and blogs, including *Clutch Magazine*, *Madame Noire*, *MyBrownBaby*, and *Sesi Magazine Online* that are geared toward an African American female audience. Many of these online sources provide a platform for affirming and empowering black women and girls. For instance, the following excerpt from the *For Harriet* website (named in honor of black female abolitionist Harriet Tubman), whose mantra is "celebrating the fullness of black womanhood,"[21] describes their mission in the following statement:

> For Harriet is an online community for women of African ancestry. We encourage women, through storytelling and journalism, to engage in candid, revelatory dialogue about the beauty and complexity of Black womanhood. We aspire to educate, inspire, and entertain. For Harriet seeks to raise the level of discourse surrounding Black women. Founder and Editor, Kimberly Foster, launched the blog in June 2010 while still an undergraduate at Harvard University to provide a thoughtful, collaborative alternative to mainstream media representations of Black womanhood. Thus, For Harriet seeks to explore all parts of who we are and who we hope to be.[21]

The blog's founder, Kimberly Foster, uses her website (which currently has over 120,000 Facebook "likes" and 33,000 followers on Twitter) to speak to many issues germane to the black female experience, like colorism.

Similarly, *Bougie Black Girl*, an online media platform designed to empower black women, has been successful in creating a space for black women's voices (in fact, an avatar of a black girl serves as the banner for the blogsite, with the caption "I refuse to be silenced"). The site's creator, navy veteran and business maven Lakisha Watson-Moore, developed a Declaration page on the blog, which states the following:

> I proudly declare . . .
> I am a proud Black woman.
> I am the original woman and true reflection of the creator's image.
> My womb birthed many nations.
> I love myself deeply, completely, and unconditionally.
> Every inch of myself is intelligent, beautiful, graceful, and amazing.
> I am limitless, fearless, and unique.
> I am a creator and an innovator.
> I am not a mule, but focused on myself.
> I am not invisible and I will be heard.
> I will not coddle those who benefit from my or others' oppression.
> I will stand up for myself and the ancient people whose blood gave
>   life to me.

I will ignore those who challenge these declarations because I know my worth and I see the truth.

I want to welcome you to this blog where I write about issues that empower the lives of Black Women.

—Bougie Black Girl[22]

According to the site, *Bougie Black Girl* boasts more than 46,000 views per month and 13,000 Facebook endorsers and caters to a predominately black female audience (87 percent) between the ages of 15 and 65 years old. At the time of my online research, the most popular post on the website was related to colorism: "30 Light Skin Privileges Light Skin Blacks Have that Dark Skin Blacks Don't." Both of these online platforms and the many others like it embody the core principles of liberation and self-definition, indicative of the growing presence of a black feminist standpoint online. As black feminist scholars remind us, everyday black women are agents of knowledge, truth, and change. We are all equally capable of the intellectual production of a black feminist perspective. And these virtual mediums give us the opportunity to connect with one another, amplify our color stories, and work together for change.

The Growth of Black Feminist Scholars and Public Intellectualism

An interconnected factor in shaping the more public discourse of colorism in the 21st century is the rise of black female public intellectuals. In 2013, I co-authored a journal article with Tamara Bertrand and La'Tara Osborne-Lampkin in which we discussed the achievements of black women in higher education in the 21st century. While black women do not yet represent a critical mass within the academy as faculty, we account for the majority—55 percent—of new black PhDs entering the professoriate.[23] This growth has several implications. Growing numbers of black female scholars in the academy means that there are more black women in the academy teaching and researching about the issues affecting black women.

This is not to suggest that all black women in the academy are teaching and researching about black women's issues—nor should they feel responsible or obligated to do so. Further, all black women do not share the same issues. Yet, the voice and reach of black female intellectuals is growing louder and stronger. There is also a growing contingency of black female scholars engaging in "21st-century public scholarship." Rutgers University professor Dr. Brittany Cooper—also known as "Professor Crunk"— describes in a March 2014 piece she wrote for *Salon* Magazine what this means in her work:

Part of what being a public scholar means, though, is a facility of writing for more than one audience. For scholars of color like myself, it means we do double duty. We write what we need for tenure. We write in obscure terms so that we can prove that knowledge about black people and people of color is "rigorous" and meets accepted academic standards. And then many of us turn to public speaking, radio, podcasts, blogs and Twitter to translate that knowledge in ways that are useful to our communities. None of that work will get us tenure, and it might come with accusations that we are being distracted from doing the more valuable work of academe. But we do it anyway.[24]

The regular practice of public scholarship enables black women to use their own experiences as academics as a platform to discuss the broader issues facing black women inside and outside the academy. The work and public presence of Brittney Cooper and other scholars such as Julianne Malveaux, Melissa Harris-Perry, and Imani Perry show the contemporary legacy of the black female intellectual tradition of scholarship and activism that began with the likes of Anna Julia Cooper and Mary McLeod Bethune. Similar to those scholars and many others, I use my work as a vehicle for debate, reflection, and discussion on the nature of discrimination and inequality for black women today. I have done this in many ways to raise awareness about the issue of colorism. One example is through a blog post I wrote about the prominence of colorism connected to the controversy over gymnast Gabby Douglas's hair during the 2012 summer Olympics (see Sidebar 2). Black female academics are in the unique position of being able to shape and enhance these types of discussions by offering both a personal and scholarly perspective.

(Black) Social Media: A Platform for Circulating Truth and Spreading Hate

I can vividly recall the "world wide web" gaining ground in popularity and importance when I graduated from Allegheny College in 1997. Roughly 18 percent of American adults were using the Internet at that time.[25] Not even two decades later, the Internet has moved from a place of limited networking to the destination for everything. With the advent of virtual communities and the growth of Internet activity, there now exists a myriad of social networking sites (Facebook, Instagram, Twitter, Tumblr, Pinterest, LinkedIn, and YouTube) that provide a platform for not only sharing information but also discussing pertinent social, political, and cultural issues.

For a long time, there was a significant "digital divide" among racial/ethnic minorities and their white counterparts. In 2000, only 35 percent of black Americans had access to the Internet, compared to 50 percent of white Americans.[26] By 2011, 71 percent of African Americans were going online.[27] There is still a gap in the number of black households with a personal computer compared to white households, yet many folks in minority communities are joining online communities with their smartphones. A 2013 report from the *Pew Research Center* indicated that 81 percent of black Americans access the Internet from their mobile phones, compared to 85 percent of white Americans.[28] Thus, smartphones have essentially "leveled the playing field" in Internet access between whites and blacks.

The digital stratosphere, specifically the micro-blogging site *Twitter,* has quickly become a virtual "ground zero" for many people in the black community to discuss pertinent issues affecting African Americans. This particular social networking medium is quite popular among black social media users. While only 15 percent of online users tweet on the networking site, 28 percent of African Americans with access to the Internet use Twitter.[29] This is responsible for the growth of "Black Twitter," a subculture within the broader population of Twitter users who create witty hashtags (#) as a platform for activism and resistance. In many ways, the Black Twitter movement of today is reminiscent of the sit-in movements of the 1960s. (Black feminist blogger Feminista Jones even compared Black Twitter to the Underground Railroad.)[30] Aimed at raising awareness about racial inequality and justice, Black Twitter functions as the social mouthpiece of the black community and is likened by some as the gateway to contemporary African American activism. Further, many of these online discussions that start on Black Twitter provide the momentum for organizing many on-the-ground rallies and protests. Many recent events, including the George Zimmerman trial; the deaths of Jordan Davis, Michael Brown, and Eric Garner; the Donald Sterling and Paula Deen scandals; and even the kidnapping of several hundred Nigerian schoolgirls have resulted in viral campaigns and subsequent hashtags including #iftheygunnedmedown, #blacklivesmatter, #dangerousblackkids, and #bringbackourgirls.

Black Twitter has proven to wield a significant amount of political influence in raising consciousness and public awareness about some of this century's most important racial matters. Notwithstanding, the networking site (in conjunction with other social media platforms) has not been so kind to the typically delicate and private matters of skin tone. An unintended consequence of the newly public discourse on colorism is the overt nature of bias, discrimination, and overall hating that can circulate instantaneously and in "real-time." In fact, through the creation (and continued usage) of hashtags such as #teamlightskin and #teamdarkskin, among others (see

Figure 2), social media platforms provide members of the black community with new ways to reinforce and perpetuate internalized racism virtually and somewhat anonymously. People can weigh in and reinforce (or, at times, dismantle) colorist ideology with a simple post, (re)tweet, or like.

This was perhaps best personified during *State of Florida v. George Zimmerman*, the second-degree murder prosecution of 29-year-old George Zimmerman. On February 26, 2012, the mixed-race, Hispanic man shot and killed Trayvon Martin, an unarmed African American teenager walking home from a convenience store. Zimmerman mistook 17-year-old Martin for a community trespasser and got into an altercation with the teen when confronting him about his presence in the Sanford, Florida, neighborhood. George Zimmerman claimed that Trayvon Martin attacked him and that he shot Trayvon in self-defense.

Undeniably one of the most significant events shaping the racial landscape of the early 21st century, the death of 17-year-old Trayvon Martin sparked a tense national debate about the nature of modern-day racism, racial profiling, the state of Florida's controversial *Stand Your Ground*

Figure 2: A Sampling of Popular Colorism Hashtags

self-defense law, and gun control. Many people believed that Trayvon Martin was murdered because he was unfairly stereotyped as a criminal.

When George Zimmerman's trial began in June of 2013, millions of people in the United States and around the world watched the various aspects of the legal proceedings unfold. Conversations about race and racism were prohibited inside the courtroom; however, outside—in the court of public opinion—"race talk" was palpable. There were many memorable aspects of the trial, but perhaps nothing amplified issues of race more than Witness No. 8, Rachel Jeantel, Trayvon Martin's close friend and the last person to speak to the young man. Jeantel, who was a 19-year-old 12th grader at the time, spent a grueling two days on the witness stand. At the end of her first day of testimony, social media—particularly Twitter—was set ablaze with negative and disparaging commentary about this young woman.

Many people supported Rachel Jeantel for her courage and grit on the witness stand, yet the bulk of the remarks (made by black and non-black folks alike) about Trayvon Martin's friend were denigrating. Rachel was vilified for her demeanor on the witness stand. Ms. Jeantel's credibility, intelligence, and morality were called into question as such adjectives as "ignorant," "hostile," and "thuggish" were used to describe the young woman, who is also a first-generation Haitian immigrant and non-native English speaker. After the first day of Rachel's testimony, Molly West, the daughter of Don West—one of the (white) attorneys on George Zimmerman's defense team—posted a "selfie" of herself, her sister, and father on Instagram, an online photo-sharing networking site. The picture showed the three family members enjoying ice cream cones. West's daughter posted the picture with the caption, "We beat stupidity celebration #zimmerman #defense #dadkilledit." The following are more examples of tweets posted on Twitter following the first day of Rachel Jeantel's testimony:

This Rachel Jeantel witness is dumber than a box of rocks. Zimmerman might get off.

Trayvons parents were like damn our son was hitting that?!?!?! #pussyfail #nastybitch #RachelJeantel

Rachel Jeantel hurt more black folks today than 1,000,000 Paula Deens singing 10 lil niggas

Rachel Jeantel has absolutely no respect for this country's judicial system. Humanity as a whole should be embarrassed. #TravonMartinTrial

In addition, Rachel Jeantel's physical appearance was mocked as many people compared her to the animated cartoon character Shrek (a large, green male ogre) and also to Precious—the 16-year-old obese, illiterate protagonist in the 2009 film of the same name. Light-skinned, biracial track star and Olympian Lolo Jones was heavily criticized for her remarks about Jeantel. On June 27, 2013, the famous athlete tweeted, "Rachel Jeantel looked so irritated during the cross-examination that I burned it on DVD and I'm going to sell it as Madea goes to court." Jones, who is no stranger to social media controversy, was referring to the fictional character Madea popularized by African American director Tyler Perry.

Shortly after Jeantel's testimony, The *New York Times* published an article on the impact of race in the Zimmerman trial. I offered my sociological perspective to the piece and specifically on the public's treatment of Rachel Jeantel:

> She was "mammyfied," said Ms. Wilder, the sociology professor, expressing disappointment over the reaction. "She has this riveting testimony, then she became, overnight, the teenage mammy: for not being smart and using these racial slurs and not being the best witness. A lot of people in the African American community came out against her."[31]

During my interview with the reporter who wrote about the case, I was careful to point out that in my mind—as a sociologist and race expert—this trial exposed not only the deep issues of race in our society but reflected vestiges of colorism as well. That piece of the conversation did not make it into the final edit of the newspaper article, but they are relevant here. When scores of people began insulting Rachel Jeantel, their invectives reinforced and normalized two historically negative images of black women. The first is the aforementioned *mammy* caricature—a dark-skinned, overweight, asexual and, at times, thoughtless (i.e., devoid of deep intellectual capacity) black woman—an image pervasive in American media and popular culture since the 18th century. The second depiction is that of the *angry black woman*, a socially constructed image of a confrontational, aggressive, and bitter woman who is always upset and has a perpetual "attitude." I shared with the *Times* reporter my personal belief that if Rachel Jeantel looked different, she would have been treated differently. If Rachel were light skinned, she probably would have been seen as more relatable and friendly. I also believe that had Rachel been thin, middle-class, and dark skinned *but* with facial features similar to Kenyan actress Lupita Nyong'o, she may have been extended more dignity and compassion. After all, the young woman was the only witness to a terrible tragedy.

As a black woman, Rachel Jeantel is already subject to multiple levels of oppression by virtue of her race and gender. This is what Kimberlé Williams Crenshaw and other feminist scholars of color refer to as the notion of *intersectionality*.[32] And regardless of skin tone, many black women are objectified (typically as hypersexual or asexual—and presumably, heterosexual) in a sexual manner. Yet, the unfortunate combination of Rachel Jeantel's race, class, gender, ethnicity (there are many negative stereotypes associated with Haiti), *and* color compounded the subjugation and pure vitriol she experienced by people of all races. However, given the internal knowledge of colorism within the African American community, many black folks were armed with more ammunition to degrade and assail the young woman's character and personhood in a particularly colorist way.

The irony here is that during this trial, Black Twitter became a veritable force in social media due to the overwhelming support of slain teen Trayvon Martin and the public cry for justice in his death. Black journalist Whitney Teal pointed to this paradox in her 2013 piece in *Clutch Magazine*. She writes: "I'm so confused. What happened to the "We Are All Trayvon" solidarity from just a few months ago? Remember? We all wore black hoodies and posted the pics on our Facebook pages. Trayvon was everyone's child, at least for a time. Why aren't we extending that same graciousness and sense of human decency to Jeantel?"[33] Teal raises an important question, one that we can look to the roots of (gendered) colorism that is deeply embedded within black America for the answer. The undue surveillance, criticism, and cruelty circulated through social media are some of the negative consequences of the increased presence of black women and colorism in public discourse. This visibility is precisely what Patricia Hill Collins discusses as the "new politics of containment" in her work, *Fighting Words*. She writes, "The public sphere becomes a curiously confined yet visible location that increases the value of private services and privacy itself. Public spaces become devalued spaces containing poor people, African-Americans, and anyone else who cannot afford to escape."[34] The high-profile George Zimmerman case, viewed in many public spaces across the globe, resulted in the erasure of citizenship, humanity, liberation, and ultimately voice for Rachel Jeantel. This young woman's broken silence did not represent freedom; rather, it reinforced the powerful negative images of black womanhood that have been persistent across time and space.

Colorism Studies: A Growth Industry in the Academy

Writers, poets, social scientists, filmmakers, and everyday black people alike have been fixated on colorism for more than 150 years. The issue of skin color in the black community has graced the pages of many literary and academic works and works of popular culture dating back to the mid-1800s. William Wells Brown, author of the first black American novel, was the first to document the complexity of skin tone in the 1853 classic *Clotel*. Since then, color consciousness has seeped through the pages of black epics such as *The Blacker the Berry*, *The Bluest Eye*, and *The Color Purple*, and films such as Spike Lee's *School Daze* and Oprah Winfrey's *The Wedding*. This robust body of work indicates the persistence of skin tone bias and discrimination over time in black American culture.

In the academy, issues of colorism in the black community have been at the center of analysis and discussion of many scholars' work for more than a century. However, *colorism studies*—a term that I use to describe the interdisciplinary field of academic work devoted to understanding the meaning, significance, and implications of colorism for black Americans and other people of color across the globe—has become a growth industry over the past 20 years. An increasing number of race scholars are specializing in this subfield of contemporary race studies. The growth of this kind of work has undoubtedly aided in transforming colorism into a public topic garnering widespread academic and social attention.

This has not always been the case. I enrolled in a terminal master's degree program in sociology in the fall of 2000. While I was uncertain about pursuing a doctorate in sociology, I was sure about completing a master's degree and even more certain that I wanted to write my master's thesis on colorism. Because I had already conducted an undergraduate thesis on this topic just three years earlier at Allegheny College, I was ready to jump right into my graduate project. I made an appointment to meet with the graduate advisor to inform her of my decision and to formalize a plan of action. As I excitedly shared my research goals with my professor, she stopped me midsentence and replied, "No, you can't do that topic. It's not sociological." Confused, I assured my advisor that colorism was indeed a sociological topic and one that warranted further examination. I even showed her a copy of Charles Parrish's classic 1946 sociological study, *Color Names and Color Notions*. Unimpressed, this professor stood her ground and cautioned me that there was not a large enough body of literature on this topic and that I would be better served by choosing another topic with a larger body of research to draw from. I was devastated. It was apparent that this sociologist—who incidentally was white—was unfamiliar with colorism and that she did not recognize its larger importance within the field of sociology, race, and the study of black life. I made two decisions that day: to pursue my PhD in sociology and to write my dissertation on colorism.

I finished my master's thesis on another topic and completed my MA in sociology in 2002. By the time I enrolled in my doctoral program at the University of Florida in 2004, the field of colorism studies was emerging as a significant field of academic inquiry. Today, there are hundreds of peer-reviewed journal articles on many aspects of colorism—skinbleaching, hip-hop lyrics, employment discrimination, sport and physical education, self-esteem, family dynamics, advertising, and school suspension. A wide range of scholars representing an even broader range of academic disciplines—from sociology to education to women's studies to public health—are examining colorism, and this "academic awakening" has been solidified in the 21st century. The vast majority of academic studies on colorism have been published *after* 2000. A fair amount of this work has been in the form of master's theses and doctoral dissertations. For instance, conducting a basic search in the ProQuest dissertation and master theses database using the terms *African Americans* and *colorism* yields 843 results of work published since 1988. When refining this search to work published after the year 2000, 723 items, or 86 percent, of graduate-level research on colorism was completed in the 21st century.

The burgeoning field of colorism studies has fashioned a new space in the academy for students and scholars to debate, discuss, and explore the contemporary nature of colorism. Perhaps more importantly, this newer body of literature has given individuals the platform to launch more work in this area. Take, for instance, the following email I received from a doctoral student in counseling psychology completing her dissertation on colorism and its influence upon life success for women of color. She writes in a communication from March 2014:

> I have been a huge fan of yours since 2009 when I found your dissertation on colorism online. I am a doctoral candidate at ["X-institution"]. I am fortunate to have Dr. X, a leading multicultural psychologist as my doctoral advisor, dissertation chair, and friend. Currently, I am working on my dissertation.
>
> I happened upon the construct of colorism during my residency research in [X], a year-long qualitative research project that involved interviews with dual-diagnosis, homeless women living in shelters in [Big City]. When asked the question, "what is the most difficult or challenging thing you have dealt with in your life," all of the women of color cited a colorism experience involving their mother or grandmother. I was deeply moved as I listened to the heart-wrenching stories of these dear women who spoke with tears flowing down their faces. I was also surprised because these women had survived every

form of trauma a woman can experience, addiction to heroin and/or cocaine and other drugs; domestic and other forms of violence, prostitution to support their habits, having their children removed from their care, on and on. Yet, **they counted their colorism experience as the most painful thing they had experienced.** There was little current literature at the time that I conducted my residency research, and I was very grateful to have found your dissertation, and the references that you cited. Thank you.

Because of the growing field of colorism studies in the academy, this student has the space and the literature to examine issues of skin tone among women of color in treatment, and her dissertation has the potential to influence the field of counseling psychology in a new way. Unlike my experience in my master's program, this woman will have the support and room to make a meaningful contribution to her specific area and the broader field of colorism studies.

Further, the existence of colorism studies within the academy has exposed individuals who may have no previous experience and/or frame of reference for color bias to important background information typically not afforded to "cultural outsiders." The above-mentioned student is white, and because she is not black, she did not have any prior knowledge—academic or personal—of skin tone bias and stratification within communities of color. Because colorism has long operated as a secret among African Americans—and black folk are oftentimes taught *not* to discuss this issue in the presence of "mixed company"—nonminority group members are unable to recognize or consider how issues of skin tone may play a role in their research involving people of color. Note this doctoral student's "surprise" in hearing about the women of color's experiences with colorism. Contemporary academic studies on colorism fill a much-needed "gap of knowledge" for students and scholars who aim to more completely understand the lives of people of color.

Furthermore, there are black female faculty in the academy—including Donnamaria Culbreth, editor of the academic journal *Journal of Colorism Studies* and founder of the Interracial Colorism Project, and legal scholar Kimberly Norwood, organizer of the Global Perspectives of Colorism professional conference—who have leveraged their unique positions as black women and academics to shape and enhance the discourse on colorism by offering both personal and scholarly perspectives to the ivory tower and our communities. The presence of their work and the growing field of colorism studies ensure that no student who wants to study colorism will be discouraged in the same way that I was dismissed in my advisor's office over a decade ago. Finally in the academy, the voice of colorism is increasingly louder and evolving.

Sidebar 2. Why Don't We Like Her Hair?

Sounding Off on Gabby Douglas, Colorism, and Why *Black Hate* Is Just as Endemic to Black American Culture as *Black Pride*

Unpublished Blogpost, August 2012

Like countless other people across the globe, I love the Olympic Games. There is just something about cheering on my fellow Americans to their quest for gold that makes me proud. As an African American, it is one of the few times in my life when my race fades to the background and my nationality—my Americanness—becomes most important. Yet, as I was watching the coverage of the women's gymnastics competition, I was quickly reminded why my blackness is so much more salient.

Sixteen-year-old Gabby Douglas made history as she twirled her way to being the first African American to win gold in the individual all-around competition. As a black woman and mother, I was so proud of our beautiful "flying squirrel." Yet, I am ashamed to admit that as a sociologist and race scholar, one of my first thoughts as I watched Gabby sing the national anthem on the winner's podium was, "Too bad there was no one in London who could do her hair . . ."

Immediately, I was jarred by this racist remark. That's right—what I thought to myself, and what countless others have taken to social media to comment on—is, in fact, racist. More accurately, this internalized criticism reflects many dimensions of *colorism,* a form of racism in the black community that has separated individuals based on their skin color, facial features, and hair texture since the days of slavery.

For many black women and girls, hair is central to our identity. Black women spend considerable amounts of time and even more money getting our hair "done." It is oftentimes a rite of passage, a site of socialization, and, ultimately, a point of pride.

The obsession with Gabby Douglas's "undone" hair reflects the long-standing history of a colorist mindset that has elevated and privileged whiteness in our society (typically DONE HAIR = ACCEPTABLE

HAIR=WHITE=GOOD), while simultaneously deflating and devalu-ing blackness (UNDONE HAIR=UNACCEPTABLE=BLACK=BAD). Having unproductive conversations about Gabby's hair (e.g. *Is there really no place to get her hair done in London? Why would her mother allow her to be seen on a worldwide stage with her hair like that?*) holds this young woman to an unfair standard of acceptance and beauty and reduces her remarkable accomplishments to a frenzy over a coif rather than her craft.

Ask yourself: did anyone care much about white swimmer Missy Franklin's undone, wet hair as she stepped on the winner's podium to claim her gold medal? Further, did we nod in approval when we saw the likes of Alison Felix, Carmelita Jeter, Sonya Richards Ross, and the Williams sisters donning fresh relaxers, perfectly gelled edges and fly weaves? Why is it so hard for us in the black community to simply be happy for Gabby Douglas?

The answer is because *black hate* is just as much a part of African American culture as *black pride*.

For centuries, blacks have received negative messages about who we are (unattractive, unintelligent, unworthy, etc.). These messages originated within colonialist white ideologies and institutions. In response to the negative imagery and stereotypes, African Americans have adopted a cultural resiliency and black pride. While as a group we have worked very hard to re-define these stereotypes, we still struggle with disabling the mental shackles of slavery that have black culture suffering from a bipolarity of sorts—a love-hate, or *black pride-black hate* identity complex.

It is no surprise, then, that black people are so pressed (pardon the pun) about Gabby Douglas's hair.

The undue attention placed on this young woman's ponytail high-lights the alarming discourse of negativity and inferiority still alive and well within contemporary black America.

As black people, we need to spend less time tearing each other down and more time elevating the accomplishments of our young people, especially young black girls. Let's celebrate what Gabby Douglas represents for the black community and for America, and let's learn from her new legacy.

CHAPTER 2

Understanding "Everyday Colorism": Theoretical Considerations

I regularly teach Sociological Theory, a class aimed at exposing students to the origins of the discipline of sociology and engaging both classical and contemporary thinkers' views of our social world. Many students come into the course with a great deal of anxiety and trepidation at the thought of having to analyze and understand material that is (in their minds) centuries old, with no relevance to life today. However, as we engage the lives and works of individuals like Karl Marx, W.E.B Du Bois, and C. Wright Mills, the connection and significance of theory becomes clear. By the completion of each class, students share how they grew to understand the critical importance and value sociological theory has to sociology today. More importantly, they recognize precisely how theory is the "glue" holding all the essential pieces of sociological research, practice, and discourse together.

The same logic applies here. In order to grasp the modern-day implications of colorism—*and* to fully appreciate the context for and advancement of colorism research—we must first engage with theory. The questions and perspectives surrounding the nature of skin tone in black America have been examined, re-examined, and revised for more than a century. From W.E.B. Du Bois's conceptualization of a *colortocracy*[1] to Jennifer Hochschild and Vesla Weaver's recent theory of the *skin color paradox,*[2] many of the key ideas and explanations of colorism have been grounded within theories of race and racism. In other words, many scholars who study colorism rely heavily on racial paradigms to situate and explain the issue; as such, colorism is viewed as a consequence and extension of racism. Because of the common scholarly coupling of race and color, social scientists have developed a wide range of empirical studies exploring color bias and discrimination in African American communities. However, conceptual frameworks of colorism have remained undertheorized over time. As sociologist Linda Burton and colleagues explain in their scholarly review of critical race theories and colorism research in the area of family studies in the new millennium,

> Nonetheless, the conceptual discourse about colorism burgeoned during this decade in response to shifting color lines in the American population, interracial couplings and childrearing, and recognition by race and stratification scholars of the global pervasiveness of colorism practices. This discourse did not lead to formal colorism theories, but it heightened researchers' sensitivities to important racial and ethnic subtexts and processes (e.g., intragroup racism) in family life that required vigilant attention of family researchers.[3]

As I share with my students, theories inform research and knowledge production. In the 21st century, as the racial dynamics of our society change, the "color line" becomes simultaneously invisible and deeper, and as the discourse of colorism increases within our societal sphere, scholars must consider how to push theories of colorism from the margins to the center of race theorizing.

This chapter aims to bridge this gap by presenting my theory of *everyday colorism*, a theoretical framework originating from my research on black women's experiences with colorism. I begin with a brief meta-synthesis of the foundational ideals of colorism theory, examining the classical and contemporary perspectives on colorism. I then move to a discussion of the work of C. Wright Mills, Patricia Hill Collins, and Philomena Essed—three sociologists whose perspectives are vital in shaping my theoretical lens of everyday colorism. Lastly, I detail the structure of everyday colorism as a critical starting point for conceptualizing the continuing significance of colorism in the 21st century.

DEFINING KEY CONCEPTS

Race, *racism*, *color*, and *colorism* are important concepts in this overview, and thus they should be defined accordingly. Highly complex and controversial, the construct of *race* and the way we talk about the concept in the United States is defined by presumed biological differences based on the phenotypic identifiers of skin tone, hair texture, and facial features. As many contemporary race scholars have noted, race is not biologically real; rather, it is a social construct. Sociologists Matthew Desmond and Mustafa Emirbayer precisely explain that race is "a symbolic category, based on phenotype or ancestry and constructed according to specific social and historical contexts, that is misrecognized as a natural category."[4] The origins of the race concept—and corresponding racial categories "black" and "white"—coincide with European colonial expansion into the Americas and, ultimately, African slavery in the 17th and 18th centuries.[5] Many scholars, including anthropologist Audrey Smedley, are quick to point out that race in the United States is also connected to a "global worldview," or set of attitudes that situates whiteness at the top of a "hierarchy of inequality."[6] *Racism*, then, is the differential treatment of individuals based upon their assigned or perceived racial category. According to race scholars Michael Omi and Howard Winant, racism involves the "creation and domination of structural domination based upon essentialist categories of race."[7] To that end, race and racism are rooted in the ideology of white domination and supremacy.[8]

A less commonly discussed aspect of race, racism (and thereby colorism), skin *color*, or pigmentation is the biological marker that anchored the "science" fueling racism. While human diversity, that is, phenotypic features—skin tone, hair texture, and facial features—is indeed real, the social and cultural meanings attached to these biological differences, especially skin color, is socially constructed. As Nina Jablonski expresses, "Skin color was the essential characteristic that gave race its social valence and established its place in an explicit hierarchy."[9] Colorism employs the same principles of race and color to reinforce a system of hierarchy and inequality based upon skin tone, hair texture, and facial features. The ideologies of colorism mirror the ideologies of racism: privilege and value are assigned to phenotypic features that are closer to white. It is important for people reading this book to understand that while the system of color prejudice operates on its own in the black community to privilege light skin over dark skin, *colorism is a byproduct of racism* and shares many of the same qualities and characteristics. For example, colorism, like racism, is deeply embedded within societal structures (e.g., education, politics, the media) and can be institutionalized. Recent commentary from black actresses including Gabrielle Union, Keke Palmer, Tika Sumpter, and Vanessa L. Williams highlight the long-standing struggle of both insitutionalized racism and colorism (and sexism, of course) for African American females in Hollywood. It is also important to clarify this point: while African Americans are not capable of insitutionalized racism (they lack the power to do so), colorism, however, has been perpetuated and rooted into our societal structures. This is due in large part to the broader system of white racial domination in American society. Black Americans have been responsible for maintaining the seeds of colorism that were originally planted (and still presently reinforced) by this larger system of white privilege.

Notwithstanding, a discrete yet unified (to race and racism, gender, and other interconnected social structures) understanding of colorism is essential. Given what we know about the origins of race and racism and, subsequently, the nature of colorism, I am offering the following five points as the distinguishing features of colorism in modern-day society:

1. Colorism operates internally *within* the black community. Referred to by some as *intraracial* colorism, this is the traditional way of understanding how the social phenomena functions among people of the same race.
2. Colorism can also operate externally and outside of communities of color. Recently, scholars have articulated this dynamic as *white colorism*, or *inter-racial* colorism. A non-black person can perpetuate colorism when they elevate or place a higher value (either consciously or subconsciously) on lighter skin, straight hair, and less "Afrocentric" facial features. (There is a substantial amount of academic research to support the notion that whites show favor toward blacks and other people of color with "white-sounding" names and "articulate" (i.e., white) diction in the areas of employment and housing.) We know that the same logic applies to skin tone. While some folks may find this hard to distinguish or separate from plain racism, there is a difference, and it underscores how racism and colorism are interconnected yet distinct.
3. Black and non-black individuals regularly participate in colorism in subtle and covert ways. Instances, experiences, and messages of skin tone bias can be blatant and intentional, yet they can also manifest in hidden and unintentional ways. There are many examples of this in the analyses that follow in Chapters 3–5.
4. Oftentimes, colorism operates within an already racialized context. That is, colorism can add an additional layer or element to an event or situation with racial implications. Take, for instance, the backlash against white disc jockey Don Imus, who in 2007 referred to the members of the Rutgers University women's basketball team as nappy-headed hoes and jigaboos. The majority of the team was comprised of black women, and his comment was not only blatantly racist but also colorist, given his

usage of derogatory terms that are offensive and particularly disparaging to dark-skinned individuals. (Director Spike Lee illustrated this is in the musical number "Straight and Nappy" in his 1988 film *School Daze*.) Imus was scolded for his racism, but fewer individuals placed an emphasis on the colorist nature of his actions.

5. Likewise, colorism can manifest itself or operate within a seemingly non-racial context. Mainstream events can appear unrelated to race or color but nevertheless cause an outpouring of dialogue and attention mediated by newer forms of public communication. A great example of this was the media attention over gymnast Gabby Douglas's hair during the 2012 Summer Olympics (see Sidebar 2 in Chapter 1).

While the above-mentioned characteristics reflect the nature of colorism, they do not unpack the important "how" questions related to skin tone bias and discrimination. The following section provides an important overview of scholarly theories on colorism.

THE TRADITIONS OF COLORISM THEORY

While somewhat small and marginal compared to the growing and robust field of empirical colorism studies, theoretical conceptualizations of colorism have nonetheless grown over time. Many of the theories used to explain skin tone bias and discrimination have been connected to either social theories of the black American experience and/or evolving theories of race and racism within a U.S. context. Although there is presently no body of work that provides a meta-synthesis of the theoretical models of colorism, this section begins this important effort. Today, the research and discourse on colorism occurs on a comparative and global scale. While these connections are both important and crucial to our understandings of the broader scope of colorism around the world, the theoretical traditions noted here are centered on the African American perspective.

Framing Colorism within Racial Epistemologies

Epistemology refers to the genesis of knowledge; it aims to explain *how* we know what we know. Moreover, epistemology helps us to understand who can know and what kind(s) of knowledge is privileged over others. Within the discipline of sociology, our epistemological framework surrounding race and racism in the United States has shifted and evolved over time. In her work, *Rethinking Epistemology, Methodology, and Racism: Or, Is White Sociology Really Dead?*[10] sociologist and colorism scholar Margaret

Hunter presents an important discussion of five key racial epistemologies and their influence upon research and knowledge production within the field of sociology. She writes:

> Each of these "ways of knowing" structures the method for conducting research, as well as for understanding race in society at large. [...] Epistemologies do not exist outside of the people who construct and use them. Individuals and groups adopt various epistemologies at different points in time to make sense of the world. Epistemologies are also not equal in status, in society at large, or in the academic community. Epistemologies are situated within political, historical, and economic contexts that can provide power and legitimacy to their knowledge claims.[11]

Hunter's objective is to discuss the diversity of racial knowledge production; however, three of the five racial epistemologies she uses in her work—the *Black/White racial* epistemology, the *Colonial Domination* epistemology, and the *Critical Intersectional* epistemology—are particularly useful in similarly framing the theoretical models of colorism. As such, I extend these models to outline the traditions of colorism theory.

Tradition 1. Colorism as a Consequence of American Slavery

Many scholars document the distinctive nature of race in the United States, which can be attributed to European colonization and the mass incarceration of West Africans into the institution of plantation slavery beginning in the 17th century. While the United States was not the only nation participating in the Atlantic Slave trade, the way in which the laws were shaped around racial mixing were indeed distinctive (refer to the Introduction for greater detail and explanation). Racial homogenization was encouraged within broader society, and strict racial classifications ensued. Although interracial intimate relationships occurred between blacks and whites at this time,[12] any mixed-race offspring born from these types of unions were deemed fully "black" in the eyes of the law. Among other things, this created a "race" of African Americans with a broad range of phenotypic differences and, ultimately, internalized divisions based upon skin tone, hair textures, and facial features within African American communities. Racially mixed blacks were afforded more advantage and opportunity before and after Emancipation. As such, slavery—and the subsequent "one-drop" rule and anti-miscegenation laws—becomes a reference point for the genesis of colorism in black American society.

In her work on racial epistemologies, Margaret Hunter identifies the *Black–White* racial epistemology as one that views race and racism within the traditional black–white binary. She writes, "This epistemology identifies the root of contemporary racism as American chattel slavery."[13] Consequently, early perspectives on skin tone bias were grounded within the same theoretical framework. From this vantage point, the institution of slavery created the system of racism and a subsystem of colorism. As a result of the educational and socio-economic privilege bestowed to fairer-skinned blacks with visible white ancestry, the black community became economically and socially stratified based upon skin tone. In many ways, skin tone shaped blacks' chances for economic opportunity and mobility. The eventual abolition of slavery only enhanced levels of stratification, as members of the light-skinned elite continued to set themselves apart from their darker-skinned counterparts by marrying and procreating with one another. Although there were no works devoted explicitly to the area of skin tone stratification at the turn of the 20th century, the early writings of Anna Julia Cooper and W.E.B Du Bois document the presence of colorism as a legacy of slavery. Additionally, early literary works and sociological studies of black Americans, such as St. Clair Drake and Hayton Cayton's 1946 classic *Black Metropolis*, or E. Franklin Frazier's 1957 text *Black Bourgeoisie*, observe the color and caste divisions within African American society. As Sydney Kronus suggests in his work on the black middle-class, slavery caused three distinct class divisions in black American society, which in turn led to the post-slavery pigmentocracy.[14]

Tradition 2. Colorism as a Function of Colonial Domination

Although slavery is a viable way to understand skin tone stratification in black American society, this theory does not adequately explain the bias and discrimination inherent in the African American community. Theoretical perspectives that evolved during the height of the Civil Rights and Black Power movements can perhaps better explain how skin color differences translate into internalized racism. A significant amount of research on the black community appeared at this time, and much of the empirical work on skin tone includes the historical significance of slavery but is characteristic of what Hunter describes as the *Colonial Domination* epistemology. She notes, "Knowledge about race and racism can only be proved or understood in the context of historical European domination."[15] For many scholars who examine race through this lens, colonial expansion (as opposed to slavery) is credited for introducing a Eurocentric racial hierarchy aligning whites at the top and blacks at the bottom. With the coining of such biological identifiers as black and white, notions of one's worth came to be associated with his or her skin tone; whiteness implied racial and moral superiority, and inferiority was equated with black skin. More recent conceptualizations of colorism extend the idea of colonial domination, situating the practices of colorism—such as skin bleaching—as a form of global white supremacy and domination among people of color around the world.

Tradition 3. Gendered/Intersectional Theories of Colorism

Perhaps the most significant theoretical contributions of colorism have occurred within the last 30 years. During this time, colorism has been a growth industry in the academy and has been the focal point of study in a wide range of academic disciplines, such as sociology, anthropology, economics, law, English, and social work. For instance, legal scholars Trina Jones and Angela Harris theorize how colorism fits within legal scholarship (i.e., critical race theory). The work of many others report that in the post–Civil Rights era, gender does make a difference when considering predictors of physical attractiveness, self-esteem, and self-efficacy. Unpacking the term *gendered colorism,* Mark Hill (2000) explains that "skin color has more bearing in the lives of African-American women than of African-American men."[16] This is not surprising given the societal value placed on female beauty. The bulk of colorism theorizing, however, falls within the realm of Margaret Hunter's *Critical Intersectional* racial epistemology:

> This epistemology is born out of the scholarship of women of color who have brought attention to the intersecting nature of oppression, or the "matrix of domination." This way of knowing about race and racism necessarily ties any knowledge of race, to knowledge of gender, class, sexuality, disability, and other intersecting identities that structure inequality.[17]

In the 1980s feminist scholars of color began to employ a critical intersectional epistemological perspective to our understandings of colorism. In doing so, these scholars investigate how skin tone intersects with other factors such as race, class, and gender. Indeed, black women have advanced our understandings on the experiences of black women and colorism. In 1983, Alice Walker penned the term *colorism* in her book *In Search of Our Mothers' Gardens*. Discussing the divisions among black women, she writes:

What black black women would be interested in, I think is a consciously heightened awareness on the part of light black women that they are capable, often quite consciously, of inflicting pain upon them; and that unless the question of Colorism—in my definition, prejudicial or preferential treatment of same-race people based solely on their color—is addressed in our communities and definitely in our black "sisterhoods" we cannot, as a people, progress. For colorism, like colonialism, sexism, and racism, impedes us.[18]

At the time of this writing, black feminism and black feminist theory were gaining ground within academia. The expansion of this oppositional framework that embraces the knowledge, consciousness, and empowerment unique to black women also highlights the mutually intersecting oppressions that shape black women's lives and experiences. Consequently, a considerable amount of contemporary empirical work examines colorism through a critical intersectional framework in a variety of academic disciplines.

THE THEORY OF "EVERYDAY COLORISM": BRIDGING MICRO- AND MACRO-LEVEL PROCESS IN SOCIAL REALITY

In his book *The Sociological Imagination*, American sociologist C. Wright Mills wrote that no sociological examination is complete without investigating the connection between an individual's private troubles and the "public issues of social structure."[19] In fact, Mills encourages us to examine deeply the intersections of history, biography, and structure. That is, we cannot ignore the relationship between large-scale (macro) institutions and individual (micro) aspects of social life. In reflecting on my own placement as a sociologist, I chose to situate myself within the field of theorists who engage both micro and macro social theories to guide their work. I am interested in understanding the everyday nature of colorism as a regular, taken-for-granted process and feature of life for black folk (women in particular). So, what are the language, rules, norms, practices, etc., attached to colorism as an everyday feature of black life?

Secondly, I am concerned with the everyday as a regular, recurring pattern of experiences for black folk individually and collectively. How does colorism map itself onto the lived experiences and interactions of black people on a regular basis? How do these micro-level patterns become reinforced and institutionalized on a macro-level? In examining black women and their everyday experiences of colorism, I turn to the work of Pierre Bourdieu, Patricia Hill Collins, and Philomena Essed—three thinkers who

articulate ideas on the interconnected processes of everyday life and practice. Each of these theoretical imprints is essential in articulating the concept of *everyday colorism*.

Theoretical Imprint 1: Pierre Bourdieu

French sociologist Pierre Bourdieu offers many contributions to contemporary sociological theory; his work as a social scientist is useful in
bridging the divide between macro- and micro-sociology. In his work,
Bourdieu suggests that sociology makes a number of connections, namely
between theory and practice, micro- and macro-sociology, and qualitative
and quantitative methods. More importantly, he is focused on the unifica-
tion of objectivity and subjectivity. As E.C. Cuff and colleagues point out,
"Bourdieu is centrally concerned with the reconciling of dualisms . . . the
dualism which occupies centre stage . . . is the classical epistemological one
between objectivism and subjectivism."[20] In Bourdieu's view, the concen-
tration of intellectuals on objectivity prevents them from knowing and understanding the social world from the perspective of the social actors
within it. Conversely, an emphasis on subjectivity leads to a reductionist
view of the social world. Despite this limitation, Bourdieu argues that the
subjective, or "soft sociology," is perhaps a more accurate representation of
the social world. He offers the following resolution:

> I believe that true scientific theory and practice must overcome this
> opposition by integrating into a single model the analysis of the expe-
> rience of social agents and the analysis of the objective structures that
> make this experience possible.[21]

In consideration of Bourdieu's numerous contributions to the area of
sociological theory, I believe his conceptualizations of *habitus, practices*,
and *fields* are most applicable to this research. Framing these concepts
within the conversation of structure and agency, Bourdieu situates these
three ideas as critical elements in how people construct life and social reality. First, the *habitus* represents the internalized thoughts and ideas that
guide the ways in which people understand and view the social world.
Habitus is acquired through socialization, and as people internalize the
rules and structures of the world, these dispositions become part of one's
consciousness. In fact, Bourdieu suggests that "the habitus functions below
the level of consciousness and language, beyond the reach of introspective
scrutiny and control by the will."[22] Further, Bourdieu notes that while each
individual has his or her own habitus (shaped by social location and

position in society), there is, however, an element of collectivity inherent within habitus. Ultimately, the habitus provides a basis for choice and action, producing the practices within society.

While habitus represents the internalization of thought, *practices* constitute the externalization of internalized thoughts and ideas. According to Bourdieu, practices represent the behavior mediated by structure and agency; practices are simply what one does. *Fields*, then, symbolize the setting of shared relations, which contextualizes group interaction and identity. Both individual agents and institutions co-exist within fields, and matters of power and position impact habitus. Bourdieu's unified perspective of habitus, practices, and fields attempts to resolve the partiality of a micro- or macro-level model explaining the social world.

Theoretical Imprint 2: Patricia Hill Collins

Patricia Hill Collins is another thinker who is useful in bridging the micro–macro divide. Like many feminist theorists, Collins employs an integrative macro–micro framework, and thus is quite capable of bridging this divide in her work. Throughout her work, Collins offers a clear and yet seamless way of understanding the interdependent nature of institutional organization and individual thought and behavior. Using the empowerment of black women as her theoretical lens, Collins employs four highly interconnected systems of power (structural, disciplinary, hegemonic, and interpersonal) operating through the matrix of domination in various micro- and macro-levels ways. As Collins reveals, although each domain functions at different societal or individual levels, each domain influences individual and collective human agency.

The *structural* domain of power reflects the ways in which macro-level processes affect the lives of black women. As Collins explains, this particular domain "encompasses how social institutions are organized to reproduce Black women's subordination over time."[23] She points to such structural inequities in housing, education, and employment that have hindered the resources and opportunity for black women and reinforced institutional forms of racism. An interplay of the structural and *disciplinary* domains of power enable the enforcement of such large-scale bias and discrimination. This second feature of macro-level power points to the "inside" enforcement and surveillance of organizations that "foster new and unanticipated forms of disciplinary control."[24] Despite legal advances (i.e., Civil Rights Act or Voting Rights Act) that impact the structural domain of power by furthering the position of women of color, large-scale discrimination is still possible at this disciplinary level.

In comparing the four models of power, Collins provides this summary:

> The structural and disciplinary domains of power operate through system-wide social policies managed primarily through bureaucracies. In contrast, the hegemonic domain of power aims to justify practices in these domains of power. By manipulating ideology and culture, the hegemonic domain acts as a link between social institutions (structural domain), their organizational practices (disciplinary domain), and the level of everyday social interaction (interpersonal domain).[25]

As she maintains, the *hegemonic* domain of power refers to symbols, ideas, and ideologies, while the *interpersonal* realm is more concerned with day-to-day relationships and communication. Although this model is complex, it does provide an alternative way to understand how the status and position of black women individually and collectively are mediated through this interrelated process of micro- and macro-level domains. These linkages are critical to the social transformation and empowerment of women of color.

Theoretical Imprint 3: Philomena Essed

In her research examining the daily experiences of racism faced by black women in the United States and the Netherlands, Dutch sociologist Philomena Essed's 1991 pioneering work, *Understanding Everyday Racism*, provides both a theoretical and empirical framework for studying and understanding the unique perspectives of black women. By using the narratives of 55 black women as her guide, Essed builds a theoretical frame of *everyday racism* that explains both micro- and macro-level implications of racism.

Similar to other theorists who engage the sociology of knowledge, Essed considers knowledge to be an integral part of everyday life and practice. Within any given society or culture, there exists a collective stock of knowledge that guides behavior and action. All members of a society acquire the knowledge needed for navigation within that particular society or culture. The acquisition of such knowledge is developed by learning the language, customs, traditions, and rules of that particular culture or society. According to Essed, knowledge used in everyday life is in many ways mediated by the institutions of family, media, and education. For many members in a society, going about daily life and interacting with these various institutions on a frequent basis results in the institutionalization and embodiment of this frame of knowledge that is oftentimes taken for granted as an objective part of reality.

Philomena Essed applies an intersectional perspective to the sociology of knowledge and uses the framework to explain: 1) how members of a society acquire a collective knowledge on racism; and 2) how black women are particularly impacted by everyday practice and interaction as it relates to racism. As she points out, "everyday practices are present and reproduced by everyday situations. The situations of the everyday world are substructured by relations of race, ethnicity, class, and gender. This introduces, finally, the notion of everyday racism."[26] Essed's specific use of the concept *everyday* is key in fusing a micro- and macro-level paradigm. As she explains, employing the term "cross[es] the boundaries between structural and interactional approaches to racism and link[s] details of micro experiences to the structural and ideological context in which they are shaped."[27] For Essed, it remains important to underscore the cumulative effects of racism. She describes that "specific instances acquire meaning only in relation to the sum total of other experiences of everyday racism."[28] To that end, everyday racism encapsulates the routine practices, attitudes, and behavior of racism that taken alone would go ignored and unnamed as racist.

Essed's framework of everyday racism is so essential to scholarly research on black women for several reasons. First, Essed points to a scholarly disinterest in micro-level practices and in the evaluation of everyday experience. "Due to this prevailing macro-sociological bias," she writes, "micro-interactional perspectives on racism . . . have been neglected."[29] As such, Essed believes that the value of everyday experience has been taken for granted and omitted from empirical inquiry. (It is important to note more contemporary studies *do* address everyday experiences of racism. Recently, there has been a proliferation of research exploring racial "microaggressions," or subtle, unintentional forms of bias occurring in everyday settings.) Secondly, Essed highlights that a "marriage" of micro-level practices and macro-level structure within research and method is necessary in order to completely understand the experiences of black women and racism. Further, she encourages future scholars to develop studies of racism that place real-life experience at the core of analysis. Essed's model of everyday racism is useful, then, in engaging a conversation on colorism.

Understanding "Everyday Colorism"

Building upon the theoretical contributions of Bourdieu's *habitus*, Collins's framework of empowerment, and Philomena Essed's notion of everyday racism, I am coining the term *everyday colorism*, a theoretical frame emerging from the data that contextualizes the voices and experiences of the women involved in this research project.

This model of everyday colorism is comprised of three elements: *language, internal scripts,* and *external practices* (See Figure 3). I define *language* in this context as the everyday vocabulary and system of meaning attached to skin tone. *Internal scripts* refer to the socially constructed ideas, expectations, emotions, and beliefs women carry with them about skin tone. Internal scripts then guide *external practices*, everyday behaviors and actions enacted by women towards themselves and others based upon their internalized views about skin color. It is important to highlight that the language, scripts, and practices of everyday colorism can yield two models: a normative framework and an oppositional framework. The most common form of everyday colorism, a *normative* model, explains the dominant nature of colorism that places light-skinned women at the top of the skin color hierarchy and dark-skinned women at the bottom. An *oppositional* model of everyday colorism yields everyday language, internal scripts, and external practices that resist and challenge the dominant ideology.

The framework of everyday colorism is significant for several reasons. First, my usage of the term *colorism* is a first step in formally naming the issue. It is important to note that despite the long history and widespread prevalence of colorism in black communities, the term itself remains largely unnamed. In fact, at the onset of this project, I found it more challenging to recruit participants using *colorism* on my recruitment flyer. After quickly recognizing this oversight, my recruitment efforts were more fruitful after I started looking for young women who wanted to "discuss issues of light skin, dark skin, good hair, and bad hair" (See Appendix). Like other scholars who readily study and understand the issue of colorism, this term is part of my everyday vocabulary; yet my researcher bias failed to consider how uncommon the term is among young black women. In fact, at the beginning of one focus group session, I asked every participant to talk about why she wanted to be a part of this research. One young woman honestly stated, "Before today, I have never really heard of this word, so I can't really give you any answer and look stupid. What exactly is colorism?" When asking participants about the relative obscurity of the term, many observed that usage of the term *colorism* was rare and directly related to the problematic nature of this sensitive subject. As Karina, a Haitian woman noted:

> I think [. . .] if we don't give it a name, then it's not really an issue, we're not considering it an issue, so we're, like, keeping it, you know,

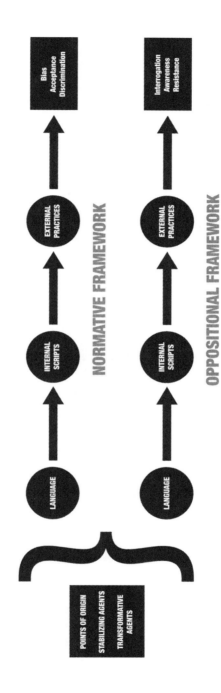

Figure 3: *The Structure of Everyday Colorism*

undercover. If we were to say you know, like racism, if we called it colorism, then that means it's an issue in our community, and I guess we don't want to say that all the time.

Throughout this project, there were no respondents who used the term *colorism* freely. Some women talked about the "color complex" (which could be a direct allusion to the popular 1992 book of the same name), yet the majority of participants did not connect their daily experiences with skin color to colorism. The irony, however, is that although colorism is not readily recognizable or easily defined, not one woman in this study had any difficulty articulating the meaning and value inherent in skin tone, or that colorism was a problem disproportionately affecting black women. As Becky so aptly remarked, "This is something that plagues women rather than men, and I was drawn [to this research project] because it's something you could never really get tired of talking about because it always seems to be an issue." Despite the fact that colorism goes unnamed in the black community, there is a unanimous recognition that colorism is alive and well in everyday life and interaction and, as Becky suggests, operates in a covert fashion, looming in the mindset and mentality of young women.

The second value of the everyday colorism framework is that this model highlights everyday experiences of colorism, yet it also points to the connection between individual behavior and institutional processes. While the empirical illustrations of this conceptual framework follow in the subsequent chapters, it remains important to underscore that this research aims to examine day-to-day, interpersonal interactions *and* the role individuals play in reinforcing behavior that becomes reproduced and institutionalized on a structural level. The manifestations of colorism remain salient yet insidious in a variety of contexts including family and personal relationships, and larger societal institutions such as the media and education. Consistent with Pierre Bourdieu's interplay of habitus, practice, and fields, or even Patricia Hill Collins's four domains of power (structural, disciplinary, hegemonic, interpersonal), perceptions and experiences of colorism rest on a fine line of individual agency/constraint that is influenced by both interpersonal and institutional domains. Evaluating one or the other does not provide an accurate description of how black women view their skin tone as a multidimensional element (in conjunction, of course, with additional interlocking oppressions) that shapes their life agency and/or constrains them within this dynamic system.

New Directions in Colorism Theory: Towards a Structural Interpretation?

While many scholars rightfully understand colorism as a byproduct of slavery, a colonialist ideology, or as a function of intersectionality, it is imperative to develop more comprehensive independent conceptual analyses of colorism that better approximate the patterns, nuances, and distinctions of colorism in the post–Civil Rights era. It is my hope that this research can serve as a starting point on how to conceptualize colorism in the 21st century.

In modern-day theorizing on social processes and structure, more contemporary social scientists who center their work on social inequalities are devising alternative theoretical frameworks that move theory beyond informal constructs that integrate micro- and macro-level paradigms. For instance, preeminent race scholar Eduardo Bonilla-Silva argues for a structural interpretation of racism, suggesting instead that racism be studied from the theoretical lens of racialization. He contends,

> after a society becomes racialized, a racialization develops a life of its own. Although it interacts with class and gender structurations in the social system, it becomes an organizing principle of social relations in itself. Race, as most analysts suggest, is a social construct, but that construct, like class and gender, has independent effects in social life. After racial stratification becomes established, race becomes an independent criterion for vertical hierarchy in society.[30]

Recognizing the value in Bonilla-Silva's structural thesis on race, feminist sociologist Barbara Risman extends the same paradigm to build a theoretical model of a gender structure. She notes:

> My argument is that race, gender, and sexuality are as equally fundamental to human societies as the economy and the polity. Those inequalities that are fundamentally embedded throughout social life, at the level of individual identities, cultural expectations embedded into interaction, and institutional opportunities and constraints are best conceptualized as structures: The gender structure, the race structure, the class structure, and the sexuality structure. This does not imply that the social forces that produced, nor the causal mechanisms at work in the daily reproduction of inequality within each structure, are of similar strength or type at any given historical moment. [. . .]

I propose this structural language as a tool to help disentangle the means by which inequalities are constructed, recreated, and—it is hoped—transformed or deconstructed. The model for how gender structure works, with consequences for individuals, interactions/cultural expectations, and institutions, can be generalized to the study of other equally embedded inequalities such as race and sexuality. Each structure of inequality exists on its own yet coexists with every other structure of inequality.[31]

In her treatise, Risman lays out a multidimensional structure of gender, inclusive of three important domains: the individual, interactional, and institutional levels. Gender relations and processes (and inequality) occur alongside each dimension.

Building upon Bonilla-Silva's and Risman's interpretations of race and gender as social structures, I argue that colorism can also be viewed as a multidimensional structure. Although colorism does exist within the larger structure of racism, it can undoubtedly be conceptualized as a structure functioning at the individual, interactional, and institutional levels. Although I am not equating colorism with gender (or race, for that matter), I consider colorism a multilevel construct existing at these three levels, at many times in conjunction with other structural inequalities. Everyday colorism examines the broader connections between these micro- and macro-level structures. These ideas represent a start point in advancing the scholarship on colorism theory. More theoretical perspectives and empirical research is needed in order to bridge the current gaps between theory and research. I return to this model of everyday colorism in the Conclusion. In the following chapters, I present the findings of analysis that are grounded within this approach.

CHAPTER 3

The Language, Scripts, and Practices of Everyday Colorism

From the time I can remember everyone was described by color, down to a half or quarter shade darker than someone else. If the person was dark, the description was negative, especially if the person was female . . . I got the message: no good, dark, ugly, not worth black men's attention, unattractive, and not wife material. I believed it.

—Virginia R. Harris[1]

In the statement above, artist Virginia Harris describes her own experience growing up as a "prisoner of color." Being called "black" on a regular basis led Harris to believe all of the negative attributes commonly associated with having a dark skin tone. There is a variety of descriptors used within African American society to refer to various skin tones, as well as a wide range of connotations (positive and negative) attached to every name. These names and ideas constitute the first two elements of everyday colorism, *language* and *internal scripts*. Referring back to the story of Virginia Harris, she notes that as a child, she was called black so many times by family members and schoolmates that by the time she reached adulthood, she unknowingly internalized the socially constructed images of the term, convincing herself and others that she *was* in fact "no good, dark, ugly." In many respects, this research aims to deconstruct the collective language and internal scripts of colorism. Furthermore, by examining how black women talk about and understand colorism in their everyday lives, this project aims to identify any shifts in color consciousness compared to previous generations of young black Americans. I use the pioneering work of sociologist Charles Parrish conducted in 1946, *Color Names and Color Notions*, to serve as a basis of comparison.

LANGUAGE: "COLOR NAMES"

Within our society, language is perhaps the most vital component of interaction and communication. As sociologists Peter Berger and Thomas Luckmann point out, "an understanding of language is essential for any understanding of the reality of everyday life."[2] The language of a particular culture or society inherently implies meaning, power, identity, and location. Sociologist Larry Crawford shares his perspective on language and its relationship to race and color:

> Language is a very powerful tool. When oral or written symbols are reinforced through entertainment, education and religion, it becomes even more potent. Words communicate meanings that are commonly understood by all participants or they cannot stand as a method for conveying meaning or order. The subconscious, symbolic reality which people speak into existence facilitates the exercise of power or reveals impotence. Words, also, are made into allies or enemies. Our unspoken awareness of the European meanings behind the symbols we use demonstrates a willing consumption of a racist reference group's seductive culture. The language we ape reveals our not so blind endorsement of another's self-benefitting cultural definitions about color, ours relative to their lack of it.[3]

The first element of everyday colorism, *language*, is defined as the everyday vocabulary attached to skin tone. This language, of course, is filled with value and meaning. Although the term *colorism* has only recently been used more frequently by members of the black community, there exists an extensive and sophisticated vocabulary for identifying and distinguishing skin color categories. Historically, blacks have designated each other as either light-skinned or dark-skinned. In addition to these two basic terms, there is an additional set of terms associated with being light or dark. As writer and colorism expert, Marita Golden, suggests it is the "more specific descriptive terms that separate Blacks and create castes and cliques."[4] Many of these terms, including *high yellow*, *brownskin*, and *redbone* are connected directly to the perceived hue of one's skin tone and have been common-place in black American culture for generations. Yet the extensive vocabu-lary of color has origins in slavery and colonialism. There are other societies, in Latin America and the Caribbean, for instance, which have similar pat-terns of color naming connected to phenotype. In the United States, white European colonialists are credited with the invention of racial terms (i.e., black and white) and are additionally responsible for developing a nomen-clature differentiating light- and dark-skinned blacks.[5] But it is African Americans, for sure, who have amplified the attention given to the nuances of skin gradations and hair texture.

Perhaps the most comprehensive attention given to the vocabulary of skin tone has been the work of sociologist Charles Parrish. In his 1946 seminal study, *Color Names and Color Notions,* Parrish explores the various names blacks use to describe people of varying skin shades. The results of his questionnaire given to high school and college students uncovers over 125 various names referring to various skin tones. Twenty-five of those color names were commonly used across the data to describe light, me-dium, and dark skin tones (see Table 1). Names such as *fair, bright,* and *yellow* are regularly cited for characterizing light-skinned individuals.

Variations of the word *brown* (e.g., *high brown* or *brownskin*) are univer-sal terms for a medium skin tone. *Dark* and *black* are commonly used names for those with the darkest skin tones. Parrish also investigates the various meanings and associations attached to these terms. He learns that the names associated with skin tone are invariably connected to stereo-types and personality traits. Those blacks having a medium complexion are favored the most and receive either neutral or positive attributes. Yet those who are both very light and very dark are subject to the most objectionable stereotypes.

> [Blacks who are very light] . . . are physically attractive—look well in their clothes. They are thought to have a superiority complex which makes them conceited; they act like White people and have little to do with darker Negroes; they are "not in the race."
>
> [Blacks who are very dark]: Most of them are thought to be ugly; they are thought to be evil and hard to get along with; they have a strong feeling of inferiority; they are quick tempered and like to fight.[6]

Although the aim of my research was not to replicate Parrish's study, it is important to gain an understanding of the names that many young women today use and hear on a regular basis. In the first phase of data collection, I noted the preponderance of different names participants talked about to describe various skin tones. In light of this, in the second phase of data collection, I explicitly asked respondents to free-list and discuss the many color names they use or hear on a regular basis. The results of the focus groups indicate that there are 40 terms that these women commonly employed to describe themselves and others in their day-to-day lives (See Table 1). Several points of significance are worth highlighting here. Each of the included terms was mentioned by at least three participants; the majority of these terms were easily identified, recognized, and understood by all of the women interviewed. There are nine terms (denoted with an asterisk) that are an exact match to Parrish's list of terms. Close to half of the names are related to being light skinned; many of these are consistent with not only the terms Parrish found over 60 years ago but resonate with many other bodies of historic and contemporary works of fiction and scholarly literature.

Reflecting the history of color language in African American culture, the terms associated with a light skin tone, such as *pretty skin*, are generally positive. However, it is necessary to mention the term *house nigga*. As Denise, a brown-skinned participant, aptly stated, "I think that the problem with the color complex is that everybody wants to be a house nigga." This comment is a direct reference to the distinctions made between mixed-race, light-skinned slaves (commonly referred to by plantation owners as "house slaves"), whose duties were relegated inside the slave master's house, and their darker-skinned counterparts ("field slaves"), who had to perform manual labor outdoors. Post slavery, these terms have evolved over time to "house/field Negro" in the 1960s, and today, some African Americans invoke the term *nigga* (a derivative of the term *nigger*) when referring to the strict hierarchy and classification of slaves by skin tone. Denise's remark, in addition to those of the other women who noted either using or hearing the term *house nigga*, reflects not only the survival of the contentious word *nigger* but the continued reification of the slave mentality within black culture.

As *light skin* and *dark skin* reflect the polar opposites of colorism, the majority of terms offered for dark skin are derogatory; names such as *burnt*, *charcoal*, and *watermelon child* point to the historical bias toward being dark and reinforced controlling images of dark-skinned black women. These labels continue to signify negativity and inferiority, standing in stark contrast to the majority of favorable labels for light skin.

Some terms listed provide direct references to more concrete instances of skin tone bias. For instance, a significant portion of participants in this study were Jamaican, and many of them offered the terms *browning* and

Table 1. Color Names Associated with Light, Dark, and Medium Skin Tones: 1946–2015

Parrish, 1946			Wilder, 2015		
LIGHT	**MEDIUM**	**DARK**	**LIGHT**	**MEDIUM**	**DARK**
High Yellow*	Brown*	Chocolate Brown*	Yellow*	Brown (Skin)*	Black(ie)*
Fair Bright*	Brownskin*	Dark*	Bright*	Pecan Tan*	Dark(y)*
Yellow*	Tan*	Black*	Light Bright*	Milk Chocolate	Chocolate*
Light*	High Brown	Blue Black *	High Yellow*	Caramel	Blue-Black*
"Yaller"*	Olive	"Tar Baby"*	Fair*		Tar Babies*
Half-White	Teasing Brown	Dark Brown	Mulatto		Jigaboo
Dirty Yellow	Creole Brown	Rusty Black	White		Purple
	Medium Brown	"Ink Spot"	Coolie		Super Black
			Pretty Skin		African
			House Nigga		Darkness
			Mixed		Charcoal
			Oreo		Sexy Black
			Browning		Watermelon Child
			Vanilla		Burnt
			French Vanilla		Midnight
			Red (Bone)		
			Red-Skinned		
			Sexy Red		
			Dirty Red		

On the left side are the color names identified in sociologist Charles Parrish's work associated with light, medium, and dark skin tones. The color names that I identified in my research appear in the three columns on the right. Color names marked with an asterisk* are consistent with Parrish's 1946 study and my own work.

coolie to denote a light-skinned individual. Both of these terms are rooted within Jamaican culture; browning is typically used to refer to light-skinned women and girls, while coolie refers to someone with East Indian lineage. In addition, the term *jigaboo*—another term with origins connected to the verbal denigration of blacks at the height of the Jim Crow era—was mentioned by several participants as the name for a dark-skinned black girl but also alluding to the divisions between black women that are played out in the popular film *School Daze*. In that movie, written and directed by Spike Lee, the jigaboos are portrayed as dark-skinned women with more kinky, coarse, or "bad" hair. Their counterparts, the *wannabes*, are represented within the film as the popular and attractive light-skinned co-eds who have long, "good" hair and more Eurocentric features. Although the film is more than 25 years old, the term *jigaboo* still persists within the contemporary language of skin color.

Interestingly, there are several terms falling within all three categories that are connected in some way, shape, or form to food. *Vanilla* for light skin, *caramel* for medium tones, and *chocolate* for dark skin may in some way point to the (hyper) sexualized and eroticized images of all black women regardless of their skin tone. Without question, historical white images and attitudes surrounding the black female body have primarily been connected to sex. As sociologist K. Sue Jewell relates, "From the early 1630s to the present, Black American women of all shades have been portrayed as hypersexual 'bad-black-girls.'"[7] Consequently, the names given to black women by larger society incorporate food metaphors. In 1984, sociologist Irving Allen published the results of a study that examined the battery of terms found within American culture that derogate women of color in the peer-reviewed journal *Sex Roles*.[8] Finding the largest number of epithets for black women, many of these terms—including *brown sugar*, *chocolate drop*, *hot chocolate*, *mocha*, *charcoal blossom*, and *honey*—symbolize food. As Allen observes, although the connection of food to sexuality may seem peculiar, there exists nonetheless this universal correlation within American vernacular for all women of color. It is no surprise, then, that many of the color names offered by respondents in this study typify various foods. The larger importance of this finding is the survival (and oftentimes embracing, e.g., *sexy red* or *sexy black*) of these derogatory terms within black American culture. Many of the same terms Allen found for black women, which are both racist and sexist, get reintroduced and reaffirmed through the structure of colorism.

Although there exists a wide range of descriptors for light and dark complexions, the women in the study do not use or hear very often terms associated with a medium complexion. As one respondent stated, "I have never heard of any names for anyone with a medium tone." This comment is consistent with the literature on colorism, which has traditionally operated from a light/dark binary structure. Despite the few names offered, there is some indication that the experiences of women who fall squarely in the middle (those individuals not categorized by themselves or others as either light or dark skinned) are quite different compared to their light and dark counterparts, suggesting that colorism operates as a three-tiered structure as opposed to a binary one. I will return to this issue later in this chapter.

It is also important to highlight the most commonly used terms. When referring to light-skinned women, the overwhelming majority of respondents used the word *red* compared to any other term, including *light skinned*. Red is synonymous with light skin and is viewed as the ideal color, holding the most value in the black community.[9] Historically, the term *redbone* has signified a person with mixed white, Native American, and African American ancestry. More recently, this term has pervaded the lyrics of many rap songs as a plethora of hip-hop artists—including Wacka Flocka Flame, Kanye West, Wiz Khalifa, and Lil' Wayne—have frequently utilized *red* or *redbone* when making reference to a light-skinned woman. For instance, in the 2010 single, "Right Above It," rap artist Lil' Wayne raps in one verse, "Uh, how do he say what's never said? Beautiful black women, I bet that bitch look better red."[10] In songs like this and many others, red is that standard of beauty.

Conversely, the term *black* is used by women in this study as the predominant name for dark skin, above and beyond the term *dark skinned* itself. As scholars St. Clair Drake and Horace Cayton pointed out in *Black Metropolis*, this word has always been "loaded with negative implications in Anglo-Saxon linguistics. Things are 'black as sin.' When you don't like a person you give him a 'black look.'"[11] Although many people of African descent in the U.S. today identify themselves as black, this connotation for a dark-skinned woman is negative and is in no way connected to a racial identity, let alone infused with black pride. Clinicians Angela Neal and Midge Wilson observe that the usage of the word *black* in this context is a "derogatory adjective . . . [and] does little to enforce the idea that black is beautiful."[12] The characterization of dark-skinned women as black further reinforces the socially constructed divisions among black women.

INTERNAL SCRIPTS: "COLOR NOTIONS"

As noted in the previous section, the names and labels attached to varying skin tones are loaded with meaning. Red, brown, and black are much more than phenotypic descriptors; these color names, of course, shape color notions. More importantly, the language of skin tone creates a collective stock of knowledge that is shared and maintained by many members of the black community. The everyday experiences of colorism are connected to the ways in which women internalize the mental messages, or *internal scripts*, of skin tone. In this context, I define this second element of everyday colorism as the socially constructed ideas, expectations, emotions, and beliefs pertaining to skin tone. Similar to sociologist Pierre Bourdieu's concept of *habitus*, internalized scripts represent a *color habitus*, reinforcing for the women in this study their commonsense knowledge about skin color.[13]

"Red Girls Get More Attention"

Consistent with the many positive terms used to denote a light skin tone, many of the internalized scripts related to light skin were also positive. When asking respondents to describe the attributes associated with light-skinned women, many used words such as *trustworthy*, *amiable*, *nonthreatening*, and *comfortable*. The most commonly held view, however, was that light skin was synonymous with beauty. As Beyoncé, a medium-toned participant, observed, "I think there's an expectation [that] when somebody's light skinned, you just automatically [assume that] . . . they're just supposed to be pretty." Monica said candidly during one focus group, "I see black men talking to some light-skinned women, and in my opinion, I think they're ugly. And I think, why is he talking to her? And it's because she's a prize. Because she has light skin it makes her attractive." The vast majority of the women in this project—regardless of their skin tones— echoed this sentiment. Equating light skin with beauty translates into the placement of light-skinned women at the top of what Margaret Hunter refers to as the "beauty queue."[14] As skin tones are placed on a continuum of light to dark, so too is beauty; a black woman's level of attractiveness corresponds to where she falls within the beauty queue. The internalization of light-skinned women as the most beautiful black women has pervaded virtually every literary, theoretical, and empirical body of work on colorism. It is no surprise, then, that this was the most universal attribute offered by the women in this study.

Because light-skinned women are viewed as the most attractive, connected to this idea is the expectation of superiority. Charles Parrish and others find that within the black community, conceit and arrogance are often internalized scripts associated with light skin. Due to their skin tones, many light-skinned blacks historically looked down upon darker blacks, distancing themselves through many social clubs and organizations.

Consequently, light-skinned women are viewed to be snobbish because of their proximity to whiteness. The same ideas emerge from the women in the study. Consider, for example, the experience of Shirelle, an eighteen-year-old who identifies her skin tone as light brown. When discussing the perceived attributes associated with having light skin, Shirelle openly discusses her frustration with constantly being stereotyped as a snob.

> People always assume that because I'm light skinned that I'm stuck up, and they say, "Oh, you'd make the perfect AKA. [. . .]" I don't think I'm stuck up, but people say that I am, and I just think it's because of my complexion. I don't *think* I'm stuck up.

Shirelle's account is a compelling example mirroring the color stories of other light-skinned women participating in this study. Before they have the opportunity to prove otherwise, many light-skinned women are often judged and evaluated in their everyday lives on the basis of their skin tone. The other assumption that Shirelle alluded to—that she would make the "perfect" member of Alpha Kappa Alpha (a black sorority historically believed to select mainly light-skinned members)—automatically places her in the mind of others at the top of the beauty queue. Although Shirelle insists that she is not a conceited individual, this internalized script of superiority leads to an inevitable disconnect in communication between light- and dark-skinned women.

Colorism scholar Margaret Hunter states, "The more beauty one possesses, the better off she will be when competing for resources such as jobs, education, or even spouses in the marriage market."[15] Hunter goes on to explain that for African American women, light skin provides more social commodity and capital. In addition to the internalized scripts shared about light-skinned women and beauty, there was an overwhelming perception by the women I interviewed that light skin carried more privilege compared to dark skin. Many of these advantages include better employment, the ability to have more interracial friendships and relationships, and overall appeal. The following response, shared by Denise, a medium-toned participant, illustrates this belief:

> Red girls get more attention [from men] than dark-skinned girls [be] cause of the [. . .] simple fact that they're just red. [. . .] It could be a prettier dark-skinned girl, the red girl may not even be that pretty, but she's getting attention just because she's red. And it's where the feud begins because some dark-skinned girls feel as though this red girl isn't as pretty as they are, and she's getting all the attention just

because she's red, the dark-skinned girls are being overlooked just because this person is red.

Inherent in what Denise has internalized about what it means to be red is the notion that being average looking and light skinned is *always* better than being pretty and dark skinned. What is more desirable (i.e., what holds more value) in dating and mate selection is being red.

Similar scripts about friendships and the business arena reinforce the idea of light-skin privilege. Consider the examples offered by Desiree and Vivica, two medium-brown-skinned women who each discuss the additional advantages of lighter-toned black women:

> . . . when we see black people who hang out with different ethnicities other than black people, a lot of times they're light-skinned girls with really nice hair. (Desiree, 20)

> . . . wouldn't you say that you have more privileges. [. . .] Would you agree or disagree that the privileges offered to light-skinned people in corporate America. . . . Wouldn't you say there is more privilege? (Vivica, 21)

Tanya, a light-skinned participant who was born in the early 1960s, agrees with the perspectives of the younger generation of black women. She readily admits that her light skin has afforded her a certain degree of advantage, noting, "I personally have found it easier to get around . . . to get into places, to do things because I'm fair skinned. A lot of people are easier to hire me because I don't, to me I feel like I don't threaten them in any way. A lot of people just kind of like you just because your skin is lighter." Tanya also recognizes the adverse consequences for dark-skinned women: "Because you are dark, people are scared of you; they don't want to hire you; they don't want to hang around you; they don't want to talk to you because you scare them."

Because these ideas about the advantages of light skin have been so deeply ingrained within the psyche of many black women, there is no question that these internalized scripts are indeed verities in their everyday lives. As Denise points out in the above statement about red girls, their value to black men and their position ahead of darker women is a "simple fact." Sociologists Berger and Luckmann argue that,

> The reality of everyday life is taken for granted as reality. It does not require additional verification over and beyond its simple presence. It is simply *there*, as self-evident and compelling facticity. I *know* that it is real.[16]

The *subjective* belief that light-skinned women are the most beautiful, superior, and resourceful of all black women becomes the shared *objective* reality of many of the women I interviewed: light skin is about more than just beauty—it signals an overall better quality of life.

Perhaps an unexpected consequence of having light skin is the question of authenticity. To be sure, the "Black is Beautiful" mantra of the 1960s invoked racial pride within the hearts and minds of many African Americans through a rejection of whiteness and an appreciation of blackness. The acceptance of dark skin as "true" blackness reverberated throughout the focus groups. As one participant, Colleen, noted, "If you're a lighter black person, you have to prove how black you are." This is a common idea highlighted in Bill Dukes's recent documentary, *Light Girls*. Those who are light-skinned also express feelings of constraint, subjection to others' stereotyping, and questioning of their identities, in spite of the privileges associated with being light skinned. Some of these feelings include the perception that they do not face discrimination due to their skin tone. In addition, there is the automatic assumption that because someone has light skin, they *must* be biracial. This can be particularly offensive for some women. As two participants, Melissa and Kira, explain, the interrogations by other black women about their blackness are rather bothersome:

> It was hard being the light-skinned girl because most people always asked me, "Are you Dominican?" "Are you mixed with something?" And I'd [say], "No, I'm just black." What does that have to do with anything? But I always got that, even to this day I still get, "Oh, what are you mixed with?" or "Where are your parents from?" "Are you Jamaican?" "Are you something?" Then I just say, "Oh no, I'm just black. My parents are just African American." (Melissa, 19, light brown)

> I've been called *white* so many times, it's not even funny. I've been called *house nigga* and stuff like that because of my complexion, and I feel like sometimes that I have to overcompensate. [...] I was brought up not to be ghetto, not to be loud. I'm not that type of person, and sometimes I feel as if I have to overcompensate to fit in with the black people. I don't want to say that I more identify with white people, but I kind of do, even though I prefer black people over white people. I feel like I have to try harder to get in. (Kira, 19, medium)

Both Melissa and Kira's discomfort of course stems from their lack of recognition and immediate acceptance by other blacks as "fully" African American. Acknowledgement as an authentic member of the black community is extremely important for these and other participants, as it is for many people of color.

The same level of frustration is echoed by Trina, a 20-year-old woman who describes her skin tone as "very light." Trina notes that she is very active in school and community activities and considers herself especially committed to issues impacting black Americans. Yet, as she explains, her commitment to activism and leadership on campus is not taken seriously because of her skin tone:

> I'm light skinned and [. . .] honestly feel discriminated against. You know, I feel like I'm more about the cause than blacker people are. You know what I mean? [. . .] And I feel it's a barrier because [. . .] I am light skinned and [. . .] my natural hair may not be as coarse. [. . .] I still feel like it's a barrier for our people. [. . .] I don't feel like I'm doing good, just because somebody calls me red.

In Trina's mind, because she does not fit the stereotypical image of a "pro-black" activist, her motives and ideas are often discredited. Rather than buying into the notion of light-skin privilege, Trina considers her light skin to be a disadvantage compared to her darker counterparts, and because of this, Trina is constantly working to prove that she is black enough and worthy of validation from the black community. In my focus group conversation with college-aged men, this same script was reflected in the perspectives and experiences of the group members. Jason, who was 22 years old at the time of our discussion, attended the same university as the college-aged women in this study. Like Trina, this young man was an active member in his campus community, and in sharing his perspectives of strength and authenticity, Jason revealed his bias against light-skinned women:

> Darker-skinned women seem to be more aggressive; that's an attribute that seems to accompany them. They're a little bit stronger . . . there's a few women that I know on this campus that are dark skinned; to me it seems like [they are] more leaders than lighter-skinned women, and even though they are darker than their counterparts, the power that they portray also seems attractive to me.

It appears, then, that Trina's experiences were affirmed by Jason's commentary. While light-skinned women are deemed more beautiful, they are nonetheless cast by men and women as weaker and less powerful (in a leadership capacity) than their darker-skinned counterparts.

"Black Girls Are Ghetto"

As the literature on gendered colorism indicates, the experience of dark-skinned black women at times creates a position of quadruple jeopardy: race, class, gender, *and* dark skin can serve as mutually intersecting oppressions shaping the experience of dark-skinned women. It's no surprise that the internalized scripts revealed by the women in this study support the vast majority of literature indicating that dark skin is inherently negative. There is one exception that is worthy of discussion. During one conversation, a respondent was adamant about the perceived differences between individuals who are dark skinned compared to those who fall into the category of very dark skinned. She explains this important distinction:

> There's a special connotation that comes along with being, you know, almost like people say "African dark." From-the-motherland dark. But there's something that, to me, what I've . . . there's something special about that versus than being darker skinned, you know what I mean, and then having combination skin or something like that. I think it's something special that comes along with being, you know, that quintessential image of being African, you know what I mean. So, I think it's important [. . .] that people understand when they are very dark and what that means; it's different from being just darker skinned.

Although it could be argued that equating extreme darkness with strength and attitude are positive attributes (as noted earlier in this chapter), the overall attitudes expressed about dark-skinned women reflect the polar opposite of the attitudes expressed about light skin. In every focus group, women with darker skin tones were typically described as "loud," "suspicious," "unattractive," and "less intelligent." The following internal scripts about dark-skinned women accurately depict this mindset:

> I don't think I can really discern any true advantages [to being dark skinned] other than the idea that you are truly black, but [. . .] there are not true advantages of being darker skin, unless you define that yourself. But I think as far as society goes, I can't imagine anything that truly makes you at an advantage for being that complexion. (Callea, 21, dark)

> I guess it's a good thing and a bad thing, but people are intimidated by you sort of; nobody is going to mess with you or anything. Nobody want[s] to talk back to you, so. That's the advantages of being more dark skinned. (Keesha, 20, dark)

I've actually heard that the darker your skin, the more militant African American women are suppose to be. [. . .] Because you are so dark, you're not pretty, you're not attractive. [. . .] Boys don't look at dark girls. (Yolanda, 19, dark)

Well, I think that people seem to think that blacker girls are more ghetto. And they are loud [and] have more attitude. (Keleechi, 18, very light)

The scripts offered here portray dark-skinned women as intimidating, militant, ghetto, and loud. Of particular importance here is the conflation of dark skin with being or acting "ghetto." The connotation here is related not only to poverty but the idea of a low-class or "classless" attitude and is possibly the antithesis of "acting white," a theory coined by black scholars Signithia Fordham and John Ogbu in relation to black students' educational achievements.[17] When one "acts ghetto," one embodies poor taste, morals, and decision-making. For the participants in this study, dark skin is the signifier of bad values or, perhaps more accurately, the lack of white, middle-class (i.e., good) values. This internalized script about dark-skinned women reflects the long-standing association in the black community of light-skin with status and morality.

Furthermore, the beliefs about dark skin more likely exemplify the controlling images of African American women. Patricia Hill Collins defines *controlling images* as socially constructed ideas about black womanhood that reinforce their subordination.[18] Defined and manipulated by members of the dominant group, negative depictions of black women have been institutionalized since slavery. Two such images are particularly relevant here: The Matriarch and the Welfare Mother. The Matriarch is the epitome of the strong black woman, but to a fault. She is represented as *overly* strong, aggressive, and at times a militant black woman who works to emasculate black men. The Welfare Mother, by contrast, is not strong but lazy, poor, and uneducated. Both of these figures, coupled with more recent images of the "angry black woman," point to the internalization of these controlling images within the African American community. This highlights the nature of colorism as a vehicle for the reproduction of hegemonic racism and sexism against black women. Via these negative internalized scripts of dark skin, the young black women in this study are supporting the same images that have been historically used in their own subjugation.

Another powerful image of black women that appears in the focus group data is dark-skinned women as objects of sexual desire. Many scholars suggest that the sexuality of black women has traditionally been presented as promiscuous and deviant. Yet, some allude to the idea that there are divergent perspectives of sexuality based upon skin tone. For instance, considering the historical representations of dark-skinned women in music and literature, folklorist Audrey Elisa Kerr notes that "the recurring questions become: Is sexuality generally defined differently for dark- and light-hued women?"[19] Based upon the data gathered in the focus groups, black women answer that question with a resounding yes. While many respondents talked about light-skinned women as the object of beauty, many also communicated internal scripts about dark-skinned women as the objects of sexual desire. It was commonplace for women like Ashley, a 21-year-old who identifies as light brown, to associate a higher level of sexuality with darker women. When I asked about the qualities related to dark skin, Ashley responded, "I would say also sexuality . . . they're more than lighter-skinned women. [. . .] Darker-skinned women (pause) they're more promiscuous and doing things." Keleechi, a participant identifying herself as "very light," makes the same connections when sharing her experience in high school. She notes that her school population had a disproportionate number of dark-skinned girls, and she noticed a huge difference in the way she was perceived by the young men in her school. She recalls that,

> Me and my sister were the only [. . .] light-skinned girls. It was mostly dark-skinned [girls], and [. . .] guys would approach us differently; if a guy came and I was with a friend, he might talk to her because she was darker. [. . .] But when he came to me, he *talked* to me. Guys would approach the dark-skinned girls in a more sexual manner, or they just wouldn't approach me at all.

Keleechi quickly recognizes this difference in treatment and attributes this difference to the perceived sexual desirability of darker-skinned girls.

It is important to note that women with darker tones recognize their classification as sexual objects in opposition to the light-skinned beauty. Some women even suggested that black men date light-skinned women for their facial features and dark-skinned women for their bodies. Take for example the ideas of Shanae, a dark-skinned participant who describes her own experiences with men:

> Well to be honest, it seems that men are attracted to black women [for] their body traits; most guys are approaching me because of the way I'm shaped rather than the way I actually look. [. . .] I don't know if I ever noticed this, but most red-skinned girls, if they're talking to a guy [. . .] and if you try to figure out why that particular guy is with

that girl, it's because she's pretty rather than she has a nice body [. . .] her face stands out more than her body.

Women in this study also recognize this pattern through the media. There was agreement across focus groups that light-skinned women are typically featured as the "prize" or point of beauty in music videos, while darker-skinned women are used in music videos to entice viewers with their overly sexualized bodies. Shirelle's comments illustrate this position:

> . . . in [music] videos, usually if it's [. . .] a love song or something, and they're talking about how they feel about a girl [. . .] she tends to be lighter skinned. And if they're talking about, oh she's got a nice body or she shake her whatever, [. . .] it tends to be a dark-skinned girl. And I think in the media, the light-skinned people are portrayed as [. . .] the prize. [. . .] And I don't think it's right, but that's just the way the world is because it's been going on for so long, and it's been a while and no one's actually doing anything to stop it.

Many focus group members like Shirelle are critical of media images and are readily able to identify the various ways in which colorism becomes highlighted within the context of music. For example, Denise's remarks about the members of singing group Destiny's Child reflect this awareness:

> Kelly [is] not even looked at. In Destiny's Child she doesn't really get the focus, but Beyoncé gets all the focus because she's [. . .] more appealing to the white and the black, the whole entire United States, all the cultures, 'cause she's fair skinned and [. . .] more appealing to both cultures, but Kelly [. . .] a lot of people find Kelly to be really, really attractive 'cause she's dark skinned [. . .] but she doesn't get all the limelight.

Similar to Denise's comments about megastar Beyoncé Knowles, other entertainers, including Alicia Keyes, Halle Berry, Tyra Banks, and the cast of popular television show *Girlfriends*, were mentioned throughout the course of this study as the most beautiful black women in popular culture.

Consistent with the body of literature on colorism that documents the struggles of light-skinned women and the perception that they are *not* authentic members of the race, there also emerged from this data similar experiences from dark-skinned women. Just as light-skinned women fight to prove that they are black enough, many dark-skinned women in this study battle to invalidate controlling images—to prove for instance that they are *not* violent and *not* ghetto. The effort to disprove stereotypes appears in a variety of contexts. Recall the experience of Shirelle, the young woman who was labeled as the "perfect AKA" simply because of her skin tone. Although Shirelle was not a part of this organization, many people assumed that she was or that she should be. Contrast Shirelle's experience with those of Yolanda and Bernice, two young women who are in fact members of this sorority. Yet because of their dark skin, their membership in this organization does not make sense to many people and is often questioned. Yolanda explains,

> Everyone around here is confused because we are [members of] AKA. We joke about it [. . .] because we just crossed into Alpha Kappa Alpha a few weeks ago and [. . .] because Bernice and I are a little bit darker than a paper bag, people assume that we wouldn't be AKAs. [. . .] But the stereotypes that are connected out there, they are hurtful, and people just perpetuate them continually.

The experiences of Yolanda and Bernice serve as good examples of how some women struggle to invalidate negative stereotypes about being dark skinned. As evidenced from their stories, dispelling myths about their skin tones is a minor annoyance because it is something that they can joke about.

This ongoing battle is one that dark-skinned women frequently engage in, and this is related to the ongoing effort in contesting controlling images. Tessa, a young woman who identifies herself as "very dark," discusses openly how her family's internalized scripts about her dark skin lowered their expectations about her intelligence. She states,

> My experience, I think, I've always seen this idea if you are lighter skinned then you are capable of education. I remember my young cousins growing up who were lighter skinned and had the good hair, [. . .] they were just expected to be smart, to say smart things, to kind of carry on the family name, versus I was never expected to be smart, but maybe they didn't expect it more from me, and when they did see it, it was a surprise and kind of different than what they thought it would be, versus the lighter-skinned kids [who] came out perfect and they were, they were manifested to be perfect. Where I had to prove [my intelligence] over and over again.

Despite being an honor student, Tessa not only experienced people in her family lowering their expectations of her but also many of her peers presuming that her "African dark" skin automatically made her less capable than others. Indeed, a majority of the respondents who identified themselves as dark or very dark spoke about the limitations of their skin tone. As Tatiana and Toni express, there are constant "self-reminders" about who they are:

> I think it's always been in the back of my head, [. . .] people see you differently. I've had to learn to realize that I love being sexy chocolate, you know what I mean? I had to tell myself that, but like, it was in-stilled in me at a young age that "there's something wrong with you." I got called all the names, "doo doo brown;" all that . . . it was hard, when you're a child and you don't know that you're different from everybody else, so I think it's always been in the back of my head. (Tatiana, 19, very dark)

> I'm an adult now, and it's something that still sticks with me even though I feel as though I've grown and matured. But I do still catch myself falling back into that mind frame of insecurity because of my skin complexion. (Toni, 23, dark)

These two young women point to the "internal work" required to decon-struct the negativity placed upon them. Like Toni and Tatiana, many of the women interviewed share a turning point in their lives that re-directs the normative internal scripts of colorism. As Tatiana shared, she had to learn to love being "sexy chocolate" rather than internalizing "doo doo brown." This process of resistance and reclamation is discussed at length in the fol-lowing chapter.

"I AM NOT BLACK; I AM BROWN": MEDIUM SKIN TONE AS A SAFE AND PROTECTED CLASS?

Much of the literature of skin tone and colorism within the black com-munity speaks to the preferences and disadvantages associated with light or dark skin, yet few studies concentrate on what it means to fall in the middle of the color spectrum. In many respects, colorism is situated within the context of a binary structure (light skin/dark skin; good hair/bad hair), yet there is some indication that being medium or brown skinned is seen as favorable and is therefore somewhat of a protected position. Although a much less reported idea, the works of some scholars find that blacks rated those who are medium or brown skinned more favorably than their coun-terparts with extreme light or extreme dark skin. In her writings on color-ism, Krystal Brent Zook suggests an element of safety inherent in the middle when she writes, "all of us but the most even-toned, chestnut-smooth browns are inevitably screwed in one way or another."[20] Results from this research support the idea that those who are medium or brown skinned are not as affected by the consequences of colorism. Yet, there is some evidence that also refutes this same idea. The focus groups do not point to a universal "voice from the middle" but, rather, various internalized scripts on what it means to be brown.

One of the first themes emerging about medium skin tone is that colorism is not an issue for those who are considered brown. As 20-year-old Lela points out,

> I would consider myself medium, and there's always been this whole thing with the red girls and the dark-skinned girls and being in the middle. I've never, you know, had any problems or anything like that. Nobody's ever said anything to me.

Lela considers her experiences very different from other black women because she is recognized as being in the middle and treated as such. For this young woman, colorism has never been *her* issue; it is, rather, "this whole thing" between those who are either very light or very dark. This sentiment is echoed by Fuze, a young woman who responds,

> I've just kind of view[ed] myself right in the middle and I think that, I feel like I kind of walk the line and can observe a lot more than a lot of other women because [. . .] when I interact with women, I don't really have a problem. [. . .]

Similarly, Fiona adds,

> I don't think people call [me] dark, and I don't think people call me light, either. So I feel kind of lucky to be in the middle, 'cause I'd say that I've escaped a lot of negative things, the extreme negative things that come with being light [. . .] or dark [. . .] I feel kind of nice in the middle.

From the viewpoints shared by these women, it is apparent that being brown often creates a unique "buffer" position that affords them better navigation among women than their light and dark counterparts.

Desiree articulates her middle position very differently from other women participating in the focus groups. She understands her skin tone to be quantifiably different than women of different skin tones. Believing that black women are indeed placed in a queue, Desiree is fully aware that her position as a brown-skinned woman affords her more advantage than a dark-skinned woman, yet less advantage than a light-skinned black woman. She notes:

> And if I go into an interview and there is a dark-skinned girl sitting next to me, I feel as though I have a better chance than her just because I have a lighter skin complexion. I'm not light skinned, but I'm brown skinned, and I don't care what kind of degree she has, I have something that appeals to other people and that's my complexion. And if I go into the interview and there's a lighter-skinned girl than me there, I feel threatened because she has something that she can use against me and that's her complexion.

Desiree goes on to explain that for black women, skin color is about the survival of the fittest. Having brown skin deems her better fit than dark women and less fit than light women. Nevertheless, for Desiree this translates into varied levels of resource and opportunity, including employment. And it is for this reason that Desiree uses her skin tone to the best of her advantage and ability in order to get ahead in her life experiences.

Despite the relative inconsequence of colorism in the everyday lives of the medium-toned women listed above, there are some in this group who, like dark-skinned women, feel a considerable amount of constraint within their day-to-day lives. For instance, Vivica, a young woman who identifies herself as "medium," recounts her experience in elementary school when she first learned that there is less value placed upon her brown skin. Recalling how many of the young boys in her class were more enamored with the "light" and "Spanish-looking" girls, Vivica explains that she quickly internalized the negativity placed upon her brownness and thus developed an internal script that regulated her outlook on life. She says:

> And so when you are in that mindset or whatever, you don't try to go out for the light-skinned people or whatever. You just try to stay amongst yourself because you feel like, "Okay, this is my level. This is what I can reach." [. . .] I mean we're just at the bottom anyways.

In light of the varying contexts and meanings attached to being a brown-skinned woman, it is useful to point out that many of the women who identified themselves as "medium" were very sensitive and particular about characterizing themselves as "brown." These young women distanced themselves from the label of *dark*, preferring instead to be considered brown. Even though these women are not light skinned, for them it was better to be brown than dark. The following statement offered by Nia is illustrative of this point:

> I've never [been called dark] until my freshman year, and people were like, "Oh [yeah], you're dark." And to this day I still don't think I'm dark, I think I'm brown. . . . I really think my perception of color is distorted because [. . .] I will think that I'm the same shade as someone else, and they're like "Oh no no no, you're darker than that," and I'm like how? [laughter] And I'm, you know, pulling my arm out and [comparing to others]. That looks the same to me!"

This story is particularly interesting because Nia speaks in the focus group about her "discovery" of being dark upon her arrival to college. Growing up, Nia's family always referred to her as brown, and that is the identity that she had internalized. There was, however, a disconnect between how her family viewed her skin tone and how she was classified in the larger African American community. This mismatch of color is fairly common among blacks, as there are varying frames of reference for classifying someone as light, dark, or brown. As Nia mentions, her perception is that she is brown, yet she finds herself in a position of fighting against being labeled as dark.

Similar to Nia, Leah—another young woman who identifies as "medium"—learned from her family that it was better to be brown than dark. During the focus group, she talked about her experience as a young girl and getting darker during the summer. After many hours of playing out in the sun, she would come home and shower in an effort to restore her brown color. Leah describes,

> [As a little girl] I would get really dark in the summertime [and I would] come home and [. . .] scrub my skin when I was in the shower, so I could get my [brown] color back [. . .] cause I didn't want to be too dark, that's what was in my mind. Don't know why, I just didn't like it, 'cause I felt like I looked, um, dry and dirty. And my mom would come home and [ask], "What are you doing?" And I'm like, "Mom, I'm black, I'm black." And she's like, "No." From that point she would tell me, "No, you are not black; you are brown. Don't let anyone call you black, 'cause you're brown."

Even as a young girl, Leah feared the condemnation from others inherent in dark skin (i.e., looking dry and dirty), by attempting to scrub her color back. Additionally, her mother's insistence that she call herself brown and not black speaks to the elevation of brownness over blackness in the African American community.

This elevation of brown over black interestingly played itself out during one focus group session. This particular gathering included a pair of best friends: Melissa, who considers herself "light-brown," and Denise, who identifies as "medium." At one point during the focus group, Melissa talked about her friendship with Denise. She said, "One of my closest friend[s], she's dark skinned and we have the best relationship. We don't, um, well she's brown skinned, sorry, brown skinned." When Melissa first described Denise's complexion as dark, Denise "cut her eye" at Melissa, indicating her disapproval of being labeled "dark." In the middle of her comment, Melissa changed her characterization from dark to brown skinned. This change was important to Denise and is indicative of the notion that brown skin is "safe" and much more desirable than dark skin. Although it is uncertain whether or not being medium translates into life experiences that are truly protected and safe from the challenges of very light or very dark skin, it is clear from these narratives that "feeling" brown is much more significant than "being" considered dark.

In comparing the findings from this study with the results of Parrish's 1946 work, it appears that in many ways, the color names and color notions present within black culture have not changed. We see overwhelmingly positive names for light skin and negative names for dark skin. There is some difficulty in naming the terms for those who fall in the middle of the color spectrum.

The contemporary language of skin tone very much shapes what ideas are communicated and internalized about light, brown, and dark skin. The internal scripts of skin tone emerging from the focus groups underscore findings from previous research on colorism yet also point to new patterns among contemporary women of color. First, messages about light skin as the beauty ideal are repeated by the women interviewed, as well as implications of light skin offering more privilege and value in the black community. Negative images of black women as unintelligent and ghetto are also reiterations of the previous research. As these findings suggest, there is a "red-brown-black" divide at work in the lives of these young women. Obiagele Lake notes a similar pattern operating within Jamaican society.[21] The majority of the women in this study are conscious that their skin tones are integral parts of their identities and are fully aware that as young black women, skin tone indeed denotes a certain social position. On defining colorism, many women mentioned issues of beauty. Light skin carries the most value in terms of physical attractiveness and desirability. Yet in the everyday lives of these women, colorism goes beyond standards of beauty, as participants consider colorism to be about "separation," "preference," "attention," and "treatment." Red women seem to occupy in the black community the same space that white women hold in greater society. Dark-skinned women, who are more typically referred to in this study as "black," occupy the same space in the black community as that held by black women in broader society—the bottom space. Perhaps what is new is the presence of a middle voice and a keen recognition of the safe space being brown provides. In addition to this recognition is a resistance to being labeled "black," as that equates into "true" blackness, especially in treatment. The internalization of the scripts indicating that light is best, brown is safe, and dark is worst creates in the lives of black women a subjective reality that influences the ways in which these three distinct groups of women go about their day-to-day behavior.

THE PRACTICES OF EVERYDAY COLORISM

I had little if any interaction with the light-skinned elite, but their codes of conduct, their etiquette, their colorist beliefs and practices, were well known in the Black community and for the most part when I was a child went unchallenged. Colorism existed like a bitter, unalterable pollutant in the atmosphere of the Black community, something of which we were all aware and yet tried to ignore.

—Marita Golden[22]

In the statement above, Marita Golden, author of *Don't Play in the Sun: One Woman's Journey through the Color Complex*, writes about the unspoken and uncontested "codes" of colorism that invariably create difference and distinction based upon skin tone. As Golden suggests, these codes manifest themselves in the form of norms, beliefs, and practices of people in a wide range of social settings. The final component of everyday colorism, *external practices*, are everyday behaviors and actions enacted by women toward themselves and others based upon their internalized views about skin color. Just as the internalized scripts of skin tone represent a young woman's identity, external practices reflect a young woman's *experience* of colorism. The following example perhaps best crystallizes the nature of everyday colorism. Melissa, a young woman who identifies as "light brown," indicates how her views about darker women influenced her behavior:

I know sometimes I can be kind of racist toward dark-skinned girls because I have been before when, in my high school days, I really didn't like dark-skinned girls, because they used to be evil, so I didn't really like them. [. . .] I used to say really hurtful comments and really bring down people's self-esteem.

She goes on to say:

I saw that their color was their insecurity, so I used that against them. So, it was basically them showing me their weakness as [. . .] their dark-skinned color being their insecurity, so I used that against them.

Melissa's racism toward dark-skinned women is based upon her perception that they are evil. This of course justified her deplorable actions. Melissa's experience provides an excellent example of how white racism becomes internalized and reified through the daily interactions of black women. Similar stories emerged throughout my focus group discussions with participants. These comments suggest that women engage in three specific areas of practice: ritualistic, compensatory, and discriminatory. Each practice is detailed below.

Ritualistic Practices

Historically, black women (like many women in general) have engaged in countless *ritualistic practices*—behaviors attached to colorism rooted in familial and/or cultural tradition—in an effort to uphold standards of beauty in the African American community. From enduring the excruciating pain of a hot comb or relaxer, or even the soreness from sitting too long in an effort to achieve braided hairstyles, many black women and girls understand the struggle. It comes as no surprise, then, that many black women and girls (myself included) have been cautioned to "stay out of the sun" for fear of spoiling (or further darkening) their color. In fact, one participant in this study shares the story of her dark-skinned cousin, who in preparation for her wedding, refused to go out in the sun a full month before her wedding in order to "preserve" her color. As English professor Audrey Elisa Kerr carefully documents, the traditions and folklore surrounding skin color are central to understanding the nature of colorism. Kerr explains:

Historically, black women, in the company of other black women, are exposed to folk beliefs and practices concerned with skin lightening, hair lengthening or straightening, and repressing facial features, including milk baths to lighten skin, exercises to tighten full lips and retract full nostrils, and home-backed concoctions to straighten hair and inspire hair growth.[23]

Although many of the above-mentioned customs are associated with practices occurring in the 19th and early 20th centuries before the dawn of the Black is Beautiful movement, there is evidence that some of these rituals have been transferred to the younger generation and are alive and well within the lives of young black women. Many of the women in this study mentioned hearing and/or participating in such ritualistic practices as: holding the nose with a clothespin in order to make it narrower; scrubbing one's knees, elbows, and neck with a *white* wash cloth in order to prevent the areas from becoming darker; "double" wrapping the elbows in gauze treated with special oils; and expectant mothers drinking "special" herbal teas in order to improve the chances of giving birth to a baby with light or brown skin.

As I discussed earlier, the birth of a new baby in many black families signifies even more ritualistic practices that reinforce the strength of colorism. Close examination of an infant's ears, fingers, and even nail beds supposedly aid relatives in determining how light (or dark) a child's skin tone will become. The following remarks of two participants further demonstrate this tradition:

> All [of] my nieces and nephews are very light, and when they [we]re babies, we could tell if they were [getting] darker by checking [. . .] their ears apparently. So a part of your ear is the shade that you're gonna be; I remember they would always check my ears. You know if it's dark [then] you're gonna be, because, I mean, all black babies are lighter when they're born; they check their ears after. (Michelle, 21, medium)

> My nephew, he's the cutest baby in the world. [laughter] And he's light, you know. And when he was born, they were like, "Do you all think he's gonna get darker?" [laughter and agreement]. And then, [my family] was like, "Well look at his ears, and look at his nail beds. Whatever color they are, that's the color he's gonna be." (Trina, 20, very light)

Although many women could relate to the customs connected to newborns, the vast majority of women in the study more commonly shared their experiences with bleaching. A multibillion dollar global industry, skin bleaching is popular in countries such as India, Thailand, Nigeria, and the United States. Many of the ingredients in many skin-bleaching agents are extremely harmful, yet many young women feel compelled to purchase and use the products, oftentimes quietly and behind closed doors. African American actor and director Lisa Raye explores the epidemic of skin bleaching in the 2014 film *Skinned*, uncovering the physical and emotional scars of a young black woman who decides to bleach her dark skin.

The ritualistic practice of skin bleaching was revealed by numerous women in this study, many of whom admit to a long history of bleaching starting in childhood. Consider for instance the parallel accounts shared by Chanel, Vivica, and Stacey—three Haitian participants who label the practice of bleaching as a central aspect of their shared ethnic culture. Chanel, a dark-skinned woman, attributes bleaching her skin every night before going to bed during early adolescence as a recommended remedy for curing her acne. Vivica, a medium-toned participant, further illuminates that for Haitian women, bleaching is a common beauty practice:

> And speaking from the Haitian part of it, women, Haitian women [. . .] put [bleach] on every time [they] take a shower, they put it on, take it off, they get a pimple and I was even at one point. . . . I mean, you know, don't forget to put that on, 'cause you [don't] want to go back, you want to be as light as possible whatever [. . .] it's still prevalent in our society.

Likewise, Stacey grew up in a family where bleaching was common among her female relatives. She reveals that her mother taught her as a child to use a bleaching soap every night before bed in order to keep her pretty complexion:

> My mom said, "Oh we're going to buy you some soap for you to [use] at night, you take a shower with [it], not like Irish Spring, but bleaching soap," and I put a bleaching lotion on. I mean there's so much discoloration in my face, I [asked my] mom, "Why is my face so white, and my neck so dark?" "Cause you didn't put your cream there; you gotta work on that." And being Haitian [that] means a lot.

A large part of the care that Stacey's mother put into her complexion was due to Stacey's position in the family as the lightest child. On her demographic sheet, Stacey indicated her skin tone as "dark" yet explained that within her family, she was faintly lighter than her brothers and sisters. Because of this, Stacey explained, she was coveted by her mother more than her other siblings, and being encouraged to use bleach every night was a way for Stacey's commodity and social capital within the family to be improved.

Outside of skin bleaching, perhaps the one ritualistic practice that almost every woman in this research could readily identify with was the sun. Staying out of the sun's damaging rays was mentioned by nearly every focus group participant. Many respondents learned early on to heed the advice of their mothers, grandmothers, or other female family members and subconsciously avoid the sun. This in fact was my own experience. Although I would describe my upbringing as full of positive ideals and practices, especially relating to skin tone, I can vividly recall my mother's repeated requests for me to wear long sleeves during the hot months of the summer. Even now as an adult, I am sometimes cautious about how long I am in direct contact with the sunlight. Many of the women interviewed share a similar concern, while others express more of a ritualistic avoidance of the sun.

Compensatory Practices

The second type of external practices, *compensatory practices*, are behaviors enacted in order to balance or counteract a perceived negative attribute connected to color. In this project, women who spoke about engaging in compensatory practices were of darker hues. These women felt that they had to alter their appearance in order to be validated by themselves and others. An example of this is the story shared by Vivica. In the previous section, this young woman cited bleaching as part of her regular beauty regimen. Yet lightening her skin also serves as a compensatory practice because she does so in order to please her boyfriend, who admits that he is typically attracted to lighter women. At one point during the focus group session, there was a discussion about where to buy certain bleaching products. Vivica said,

> It's a huge section. [. . .] You know there's [a store] across the street from Winn Dixie. [. . .] Go right in there and just go to the aisle. [. . .] I know exactly what aisle it is because I used to. . . . I mean there's no reason to lie because you use [bleaching crèmes]. . . . Sometimes you feel like, you know, if you were just a little bit lighter, and, you know, what's so bad about it, because my boyfriend did like me when I was that color. [. . .] That cream makes you lighter, and he likes it.

As Vivica explains, she gets a better response from her partner when she is lighter, so in her mind, taking the extra step in bleaching is worth it.

Like Vivica, there are other women who feel compelled to pay close attention to their appearance in order to be on the same level as women with lighter complexions. Monica, a medium-toned woman, suggests that one of her best friends (a dark-skinned woman) employs various compensatory practices when she is around a mixed group of black women. Monica describes that her friend "feels like she has to do extra things to make herself look more appealing . . . Her hair has to be extravagant, make up, nails, everything has to be perfect because she feels like she has to balance that out with her dark skin." This idea of settling the "color score" is reiterated by the experience of Stacey, a 24-year-old dark-skinned participant who readily acknowledged that because of the negative ideas that she and others carry about dark-skinned women, she has to do things in order to redress her position:

> I feel because [I am dark], I always have to step up my game and [. . .] always have my dress code, doing things, always trying, mak[ing] sure that I have the knowledge or trying to play up yourself more and do more and exhaust yourself to the point of depression because you just want to be the best because you're a dark-skinned black woman.

The kinds of compensatory practices that Stacey and other women engage in are in fact noticed by some men. Consider, for instance, the observation offered by Pablo, a young man participating in the men's focus group:

> I just want to say that I noticed some women . . . especially the dark women, feel like they have to make up for the darkness, that they have to look better than the lighter girls, that their fashion has to be better, their earrings and their clothes have to be, that they have to be done up to make up for the darkness. Um, that's because the darkness might, they seem to think, and it's an attitude that darkness is detracting from their getting attention from men.

(An interesting point to note here is that few of the men participating in the focus group discussion on colorism connected their observations and perspectives back to the broader landscape of patriarchy, sexism, and racism operating within black communities. Rather, the men I spoke to viewed colorism as solely a symptom and circumstance of black female relationships and interactions.)

There are other women in this study who, like Stacey, believe that carrying out these kinds of practices are necessary in order to successfully navigate within larger society. It is not until an oppositional knowledge of colorism is gained that Stacey and others no longer feel the pressure or need to engage in such behaviors.

Discriminatory Practices

Perhaps the most common (and hurtful) types of practices mentioned throughout this research project, *discriminatory practices* are those behaviors that function to include or exclude someone based upon their skin tone. They range from small incidents such as joking or teasing to larger-scale practices that preclude certain people from forming friendships or relationships. Within the domain of discriminatory behavior, bias occurs from all points of the color spectrum.

As previously noted, on a smaller scale discriminatory practices include taunting and excluding someone on the basis of their skin color. Many women in this study recollect these types of experiences happening in grade school. Shanta, a medium-hued participant, recounted her experience in the fifth grade of being snubbed by another classmate for not being the right shade:

> [. . .] the other girl was mainly like two shades lighter than I was, [but] I was told, "You can't hang out with us because you're dark, [. . .] you should probably drink from the other water fountain."

Shanta's memory of her grade school experience demonstrates two important features of colorism. First, this story highlights the meaning and significance of "shades." Throughout the focus groups, many participants spoke about being included or excluded for being one or two shades too light or dark. Minute delineations in skin tone (i.e., one shade), as indicated by Shanta's account, translate into large-scale differences in treatment.

Second, being told that she should drink from another water fountain is a direct reference to Jim Crow segregation practices that relegated people of color to separate and substandard facilities prior to the Civil Rights movement. Although 20-year-old Shanta is recalling an experience that occurred in the late 1990s, it is a stunning example of what race scholar Patricia Hill Collins refers to as the "past in present" occurrences of the "new" racism. Collins is speaking specifically to the ways in which old patterns of Jim Crow racism continue to manifest and reappear throughout our contemporary society. As colorism is a form of internalized racism, the same reasoning can be applied to the modern-day experiences of colorism. Separatist practices such as the brown paper bag test are no longer a reality for many black Americans, yet everyday discriminatory practices resembling "old-school" colorism are still very much commonplace in African American culture.

On into adulthood, the women in this study noted that discriminatory practices become more substantive as their experiences and ideals of colorism grow more solid. For instance, Shanae suspects that her dark complexion causes her to be profiled on a regular basis:

> Well, being dark skinned, I have been called "burnt" and "midnight." [. . .] People seem to think that I'm ghetto and have an attitude because I am black. I have always been discriminated against because of my skin color, for instance, say I go into a store, you know, people tend to follow me because of my skin color. [. . .] I don't know why, but you know.

Although Shanae cannot explicitly prove that her skin complexion was the reason for being followed in stores, it is evident that she has a clear grasp of the effects of not only her race but her skin color. *Everyday racism*—a concept introduced by Dutch sociologist Philomena Essed—is characteristic of the more subtle, daily occurrences of mistreatment that are typically not intended to be harmful but are viewed as such. Everyday colorism, then, embodies the same characteristics; in Shanae's case, "looking" suspicious and being discriminated against is part and parcel of being dark skinned.

In this project, the area of relationships—specifically, friendships with other black women—are the root of the majority of discriminatory practices. The language of skin color, combined with the internal scripts associated with light skin and dark skin, work to create barriers in forming friendships with women of opposite skin tones. Tessa discusses openly how her views about her darkness serve as an impediment to developing meaningful relationships with light-skinned women:

> It's not like I go out and say I'm not going to be friends with white-skinned women, but definitely, even though you don't want to be doing it in your head, you definitely say okay, this girl is light skinned and maybe I shouldn't be friends with her because she might not understand where I'm coming from or want to be my friend because I am [dark]; I'll bring her down basically.

Tessa's perception that she will "bring down" a light-skinned woman is rooted in her family's negative attitudes toward her dark skin. Recall that earlier in this chapter, Tessa talked about the low expectations conveyed to her as she was growing up. As this excerpt suggests, although she tries hard not to let the same pessimism continue to control her internal scripts and external practices, Tessa nonetheless perceives herself as unworthy of the friendship of a lighter-toned woman.

Similar to Tessa's, there are other cases in which discriminatory practices take the form of complete evasion of women of differing skin tones. In some instances, women avoid making friendships with women who share the same complexion. This is the case for Rachel, a young woman who describes her skin tone as "light brown" but confesses that her peer group is intentionally darker skinned.

> I have to say, I don't have a lot of lighter-skinned friends. [. . .] But I think that some of them, I won't name names, I've seen the lighter-skinned girls and they're all in the cliques, they're the fashionable ones, and I don't really care for that kind of lifestyle at all.

Rachel implies in this statement that most light-skinned women are aloof and exclusionary and notes that she would rather spare herself by intermingling with darker-skinned women. This is the same sentiment of Ashley, also a young woman who identifies as "light brown"; she admits to having negative internal scripts about light-skinned women and therefore choosing to make friendships with women who are darker, because she considers them more "real."

> All my best friends are of darker skin tones. I think when I've had, you know, situations with women who are [. . .] lighter than me, it's become catty. [. . .] I wouldn't say that all light-skinned girls are catty, but it's just from my experiences it's been a lot of, "Oh, yeah, I got you, I got you," and then something happens and they were the ones who disappear. [. . .] In comparison with my relationships with darker-skinned women, they've never really pressured me about stuff, [. . .] they're real with me, honest with me about stuff. [. . .] That's the type of people I like to surround myself with. My experience with lighter-skinned girls has not been that real to me.

We learn from these statements that light-skinned women are viewed as less authentic in the area of friendships as well. Although Rachel and Ashley are light skinned, they too believe the socially constructed ideals about light skin.

To be sure, negative internalized scripts are shared by women of all skin tones and can in many ways function to create hostility and tension among women of contrasting complexions.

This notion is perhaps best displayed during a focus group session in which participants candidly discussed their reasons for avoiding their lighter and darker counterparts:

Monica: I think personally, with myself, just being honest, sometimes when I see someone who is really dark, I'm kind of hesitant. In other words, I'm wondering where they're coming from, do they come from the same place that I'm coming from. Are our personalities going to be compatible? Um, light-skinned women, I don't really approach either. [. . .] So I tend to seek out women that look like me, that are medium skinned, same kind of tone, you know.

Shanae: Okay, for me, most of my friends are red boned; before we became friends, we had a feud because of the whole red and black thing.

JeffriAnne: Give me an example of a feud that you had.

Shanae: Okay, I remember a fight in my ninth grade year with my best friend, who was very light skinned, and if you see her you would think that she was, well, I wouldn't say white, but she is light skinned. [. . .] Yeah, and we both had this attitude to where we thought, you know, walk with our heads up high, bad ass or whatever. [. . .] We sat next to each other and we would not talk to each other. [. . .] I don't know how to explain, it was just always like that with me and my friends that are red skinned. But now, it's all good.

Kira: I'm also going to agree with what Monica said. [. . .] I am more hesitant, I guess, to go up to someone who is lighter skin, just because of that stereotype. [. . .] I'm not going to go up [to them], in the back of my head, I'm like, I hope they're not rude. [. . .] Vice versa for a darker-skinned person, I hope you're not extremely ghetto, trying to hit me in my face or something crazy is going to happen. But it's just always in the back of my mind, [. . .] it affects how I speak to them or how I view them right off the bat, it's just there.

Asia: I'll finish what I was saying. I really, I don't have problems with anybody, but I don't really approach black women because sometimes I don't find that they're easily approachable.

JeffriAnne: What about just in your day-to-day interaction? Not necessarily with your friends. But just walking on campus or being somewhere, do you think that the way that you interact with other black women who aren't your friends, do you think that skin tone plays some sort of role?

Keleechi: Yes because when I approach, like, I try to be nice to everybody, just so I don't get any stereotype put on me. [. . .] If I approach someone of darker skin tone, I try not to talk too much because when I talk, I sound like a white girl, so they say, so I try not to talk that much.

This dialogue speaks to the complexity of relationships between young black women. Monica, a brown-skinned participant, believes that initiating friendships with women of similar skin tones is best and further speaks to the distrust and perceived lack of connection she has for dark-skinned women. Shanae, on the other hand, has a close friendship with a "red" girl but admits that their differences in skin color initially necessitated a fight in order to get over each other's hang-ups about women of opposite skin tones. Kira confessed that she is cautious of her light *and* dark-skinned counterparts, citing the expectation of cruelty from light women and the fear of violence from dark women. Asia, who also identifies as medium, pointed out that she has no problems with any black women but nonetheless avoids approaching "black" women. These young women are readily aware that their internalized viewpoints are influencing their behavior and potential for building true bonds of black sisterhood across skin tones.

There are some cases in which women actually make attempts to forge relationships with their lighter counterparts but are rejected. As a result, a type of retaliatory discriminatory practice is enacted against members of the "opposite" skin tone in an effort to challenge the system of hierarchy and stratification. For example, Toni recalled numerous occasions of being slighted because of her darker skin tone. Despite being openly discriminated against by her lighter-skinned counterparts, she often seeks to counteract the treatment she received in the past by establishing exclusionary friendships with fellow dark-skinned girls in college:

> My roommate was [. . .] also dark skinned and [. . .] we kind of did a reverse kind of thing, where we only hung out with dark-skinned girls, our whole clique was dark-skinned girls. And [. . .] it wasn't necessarily like "Oh, if you're light skinned you can't hang out with us" but it was kind of on purpose, you know, and I think it was just kind of our way of [. . .] turning up our noses at the way that things typically are, which is, you know, light-skinned girls, oh they stick together and they're bougie and [. . .] we were like, oh okay, cool, so we're all going to stick together, and we're fly and we're dark skinned and, you know, we roll together.

Toni's experience provides a useful example of how those who are initially *victims* of colorism later become themselves *culprits* of colorism; the only way for Toni to combat skin tone discrimination was to take part in the same discriminatory behavior.

The findings from this section reinforce just how strongly racism is internalized and inculcated within the minds of young black women. The ways in which these young people formulate negative opinions about women of differing skin tones and then discriminate against light, brown, and dark women is surprisingly similar to the documented experiences of racism. Consider, for example, the 1991 study conducted by scholar Joe Feagin.[24] In his research examining the contemporary significance of race for middle-class blacks, Feagin found that through day-to-day contact with whites, African Americans are discriminated against in five specific ways: through avoidance actions, rejection actions, verbal attacks, physical attacks by police, and attacks by other whites. Although I am careful *not* to equate the experience of the black Americans featured in Feagin's research with the young black women in this study, the parallels of racism and colorism are striking. The resemblances lie between the kinds of discriminatory practices highlighted in the everyday experiences of racism with those of everyday colorism. Similar acts of avoidance, rejection, and verbal attacks are noted in the stories shared by the young black women in this research. The next chapter addresses how the language, scripts, and practices are learned, perpetuated, and, at times, transformed.

Sidebar 3. Searching for Love and Finding Colorism Instead

The following color story is from a former student who sent me this email after attending a lecture I organized on campus regarding race relations. During this lecture, I did not discuss colorism at all, but this 29-year-old African American woman decided to use the opportunity to share her struggles with colorism.
(October 2014)

Hello Dr. Wilder,
I'm really glad I came to the lecture last week. I learned a lot about myself as far as mentalities and certain ways that I think of myself as a result of my race. Up to this point, I've never said these things that I'm about to mention because I think I have gotten so used to thinking this way that I didn't realize how bad it is and how it is something I need to change. Please understand that what I'm saying is what I have spent years thinking about myself, I'm not saying it applies to all black women or anyone in particular.

So, there are times where I think if I was light skinned with nicer eyes and longer hair I would be accepted more and more men would find me attractive. Back in 2011, I was on this dating website. Yeah I know Dr. Wilder, can you say desperate? Lol! Anyway, I'm on this site and at this point I'm writing guys and none of them are really responding to me other than a quick hello or "ok" and some are not responding to me at all or even blocking me right off the back. I had one write back and say "Sorry, you're not pretty enough." I started thinking, if I was lighter guys would be coming after me and I wanted to prove myself right so I went on the site and made a fake profile and used a google image of a woman who was around my age that was light skinned with long hair and hazel colored eyes and I set the account up and I didn't do anything. I just waited.

Guys began to write me left and right, even guys who had rejected me before were sending me messages wanting to talk to me, meet me or get to know me better. I got all these compliments and attention from men that weren't really coming before when I was trying to be myself. I deleted the account once I proved my point and I remember crying and asking myself why was I born this way and why don't I look pretty.

After days of tearing myself down with my own words, I stopped crying and even though I didn't feel it I told myself that I'm beautiful the way I am and God made no mistake when He created me. I honestly need to get back to saying those things over myself but it is hard to do when still today I struggle with feeling this way. There are days where I'll take the extra time with my hair or even go to the salon to get it done and as good as people may tell me I look, I'll still in the back of my mind think that if I was this shade or that, I would look a lot better. I should probably be more proud of my race but I'm not as proud as I should be at times and I don't know how to really fix it.

CHAPTER 4

Getting to the Roots of Colorism: Family, School, Dating, and Relationships

Often it is within the family, where a variety of skin colors may be represented among individual members, that black children first learn the values attributed to differences in skin color. When the child enters the larger social world, she carries these color conscious attitudes beyond the confines of the home, and in turn, those attitudes are reinforced by that world.[1]

— Margo Okazawa-Rey, Tracy Robinson, and Janie Victoria Ward

The previous chapter detailed the ways in which black women perceive skin tone differences in their daily lives. Emerging from the data is the theory of *everyday colorism*, or the day-to-day experiences of skin color bias and discrimination, and how it appears in these young women's lives via language, internal scripts, and external practices. Throughout the process of data analysis and interpretation, however, there were several recurring questions surrounding the nature of everyday colorism: *How does the discourse of colorism begin? How is it maintained? Does it ever change; can there be an oppositional discourse of colorism?* This chapter is focused on addressing these important inquiries.[2] Results of the analysis suggest that there are three factors impacting everyday colorism: *points of origin, stabilizing agents,* and *transformative agents.* By taking a deeper look inside the color stories of the women in this study, I examine how everyday colorism starts, is maintained, and in some cases transformed.

DEFINING POINTS OF ORIGIN, STABILIZING AGENTS, AND TRANSFORMATIVE AGENTS

An overwhelming majority of the women in this study share a strong sense of colorism in their day-to-day lives. The language, beliefs, and practices attached to the discourse of skin tone are learned through points of origin, reinforced by stabilizing agents, and challenged by way of transformative agents. Simply stated, a point of origin is the way in which colorist ideology is first introduced to an individual. Serving as the primary means of socialization, points of origin provide the foundational knowledge base (i.e., language, internal scripts, and external practices) for understanding the socially constructed meaning of skin tone. As many sociologists explain, primary agents of socialization (family, school, and the media, for example) are the most important for an individual and signify one's membership in a particular culture or society. Because primary socialization occurs in childhood, the majority of women in this study reveal that colorism was introduced to them by their families; others cite school and the media. For nearly all the women, colorism is introduced within a *normative* framework; that is, young women learn the dominant views of skin tone widely held within the black community. Yet, for a small number of participants, an *oppositional* framework of colorism—one that does not devalue or elevate one skin tone over another—is laid as the foundation of knowledge. In these instances, individuals are socialized to embrace positive aspects and attributes of all skin tones. Although very few women in this project share learning about oppositional perspectives early in life, many strive later in life to establish this alternative ideology in resistance to the mainstream principles of colorism that deem lightness as the criterion for importance and worth.

Sociologists Peter Berger and Thomas Luckmann explain that unlike primary socialization, secondary socialization is "any subsequent process that inducts an already socialized individual into new sectors of the objective world of his society."[3] Once the ideology of colorism (normative or oppositional) is introduced, the analysis suggests that there are points of secondary socialization that work to either strengthen *or* shift a young woman's identity and experiences with colorism. I am defining these elements as stabilizing and transformative agents. *Stabilizing agents* are defined as people and/or

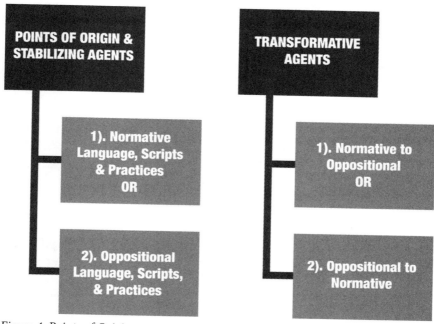

Figure 4: Points of Origin

events that legitimize one's primary understanding of colorism, confirming internalized scripts and justifying the external practices of everyday colorism. *Transformative agents* represent people and/or events that change one's primary understanding of colorism. These agents either work to a) introduce the dominant discourse of colorism, representing a shift from an oppositional to a normative framework; or b) work to challenge the normative framework, resulting in a redirection of language, internalized scripts, and external practices (See Figure 4). In essence, points of origin signify the foundation of knowledge, stabilizing agents confirm old knowledge, and transformative agents create new knowledge. In this chapter, I examine how family, school, friendships/intimate relationships, and the media play significant roles in the socialization of normative and/or oppositional ideologies of colorism.

The Black Family: The Ultimate Point of Origin

The family is regarded as a powerful force in the lives of black Americans. For many, the black family represents the bedrock of survival, resilience, kinship, and community. Black families have historically served as an institutional buffer against the external forces of racism. It is oftentimes within the family unit that black consciousness and black pride is learned

and celebrated. At the same time, however, the black family can simultaneously work to indoctrinate colorist ideology. This notion is well documented in contemporary literary works such as *Our Kind of People, Don't
Play in the Sun*, and *The Color Complex*, yet these family stories of black
women and colorism are largely absent in scholarly research. Although
there is an extensive body of revisionist literature on black families *and* a
growing body of scholarship on the contemporary nature of colorism,
there is a need for more empirical research—particularly within the field of
sociology—addressing the role of the black family as it relates to colorism.
This section of analysis begins to fill this gap.

Women in this study cited their family more than any other individual
or institution as the most influential factor in shaping their views and ideas
about themselves and others as it relates to skin tone. As one participant
observed, "I've always been affected by colorism. The majority of the members of my family are light skinned, there is a couple [who] are dark skinned,
it's just always been a big issue." When sharing their stories, many participants began their narratives—even if they were not about the family—by
describing the skin tone of their family members, at times even mentioning
great-grandparents. Further, women were very honest about the color di-
chotomies existing within their families, often referring to the "light side"
or "dark side" of the family or placing emphasis on family members with
distinctive features, such as "the cousins with the curly hair," or the "gray-
eyed" nephew. Almost every person shared this type of information at
some point in the focus groups. It is clear, then, that the language, scripts,
and practices of everyday colorism start in the family, the ultimate point of
origin for skin-color hierarchy and division. The findings point to two specific patterns in the black family: 1) the instillation of the normative discourse of colorism via female family members; and 2) the creation of an
oppositional ideology.

Bloodmothers and Othermothers

With very few exceptions, women in this study note that female family
members play a significant role in the production and socialization of a
skin color hierarchy within their respective families. This is not surprising
given the matriarchal-centered family structure that has dominated African American culture since slavery. Part of this centrality is referred to as
the power of motherhood.[4] Although this idea is raised in the context of
the politicization of motherhood as a source of activism and empowerment, in this research, the power of mothers—*bloodmothers* and *othermothers*—also lies in their ability to shape a young woman's perceptions

about skin tone. Bloodmothers, or biological kin, and othermothers, extended family or non-kin, play integral parts in childrearing and childcare and thus play a significant role in handing down colorist ideology to the next generation. As cultural critic bell hooks observes, "It is crucial that we look at the black female experience. For if the majority of black children are being raised by black females, then certainly how we perceive ourselves, our blackness, informs the social construction of our individual and collective identity."[5] Each woman in this study understands herself as a direct reflection of her mother, grandmother, or other female family member who in many ways serve as the source of her identity construction. For many of the participants, making this connection was not an easy one, as talking about their families in the focus groups made them realize that women were responsible for enabling normative ideas of colorism. Consider the story of Luann, a 21-year-old that initially had difficulty pointing to female figures as points of origin within her own life. At the beginning of her focus group, the medium-toned respondent did not consider skin tone bias to be a problem, saying, "I don't think my life has been shaped by colorism. I think I'm medium, right in the middle." Despite her initial misgivings about the impact of colorism in her life, Luann later recognized that she was wrong. Like many other participants, she shared stories of the women in her family doing a range of things from cautioning her to stay out of the sun to influencing her attraction to light-skinned men. By the end of the discussion, Luann confessed, "I don't think colorism will ever go away." She went on to say,

'Cause we all know about it, and the moment we started talking, I didn't even realize [. . .] what I said at the beginning. When I started talking, I said I don't think [colorism] should [matter], well not that much. And then I kept talking [and thought] well, you know what, my grandma said this to me, my auntie said this, my mom has said, it's all, it's the women. It's how you internalize [colorism] is in Black women. I didn't even think about it. Wow.

Luann's participation in a focus group conversation with other black women caused her to understand the oftentimes covert nature of colorism, particularly within black families.

Another woman who shared in the same mental voyage connecting family to her first awareness of colorism was Karina, a 21-year-old Haitian woman who identifies herself as "medium." When thinking about her first memories of colorism, Karina initially attributed college life to exposing her to skin tone differences. She began,

For most of my life [. . .] with me, it was more, you're either white or you're black. [. . .] There were two black kids in my school. [. . .] But when I got here to [college], that's when I [. . .] first noticed it.

As Karina explains, attending predominately white schools served as a reminder of racial differences rather than distinctions based upon color. She also pointed to her diverse circle of friends for making her less aware of colorism. However, similar to the experience of Luann, it was not until the stories of other women are shared in the focus group that Karina recognized the differences her family made about skin color. She continued,

But my family, well, now that I know about it and I look back [. . .], you know my family had roots into colorism. [. . .] A lot of them are mixed and [a lot of them are] the darkest of dark. And there were little competitions, like, you know, my child came out lighter than your child, or my child had better hair, you know, little things like that. And I didn't notice it when I was younger. [. . .] I didn't care about that, 'cause my mind was focused on other things. Now that I look back on where all this [is] coming from, it's like now I notice [that] it's probably coming from family.

Karina goes on to share that as a young adolescent, she stayed in "constant competitions" with her cousins, whom she considers to be more color-struck because they migrated to the United States from Haiti in their late teens. Noting that class and color is a "pretty major" issue in Haiti, Karina admitted that her cousins (who have darker skin tones) were socialized to concentrate more on skin color differences than she, and that resulted in small battles over who was prettier or who had the better hair. Like the African American community, Haiti has a similar history of colonization, yet the socially constructed differences based upon phenotype translated into a more rigid caste system of hair, skin, and features. As such, class and color differences are more pronounced, which explains why Karina's cousins were more concerned about skin color and hair. Several other participants of Haitian, Jamaican, and Bahamian heritage comment on more exaggerated notions of colorism in those Caribbean societies compared to the U.S. A more detailed discussion of this matter follows in the next chapter.

Despite the fact that some women were completely unaware of the impact of female family members upon their views on skin color, there were quite a few participants who readily acknowledged the authority of women in their family, particularly their mothers. The majority of women in this study identified experiences with their mothers as having the most influence over their identity, ability, and relationship choices. Consider the color story of 21-year-old Regina, a college student whose parents migrated to the United States from Jamaica. The young woman, who categorizes her skin tone as "dark," shares with the group how her mother—a light-skinned woman—made frequent jokes to Regina about having her father's dark complexion. She explains how the constant teasing made her connect negativity with her skin tone:

> My brother and I used to always run around outside all the time, and my mother always used to say, "Get inside the house, because after a while you are going to be dark just like your dad." She would say it jokingly, but my mom is really light skinned, and she always made us feel like, to look dark like my dad was a bad thing. . . . She would always, like, mock his dark skin. . . . [She would tell me] "You don't want to be too dark because that's not good, it's not a good thing to be dark skinned." I don't think that she meant for it to give that impression, but that's what I got from her.

Regina was quick to point out that her mother's disparaging remarks did not deeply impact her psyche. As the young woman later explained, "I was fine looking dark, I don't care."

For two focus group participants, Rachel and Brenda—18 and 19 years old respectively, colorism was deeply embedded into their mothers' parenting and disciplinary practices. Rachel, who identifies as "light brown," spoke openly and honestly about the preferential treatment she receives as a light-skinned woman and vividly remembers that her mother would make differences between her and her older sister when they were children. Clarifying that having different fathers contributed to their differing skin tones, Rachel suggested that even in the smallest things like housework, her mother would elevate and praise Rachel more than her darker sister:

> I don't know if it's just my imagination, but my mom would yell at her more than me. [. . .] Growing up doing chores, I would do my chores better than my sister and it just didn't make sense, but that's how it is in my family.

Brenda's story mirrors Rachel's experience. Growing up, Brenda—who classifies her complexion as "medium"—was aware of the relative privilege she had in her family. As she noted, "I was on the preferential side . . . to me, life was good." Brenda mentioned being treated better by her mother compared to her darker-skinned sister. She explained: [My mother] didn't scream at me, yell at me, and I got more money and I got more trinkets."

Eighteen-year-old Amy vaguely recalled overt experiences of colorism in her family, yet shared that her mother regularly encourages the medium-toned participant to bleach her skin. Amy described, "My mom is always trying to get me to use products to lighten my skin color because my mother is also pretty light, and she wants me to be more like that. [. . .] She sees that other people look at darker as a bad thing, [and] she doesn't really want me to go through that stereotype." Amy explained that although her mother's actions are rooted in wanting to protect her daughter, she does not recognize that she is at the same time reinforcing the socially constructed value placed on lighter skin. Amy, Brenda, and Rachel's color stories offer small yet noteworthy examples of how mothers can subtly reinforce the normative ideology of colorism.

There are, however, more significant instances of mothers making blatant references to skin tone. Take, for instance, the experience of Leah, a young woman who considers herself "medium." As a young child, Leah was preoccupied with her skin tone, partially due to her mother's insistence that Leah identify herself as "brown and not black." Her mother, a light-skinned woman, was also influential in shaping Leah's relationship choices. She admitted to being more attracted to dark-skinned men as a teenager. Leah stated, "I had this infatuation with men that were darker than me. I don't care how dark, just as long as you were darker than me, 'cause it was something that made me feel good that they were darker than I was." From this statement, it appears that for Leah, dating darker men was a way to affirm her skin color. Yet as Leah further explained, her mother was not happy with this decision and strongly encouraged Leah to "date up" within the color hierarchy as opposed to "dating down":

> So one day my mom, being red, being light skinned, she comes [and] I'm telling her about my current choice. We were driving down [the street], and he was walking past, [. . .] and I was like, "Mom, that's him right there." My mom turns to me and stops the car and says, "Who? That black boy there?" I was in complete shock [laughter]. I was like, "Black boy?" I was like, "Mom!" [. . .] You know? She [said], "I'm tired of you dating these black-skinned boys." And I was like, "black-skinned?" [. . .] And then she told me, [. . .] "I want my grandchildren to have nice hair and a nice skin tone." And I'm looking like, "Are you serious? [. . .] How is it that you're with Daddy, and Daddy's darker than me?" She was like, "Well that's how it's supposed to be, that the

light-skinned and dark-skinned are supposed to be together and not dark on dark and light on light."

This exchange between Leah and her mother speaks volumes to the ways in which mothers promote the negative ideals of colorism. Although Leah's mother attempted to guide her on the "right path" in relationships, she did so in such a way that reinforced the rules of the color hierarchy. The idea that it is only natural for people to date and marry people of opposite skin tones was a common theme mentioned throughout the focus groups. Inherent in this popular adage is the idea that a mixed-tone couple (one light skinned and one dark skinned) will ideally produce offspring that are brown and exempt from the negative experiences of being extremely light or dark. This example shows how powerful maternal influences can be in shaping self-perception and intimate choices.

Some respondents acknowledged the impact their grandmothers had in forming their perspectives on skin color in addition to mothers. This is not surprising, considering the special place grandmothers hold in many black families. As Nancy Boyd-Franklin points out, "The role of the grandmother is one of the most central ones in African-American families. . . . Grandmothers are central to the economic support of Black families and play a crucial role in childcare. . . . They represent a major source of strength and security for many Black children."[6] As a main figure in families, grandmothers are oftentimes responsible for the transmission of values from one generation to the next. In some instances, respondents noted that having a fairer-skinned and/or racially mixed grandparent provided a considerable amount of social currency and capital for the entire family. This was the experience for Gloria, a 30-year-old woman who was born and raised in Jamaica. Noting that Jamaican culture contextualizes skin tone somewhat differently than African American culture (this is explained further in Chapter 5), Gloria shared that having a grandmother who was Indo-Jamaican gave her an added sense of security and worth, despite having a medium-brown skin tone:

My grandmother's father was white, and her mom was Indian, so she was like a white-Indian looking person, and then my mom came out really, really dark 'cause [my grandmother] married a black person, but my mother had Indian hair . . . so I think that externally, that's what was put on me [by others]. . . . You're dark, but you have certain things, so maybe your skin tone is not that big a deal. . . . It made me internally, as a child, start to think, well maybe I'm not that bad because my grandma is white.

Gloria explained that whenever anyone saw her with her grandmother, the response was usually, "Well you're okay because of your grandmother." She went on to explain that "regardless of the fact that my hair didn't turn out as Indian as it should have . . . it didn't matter at that point . . . I was defined based on my family."

For other women, darker-skinned grandmothers can expect their lighter grandchildren to transfer the perceived currency of light skin privilege onto the entire family. This was true for Janice—also 30 years old at the time of data collection—who shared her riveting color story centering on her grandmother's expectations:

> My mother and I were the only light-skinned people in my family and my neighborhood, so it was always an issue. . . . My grandmother's really dark, and she would always tell me. . . . You're light skinned, you're going to make it out of the ghetto, you're gonna get the good job, you're gonna be able to take care of us. My mother failed because she didn't make it out, so then my grandmother would always look at me, and it wasn't something that I realized until I was older, but as I thought about it, I would realize the things that my grandmother would say . . . "Don't marry a black man."

Janice talked openly about the enormous amount of pressure she felt growing up, by being expected to not only "make it out" of poverty but to also bear the financial responsibility of taking care of her family. When Janice shared her experience, she was on the verge of completing her doctoral studies, and in many ways, she had indeed accomplished the goal laid before her as a very young girl. However, Janice, who admitted to crying to her grandmother as a child and asking questions as a child like, "Why don't I have hair like yours?" or "Why don't I look like you?," revealed that skin tone still plays a significant role in her life, shaping her relationships, professional experiences, and ultimately, her view of the world.

More often than not, when the women in this study mentioned their grandmothers playing significant roles in shaping their views on colorism, the grandmothers were distinguished as the fairest members of their families. It can be argued that they have more at stake in the maintenance of colorism compared to mothers. Coming of age in an earlier generation and time when skin tone stratification was more structured and overt, these grandmothers may feel a greater obligation to uphold color divisions and to draw sharper lines between their families and darker-skinned black families. Indeed, this was the case for Trina, Missy, and Monica—three young women who shared that their grandmothers of mixed ancestry were responsible for transmitting the dominant language, scripts, and practices of colorism to the women and girls in their respective families. Trina, a very light woman, revealed that growing up she recognized that her grandmother was very color conscious:

> And what I noticed was that my grandma would [say], "Don't bring no black niggers here." She would [say], "I don't want no blackeys around here." [. . .] My mom used to date dark guys, and for whatever reason [she] was attracted to really dark, husky black guys, and my grandma would [warn], "No black gorilla ghosts around here."

The harsh warnings Trina received from her grandmother contradict the popular belief that light-skinned and dark-skinned blacks should couple together. Instead, it is clear from these admonishments that dark-skinned people are demonized and/or characterized as inferior and, in the mind of Trina's grandmother, a threat to the purity of her light-skinned family. This is strikingly similar to the opening pages of Lawrence Otis Graham's *Our Kind of People*, an autobiographical account of life within the black elite. Graham recalls his well-to-do, fair-complexioned grandmother referring to darker blacks as "niggers" during his childhood.[7] This type of blatant colorism may be more common among older generations of black Americans.

Although Missy's grandmother did not impact her decisions on who to date, she did, however, have considerable control in how the 25-year-old viewed herself. At the beginning of her focus group session, Missy explained:

> My grandmother [. . .] is almost as pale as you are [pointing to Colleen, a white co-facilitator], and she's black. And she calls all her grandkids from my family "colored." [. . .] We're [the] *colored* children, the darker ones in the whole family.

As a result of being called colored and categorized by her grandmother as the darkest one in the family, Missy identified and understood her life experience as a medium-toned individual. However, Missy is one example of the discrepancies I sometimes found between my perceptions as a researcher and the participants' own perceptions of their skin-tone category. On her demographic sheet, Missy identified herself as "medium." Yet I noticed that she was one of the fairest women in her focus group; she had a "yellow" tone and could be easily classified as light brown. Although there are at times variation and disagreement as it relates to who belongs to what skin-tone category (light, brown, or dark), there is no mistake that Missy rated her skin tone darker based upon her grandmother's influence and construction of her as dark. Each time an inconsistency of this kind occurred, it was readily traceable back to the family.

Finally, Monica, a brown-skinned woman, described that her grandmother is notorious for creating divisions and hierarchy among her sisters. She explained that even though her mother has never raised the issue of skin tone to her or her siblings, it is instead her father's mother (whom she describes as very light and passable for white) who holds the most colorist values in the family. As Monica informs the focus group, her grandmother's fair skin and her views about skin tone dictated how she and her sisters were treated:

> . . . my mother is very dark, and [. . .] my sisters happened to come out dark, and I came out more of a different skin color. And my grandmother prefers me to the two of them because [of] my features, you know, my straight nose or whatever. [. . .] My skin color is more acceptable to her; she likes me better than them.

She continued,

> Well, like I said, [. . .] my grandmother had issues. [. . .] But she was always *okay* with my other sisters because of the features they had. One of them is dark, but she has really curly hair. That made it *okay*.

A number of lessons can be learned from Monica's narrative about her grandmother. First, Monica was the preferred sister due to her lighter skin tone in comparison to her darker sisters. She was favored more and got treated better. Yet in her grandmother's eyes, her sisters' European features and "good" hair served as redeeming qualities in spite of their dark skin. Unfortunately, Monica's experience with her grandmother is all too common, as her story resonates not only with other focus group participants but also with previous literature.

Tessa also shares a family story of how her grandmother influenced her early romanticized ideals of colorism. Although the narratives of Trina, Missy, and Monica point to their grandmothers as having a palpable role in producing colorism within their families, Tessa's grandmother has a common reaction to the birth of a light-skinned baby that resonates throughout her entire family. According to Kathy Russell, Midge Wilson, and Ronald Hall, authors of *The Color Complex*, within black families there exists a great deal of excitement and obsession about a child's impending skin color, hair texture, and facial features that begins well before birth. Tessa, who classifies her complexion as "very dark," explained how the birth of her biracial cousin's youngest child created a "color commotion" in her family:

[My cousin has] two sons and a girl, and his daughter in the middle is darker skinned—she takes after her mother—and his younger son [. . .] was born with gray eyes and, you know, turned out to be this beautiful light-skinned child. And I just remember [. . .] in my family a mass flocking to the hospital to see this child, and my grandmother, she still to this day will go to the house and pick up this little boy and leave the daughter there, just leave her there. And I mean, there's no other reason to explain it other than it's just . . . everyone wanted to babysit him, everyone wanted to take care of him. I even fell into the trap as well, and you know, I want to have a little gray-eyed baby my-self. And [my grandmother would say], "How can we be so lucky to have a beautiful gray-eyed child?"

Tessa openly discussed how members of her family discriminate against each other based upon skin tone, and the birth of this infant boy reinforced the negativity inherent in dark skin and the praise and elevation accompa-nying light skin. People in her family—Tessa included—provided extra at-tention to this "beautiful" baby, while disregarding the other child with darker skin. Internalizing the favor given to this baby, Tessa admitted that she "fell into the trap" of colorism and wished for a light-skinned baby of her own. She later realized her error, noting, "This is the wrong line of thinking to have." Like other participants in this study, Tessa recognized that replacing the normative language, scripts, and practices of colorism with an oppositional line of thinking and behavior is, at times, very diffi-cult. "It seems so powerful," she confessed, yet Tessa remains insistent on moving from a place of compliance to a point of resistance.

Although mothers and grandmothers are most commonly mentioned as the main purveyors of colorism in families, it is important to note here the role of other female family members in creating a color consciousness for some of the women in the study. This is perhaps best illustrated through the compelling narratives of Chanel and Jasmine, two focus group partici-pants who, in their childhoods, were impacted by female cousins in two very different ways. Chanel, a 21-year-old college student, shared that she was first made aware of the negativity placed upon her dark skin at a family reunion. Up until that point, Chanel admitted, she was not cognizant of skin tone differences because her immediate family was fairly homogenous in relation to skin tone. Yet the sharp words of a lighter-skinned cousin permanently change her perspective:

> I remember I was about eight years old, and I went to one of my family reunions. [. . .] One of our cousins married a really light-skinned woman and [. . .] the matriarchs, the heads of the family [. . .] made her this supposedly most beautiful person because she was light skinned, and it just used to bother me 'cause I could never understand. [. . .] And I remember her sitting next to me. She just looked at me [and] said, "Why do you look like *that*?" I'm just confused. I'm like, "What do you mean?" You know, she left the question alone, but I really felt that she was talking partly because of my weight, but also too because of my skin tone. Because, you know, most of my family is darker skinned, and she really thought she was important because she was light skinned because many people made her believe that. So that was one of the first real experiences I got from my family.

Chanel honestly noted that her cousin never explicitly degraded her dark skin. Yet this small exchange set the tone for how Chanel would evaluate, perceive, and judge herself in the future. She admitted this internalization impacted her intimate relationships with men. Because of her dark skin, she didn't believe she was worthy of a good relationship and discussed how she had to unlearn this crippling mentality:

> I didn't really see myself as being desirable, because that's the way, you know, men treated me. [. . .] So when I got older and the time came [when] men were showing interest in me, I really had a significant problem accepting that. I thought they were crazy, and I thought that I could never accept it, and still to this day, I'm working on it. It's okay, I can actually talk about that. But I know, personally, it's just been . . . emotionally it's been more difficult for me to accept that men would find me attractive because that's not what I experienced growing up.

As we learned from Chanel's story, moving to a point of acceptance and self-love can at times be complicated.

The narrative of focus group member Jasmine provides a good example of the black family serving as both a point of origin *and* a stabilizing agent for the normative model of everyday colorism. A 19-year-old young woman who identifies as "light brown," Jasmine has a keen sense of colorism within her life and attributes the development of her normative ideals of skin tone to her early family experiences. Similar to other women in this project, Jasmine cites her mother as an influence upon her identity but also credits the elevated position of two light-skinned cousins in her family to the development of her own self-image:

> I have two older cousins [. . .] who I'm closer with, and they're very light. [. . .] They are a lot lighter than me, and they have [. . .] brown-grayish eyes, you know, and I really admire them. [. . .] And that really legitimized [my] skin tone because how I view myself, I guess I kind of want to be just like them because they are really beautiful and I really admire them, so, you know, that really influences me. [. . .] My family used to say how I always looked like one of my cousins, [. . .] so I guess I just don't want to get darker because I just want to seem more like my cousins.

Jasmine did not mention any particular action or behavior on the part of her cousins that served as the trigger of her color awareness. Yet being compared to her light cousins with the "brown-grayish eyes" creates internal scripts that connect light skin to beauty and privilege.

Jasmine's early ideals of skin tone constructed by her mother and cousins became even more solidified when she encountered a stabilizing agent in high school.

> When I was 15 or 16, I did color guard in tenth grade, and I got so dark, [. . .] I even got sun burned. I did not know that I could get sun burned until I woke up one day and my skin was peeling. [. . .] I remember taking pictures with one of my friends and getting them developed. [. . .] My mom [saw the pictures] and said, "Wow, you're really, really dark," and I don't know, I guess it just hit me because I didn't like the fact that my mom called me dark because I was so used to being called light. And, you know, I also associated that, back then I was also like really fat, so, you know, I kind of associate being dark with not being as attractive because I noticed that in eleventh grade, after I lost weight and I was lighter, I got a lot more attention from males.

Joining the marching band represents a critical point in Jasmine's life for a number of reasons. Participating in an outdoor activity like the color guard may be regarded as a fun experience for many teenagers, yet for Jasmine, the constant exposure to the sun threatened a demotion in the color hierarchy. The terms her mother used to describe her changed from "light" to "really, really dark." In an earlier point in her focus group, Jasmine re-called that her mother never called her dark and that she typically used the word *dark* to refer to Jasmine's younger sister. At one point, Jasmine mentioned that to her, being called *red* symbolized "total affection and beautification." Her internal scripts significantly shifted from attractive to unattractive, from being likened to her beautiful light cousins to feeling dark and fat. The response Jasmine received from her mother deeply impacted her experience and thus precipitated the need for a change. Her behavior (external practice), then, is guided by these two factors. This event served as a stabilizing agent because it re-affirmed her ideals about being light skinned and fueled her aspirations to get her color back. As Jasmine explained, the following year she quit color guard, lost weight, and restored her redness—and beauty. Consequently, she attributes the attention she gets from young men to her lighter tone.

Family as the Point of Origin for Oppositional Colorism

A considerable share of women in this study admit that their families are responsible for instilling within them a belief system of bias and judgment as it relates to skin tone. Many respondents learned early in life to associate negativity with darkness and to equate goodness with lightness. Yet there were some women involved in this project who talked about a different pattern of family socialization. Several participants spoke of being reared in black families that espoused the ideals of *Afrocentricity*. Nancy Boyd-Franklin observes that "The Afrocentric movement has been a process by which many African-Americans have reclaimed the cultural strengths of their African heritage while offering them a positive alternative to negative messages and stereotypes perpetuated by the dominant European American society."[8] For the women who learn from their families to celebrate all the various hues of blackness, an oppositional knowledge of colorism serves as their point of origin. Illustrative of this notion is the case of Kira, a 19-year-old participant who credited the wide diversity of hues in her family for her oppositional foundation of colorism:

> My family always taught me to accept everyone. [. . .] There was never any type of differentiation with anyone in my family. Everyone was always welcome in my house no matter [what] skin tone you were. And in my family alone, there [is] a wide range of people. [. . .] My dad's side of the family is really light skinned. [. . .] They have green eyes. [. . .] My mom's side of the family is very dark, so there is a very big mix between everyone in my family.

Being exposed to the positive attributes of both light and dark skin, Kira learned from her family members not to discriminate on this basis and to treat everyone the same.

U-Neek, a 21-year-old college student from Miami, Florida, revealed that as a child she was never exposed to colorism. As the medium-brown participant noted, "I didn't think that I was ever affected by colorism because my family was so pro black, and 'Black is Beautiful' is how they talk to you. My mother is really dark skinned, my aunt is light, so we have these different variations in my family, and it was never noticed." U-Neek stated that her family's appreciation of everything black influenced her positive viewpoints on all skin tones. However, like many women in this study, upon entering all-black environments *outside* the home, U-Neek was introduced to the normative viewpoints of skin color:

> And then I went to black schools [where] everyone was always focused on fashion. [. . .] Talking amongst my friends, we were very focused on the color contrasts and stuff like that, and now I'm realizing that yeah, even when you meet somebody, [skin tone is] one of the first things I notice.

High school, then, served as a transformative agent that made U-Neek more aware of colorism and enact the scripts and practices attached to the normative discourse.

Callea shared a similar experience in her family. Similar to U-Neek, she recalled no formal knowledge of colorism as a child. Callea confessed, "I didn't really know colorism, I just knew that I was black." This young woman credited her father's strong Afrocentric values as central to shaping her positive self-image. Yet, similar to other participants, her positive valuations of dark skin and African features were challenged when she entered high school:

> I had African ancestors. [. . .] That is what my father really focused on. He always told us (my sister and I) that we're beautiful, natural hair is African silk, and you are beautiful the way you are. I guess that is because he knew how society is. [. . .] Because when I went to high school, it was the lighter you are, the prettier you are. If you had long hair and you're light skinned, you're beautiful as opposed as to if you're dark. [. . .] I'm not that pretty [now] because my hair is short and it's not long-flowing or straight because I'm darker. [. . .] I play[ed] basketball when I was in high school, and we were out in the sun five times a week, and I got really dark. And I liked that because my skin

was even, so I was pretty happy, but it was because I was dark skinned I wasn't considered beautiful [compared] to other girls who stayed out of the sun and who were lighter than me.

Contrast Callea's narrative with the story of Jasmine, the young woman featured earlier in this chapter. While Jasmine was raised with the normative beliefs of colorism privileging light over dark, Callea instead learned at an early age to value all skin tones. Both young women entered high school and decided to participate in outdoor activities (color guard and basketball), causing their skin tones to deepen. Pressured by the desire to be accepted, Jasmine gave up her extracurricular activity. Unshaken by dominant standards of beauty, Callea stayed involved in a sport that made her darker and admits to being "pretty happy" despite how unattractive she was as viewed by others. Both women's high school experiences functioned as stabilizing events that yielded different results. Jasmine learned from her mother that light skin is beautiful, and this ideology dictated how she viewed herself and others. On the other hand, Callea learned early on from her father to celebrate her dark skin and has no qualms about getting darker and challenging normative ideologies of skin color.

There are certain cases where respondents noted being socialized with both a normative and oppositional framework of colorism. For Vivica, her experiences with colorism were more complex because within her family, she was presented with competing ideologies of skin tone from different family members. Vivica describes her skin tone as "medium," but as many women in the study revealed, she was much lighter as a young child. "I was born the fairest of all the children," Vivica explained. It is through her aunt that she learned the dominant ideals of colorism, as she was regularly admonished for "turning."

> My auntie [. . .] was like, "Why you keep on going in the sun? You keep on turning!" [. . .] You know kids like to go outside [and] you will turn, especially if you go in the pool and stuff. We had a pool at our house. And my aunt would always say, "Every time I see you, you turn darker." [. . .] And it's true because I [. . .] come from this light, light child and then, you know, slowly but surely, I became darker.

Despite the frequent references Vivica's aunt made to her changing skin tone, her parents refused to "play color" and make a difference between her and her siblings. Unlike this young woman's aunt, her parents were instrumental in countering the dominant notions of skin tone and providing Vivica with an oppositional framework. She recounted a different childhood story where she learned that divisions among skin color are not accepted within her family:

> My little sister [. . .] remained her color 'cause she's stayed more inside or whatever. She has my grandma's [. . .] long hair, and she's kinda. [. . .] She's not light, light skinned, but one time she told my older sister, who took after my father and is very dark, she was prancing through the house, and she was like, "Vivica and I are the lightest ones, Vivica and I are [the] lightest ones. We're the prettiest ones" [. . .] and I remember my father, [. . .] he came running inside 'cause he's dark and my older sister is dark, [. . .] and he was upset. He was just like, "No! You know you don't say this." [. . .] "Don't make her feel bad because [. . .] she is the darkest."

It is through her father's reprimands that Vivica became keenly aware that making distinctions is neither valued nor welcomed within her immediate family. Although she admitted that both her mother and father were adamant about challenging colorism, it was her subsequent exposure to extended family members, schools, and relationships that overrode what her parents initially fought so hard to instill within her. Vivica conceded to the dominant language, scripts, and practices of colorism, openly admitting that as a brown-skinned woman, she feels there are "still more mountains to climb." This respondent was candid about the struggle she has with color hierarchy; at one moment she is being critical of colorism and the larger system of racism, and in another instant she is hoping that her young niece—her older sister's daughter—does not turn out to be her sister's dark color. Vivica's conscious battle with the normative and oppositional forms of colorism is typical of several women in this study. Yet like with so many others, it is difficult to decipher which one will ultimately win out.

School

Even though an overwhelming majority of participants cited their families as the foundation for their views on colorism, a large number of respondents further admitted that they were not consciously *aware* of skin tone difference until they were regularly surrounded by other people their own age. It is usually in school settings where colorism (similar to racism) is institutionalized and black women begin to understand just *how* skin tone makes a difference in their lives. Consider Toni Morrison's classic, *The Bluest Eye,* a fictional story dealing with the topic of skin tone and standards of beauty. Deeply embedded within the pages of this novel are the pain and heartache of colorism as narrated by two young girls, Pecola Breedlove and Claudia MacTeer. At one point in the novel, the arrival of a new schoolmate provides a tough lesson in how colorism operates among young people. As told through the voice of Claudia,

> The disrupter of seasons was a new girl in school named Maureen Peal. A high yellow dream child with long brown hair braided into two lynch ropes that hung down her back. She was rich, at least by our standards, as rich as the richest of the white girls, swaddled in comfort and care. . . . She enchanted the entire school. When teachers called on her they smiled encouragingly. Black boys didn't trip her in the halls; white boys didn't stone her, white girls didn't suck their teeth when she was assigned to be their work partners; black girls stepped aside when she wanted to sink in the girls toilet. . . . Freida and I were bemused, irritated, and fascinated by her. We looked hard for flaws to restore our equilibrium. . . . But we had to do it alone, for none of the other girls would cooperate with our hostility. They adored her.[9]

From this story, we see that not all black girls are treated the same. The elevation, praise, and privilege bestowed to light-skinned Maureen Peal substantiate young Pecola's longing for blue eyes. Similar to the young girl featured in Morrison's work, data from the focus groups also suggest that school experiences are critical in shaping, reinforcing, or redirecting young women's views about skin tone. Earlier sections of this chapter document that for some participants, entry into high school challenged or reiterated their foundational beliefs of colorism. Yet a larger portion of participants cited various points in their educational experiences—grade school, high school, and college—as stabilizing and transformative agents impacting their awareness of colorism.

Although women on both sides of the color spectrum recall being taunted or shunned by their schoolmates for their skin color, focus group member Shanae attributed her frequent trips to the principal's office in middle school to her darker skin tone.

> [In] elementary school, I would always stay in the pool and, you know chlorine makes you darker, so once I got to middle school, I got in a lot of trouble with other kids because the first thing they would say was, "Oh, black." [. . .] So I got into a lot of fights because [. . .] they called me black. So that's when people started telling me, "Did you know the saying 'the blacker the berry, the sweeter the juice?'" and that's when I accepted my skin color more. [. . .] Now I'm proud of it.

Shanae's experience is so noteworthy because she moved from a young girl who resorted to physical violence in order to defend herself against name-calling and harassment to a young woman who learned to appreciate who she is. She mentioned a schoolteacher who exposed her to the adage "the blacker the berry, the sweeter the juice." Although the origins of this saying are rooted in sexuality, the context in which Shanae discovered this idea was rooted in black pride and appreciation. This transformative event enabled Shanae to transition to an alternative understanding of colorism where she was better able to handle subsequent experiences of ignorance and prejudice.

For some participants, school experiences reinforced the normative values of skin tone that were originally learned in the family. Keesha's story is one such experience. The young woman, who describes her skin color as "dark," related that members of her immediate family were recognized by her extended family as the "the black sheep" because they were darkest. The knowledge she gained in her family was solidified when she started high school. Keesha realized immediate differences when she was jokingly compared to her lighter brother as "night," while he was referred to as "day." However, one specific incident served as the most stabilizing agent of normative colorism:

> I remember hearing a group of black guys talk about who the prettiest girls in school were, and what I noticed now is that either the girls were light skinned [. . .] or had longer hair. And that's a really big thing. Those two, it's either one or the other. If you have longer hair then it's great, and if you have lighter skin then it's great too. So, it wasn't the darker girls in school that were the prettiest to them. I think that was important. And that kind of hurt too, because I didn't make that list.

It was in high school that Keesha grasped the concept of the "beauty queue" and learned her position within the socially constructed hierarchy of skin tone and attractiveness. As a dark-skinned girl, she came to understand the rejection and exclusion associated with not having the right skin tone or hair length. Keesha's opening comment in the focus group aptly captured what she uncovered while in high school: "It seems that the lighter you are, the better you are, the prettier you are perceived."

While school experiences are noted as central in shaping views on colorism, there are several women who specifically mentioned that changing from a predominately white school environment to an all-black school created a transformative experience that propelled them into a larger-scale exposure to colorism. Whereas concerns about racism are more evident in all-white settings, colorism holds more significance in places that are exclusively black. Take for instance the narratives of Beyoncé, Tessa, and Tatiana, three young women who observed substantial differences upon making the transition to all-black surroundings:

> Coming from my high school, it was predominantly white, [. . .] and then coming here [to college], to be honest with you, it doesn't feel like I'm at a predominantly white school. I know we are, but it doesn't really feel that way just because the black community is so tight-knit. [. . .] It's an all-black high school almost. [. . .] So the reason why I said earlier that I don't really know how to define myself, you know, light, dark, medium, whatever, is because I've never had to talk about it before. But here, it's like, people are describing people as high yellow, red bone, I'm just like, "Okay, well what exactly is that?" [. . .] I didn't really even hear some of the terms until I got here, and it's because I was around more black people. (Beyoncé, 21, medium skin tone)

> This focus group made me start thinking about school and everything, and I went to a predominantly suburban school in the South, and about sixth grade [moved] to inner city schools and from then on, I noticed that I never even understood what color *I* was until I went to inner city schools. That was the first time that I understood in relation to our value into our society. [. . .] And I found that so funny because I had always felt that in my family, but it had never been so explicit as when I went to school around my peers. (Tessa, 20, very dark)

> I grew up in a suburban community. I went to private school my entire life. And I started off in [. . .] a majority white elementary school. So it was never an issue for me until I got to middle school, and the only people who have said anything about it or made me think twice about "you are very dark" has been black people, and they're only about two shades lighter than me. (Tatiana, 19, very dark)

It is clear from these narratives that being in all-black environments can create a more intense focus on skin tone and a heightened sense of color consciousness rather than race.

Without a doubt, classmates—whether in the form of friends or adversaries—play a role in perpetuating skin tone bias and difference within school settings. Yet findings from the analysis also point to adults within educational settings—specifically teachers—who further reinforce the stratification and hierarchy of colorism. Sociologist and colorism scholar Margaret Hunter asserts that teachers, who "exert a powerful influence of student achievement," are indeed responsible for highlighting color difference in the classroom. "If teachers, of any race, expect their light-skinned students of color to be smarter, more academically prepared, from better families, and better behaved than their darker-skinned classmates, the students may rise and fall to meet those racialized expectations."[10] Commonly, differential treatment appears in the form of light-skinned children being chosen as the "teacher's pet." Charles Parrish finds in his 1940s research on perceptions about skin tone that "favoritism is displayed by teachers toward the light colored pupils according to 63% of the persons questioned."[11] Although this conclusion was reached more than 60 years ago, there are similar beliefs and experiences shared by members in the current study. For instance, Chanel, a participant with dark skin, jokingly recalled her perception that her elementary school teacher was "much nicer to the light-skinned people in the class. [. . .] She would give them more treats than the rest of us." Although Chanel made light of this remark because she is not sure if, in fact, the lighter children were really preferred, Kira noted a different experience in which she distinctly remembers being singled out by her fifth grade teacher:

> I remember when I was in fifth grade, I had this one teacher [. . .] who was black, and she would ride me like no one else in my class. My handwriting had to be perfect, everything had to be perfect that I turned in. Everything. And if it was not perfect, she would fail me. She called my parents daily. [. . .] She was crazy.

Kira said that it is through this experience that she became more consciously aware of the differences people make in relation to skin tone.

Teresa, a 21-year-old participant who identifies her skin tone as "dark," shared an interesting experience involving her grade school teacher and her dad. Similar to other participants, Teresa recollected that many of her elementary and middle school teachers assigned seats and placed the lighter-skinned children at the head of the class. As she described, "It was every class that was this way. I had a few teachers who had the light-skinned or the rich family kids up front." Acknowledging that her darker skin relegated her to "the back row with all the other kids," Teresa noticed that it was not until her teacher met her father that she was awarded a new place in the class.

> One day [. . .] I was talking to my dad casually, and he goes, "I don't really like this teacher, I'd like to come in and meet her." My dad's a

light-skinned black male, [. . .] he's a couple shades lighter than I am. And he went there, and he spoke to the teacher, not about racism or anything, but what about [my daughter's] grades and [. . .] about her being in the back, and then, you know, she pushed me up to the front. But every day up front, she'd always be asking me about my dad, is he single, how in love is he with my mother, and stuff like that. And it was definitely crossing the line, and I had to think to myself, why is this? [. . .] She obviously favored the light-skinned kids, and here she was trying to be my friend, just to get some of my dad. And I figured she put me in front of the class [. . . because I] had some light skin in [my] family.

Like Teresa, many respondents were careful to highlight that not every teacher or class experience was one in which skin tone was of premium significance. But as these narratives suggest, all it takes is *one* bad incident involving colorism to leave a lasting impression upon a young woman's perceptions and life experience.

While grade, middle, and high school occurrences are mentioned to serve as transformative and stabilizing agents, college life was more often noted by the women in this study (the majority of whom were college students at the time) as a transformative experience relating to colorism. For Gloria, the dual experience of migrating to the United States and attending a historically black college/university (HBCU) served as a transformative moment. Gloria came to the United States from Jamaica to attend an HBCU in the Northeast. The medium-toned respondent, whose experience of using her light-skinned grandmother as a point of status and leverage was highlighted earlier in this chapter, recalled moving to the United States and learning very early on that her skin tone made more of a difference here. She explained: "My experience in the States is a lot different, compared to back home . . . When I came here and I went to an HBCU, that was a defining moment in terms of my color, and I really didn't have any of that support. . . . The experience definitely shifted a lot." Being away from home, without familial support—namely the absence of her grandmother and other lighter-skinned family members—disabled Gloria's ability to access the social capital and benefits previously afforded to her back home in Jamaica. As Gloria described, her brown skin became more salient as she navigated the social and cultural terrains of an all-black college.

To be sure, the history of colorism documents the various ways in which historically black colleges and universities routinely discriminated against darker-skinned African Americans via fraternities, sororities, and even college admission. Within this study, young women noted the persistent divisions of skin color along sorority lines, as numerous women referred to the color stereotypes present on campus, including the idea that most light-skinned women are members of Alpha Kappa Alpha (typically referred to as "AKA") and Delta Sigma Theta (commonly referred to as "Delta") sororities, while darker-skinned women are expected to pledge sororities such as Zeta Phi Beta and Sigma Gamma Rho. For one participant, Meeko, a 20-year-old African American woman who shared that "colorism basically goes unsaid" within her family, attending college reminded her of the film *School Daze*, and she described how this impacted her understanding of colorism:

> I still remember the night that I was watching HBO and *School Daze* came on. [. . .] I was really young. And I remember the beauty shop scene where they're just running around, dancing, singing jigga-boo and wanna-be and, you know, I just remember that so vividly because I never knew that there was, you know, that type of classification. I mean, they're calling the other girls, oh, wanna be, "You want to have blue eyes, you want to have straight hair, and you think you're all that, and you're stuck up." And then, the jigga-boos, they were just, "Oh, you're ugly and your hair is knotty," and that was the first time I knew that colorism existed.

Released in 1988, the film *School Daze* was written and directed by filmmaker Spike Lee. The movie, which showcased the tensions among black women as it relates to skin color and hair, was pivotal because it was one of the first contemporary films explicitly addressing colorism among young black college students. "Straight and Nappy," the specific scene Meeko alluded to, is a musical number that draws attention to the various color names—such as *high-yellow* and *tarbaby*—and color notions that are pervasive in black culture. The entire performance is comprised of the name-calling and hostility often accompanying the divide between light- and dark-skinned women. As such, the film can function as a point of origin (as in Meeko's case), and undoubtedly a stabilizing agent—upon enrolling into college—reinforcing the politics of skin color among black women.

It is important to point out that while the college experience served as transformative moments and/or stabilizing moments for the vast majority of the women in this study, the group of men that I spoke to contextualized their college experience as *points of origin*. In other words, the black men participating in this study were not aware of color differences in their lives until they got to college. Ironically, experiences of colorism—normative or oppositional—were muted or largely unrecognized by the group of six young black men who shared their views and perspectives of colorism with me. Consider the following two statements:

> The institution of colorism and skin bias has been around for some time. . . . I think, for at least all the men in the room, since we're exposed to colorism quite late, I don't think it's that big of a problem for men. (Stewart, 21, light brown)

> Recognizing colorism? I'd have to say it was pretty late for me. Probably either my senior year in high school or first year of college, because when I grew up in Miami, there were a lot of Hispanics and dark women, and to me that wasn't any difference . . . so it wasn't until I got to [college], here—freshman year that I started realizing the color clashes that were going on. (Bobby, 19, dark)

Though I only conducted one pilot focus group with the men, it became apparent from the discussion that there are divergent perspectives of black men compared to black women. Given this stark contrast of experiences, it will be imperative for future research to explore the topic of colorism among black men (See Sidebar 5).

In spite of the obvious differences expected to reinforce colorism on a college campus, a larger majority of women in this study noted a different connection to their college experience; it was through the institution of higher education that an oppositional knowledge of colorism was acquired, developed, and matured. This is exhibited through the language used within the focus groups. Without prompting, a number of participants situated the following concepts within their narratives: *white racism, colonialism, slave mentality, Willie Lynch, the one-drop rule, octoroon, quadroon, Eurocentric* and *Afrocentric standards of beauty*, and *controlling images* of black women. As college students, these young women were exposed to scholarly literature, arming them with an oppositional knowledge of colorism. This is perhaps captured best by the opening remarks of Meeko, a participant who revealed that taking a class in women's studies and learning about colorism in the course changed her entire perspective and fueled her interest in colorism:

> What sparked my interest was a summer course that I took, it was women's Studies, and [. . .] I had a lot of unanswered questions, and I felt that coming to this focus group would help me gauge more on how people see this issue, because it's a big issue in my life, and I never thought it was that big until taking the course, because it basically involves every part of my life, and I never knew that.

Majoring in and/or taking classes in women's studies, English literature, African American studies, and sociology (as participants mentioned) provided an alternative stock of knowledge on black women and skin color that easily enabled many respondents to develop a critical consciousness of their everyday experiences with colorism.

Relationships

Kelly, a biracial participant explained, "My skin tone has been the theme of my life when it comes to dating black men." Although they do not function as points of origin, friendships and intimate relationships do serve as stabilizing and/or transformative agents for the women in this study. A large part of the scrutiny black women give and receive is owed to European standards of beauty and the long-standing belief in the black community that light-skinned women are the most suitable dating and marriage partners. This, of course, impacts the relationships between black men and black women, but the underlying threat of competition invariably shapes the context of black female relationships. Margaret Hunter expounds on this issue:

> The demographic reality of the African American community today exacerbates the perception (and reality) of competition for scarce male partners because of the unbalanced sex ratio of African Americans. . . . This scarcity leads to increased tension and competition among African American women for the limited number of male partners, thus increasing animosity over issues of beauty and skin color.[12]

On the issue of relationships with black women, a considerable number of women revealed circumstances where their skin tone impacted a friendship with another black woman. The previous chapter detailed how the internal scripts related to light, medium, and dark skin tones at times prevent women from making friendships across skin tone lines. Yet in the instances where friendships are forged between women of varying hues, differences in skin color may cause some friction. For Stacey, building bonds with all types of black women is easy. In fact, similar to many other participants in this study, she indicated that initially, skin tone is "never an issue." This young woman noted that her current group of close friends falls on various places of the color spectrum. Yet, as she describes one particular incident when she and her friends were preparing for a night out, Stacey quickly realized that colorism indeed plays a role in their relationship:

I was going out, and my hair, I didn't like my hair style, so I just didn't want to go out, and my friend who is half black and half Puerto Rican was like, "Well, it doesn't matter what you look like, you know, let's just go out because, you know, your hair is never that great looking anyway." Hurt by that comment [. . .] I [asked her], "Are you trying to call me your Ugly Betty?" and we got into this huge disagreement. [. . .] There is this issue that I would call "the Ugly Betty." She needs to be a part of the group in order for the other women who are a shade lighter or a tone lighter to feel better about themselves, and [she] is always a dark-skinned black woman. [. . .] I consider myself a dark-skinned woman, [and . . .] I have to always make sure that I wake up in the morning and look in the mirror and be like, "I'm a beautiful dark-skinned black woman," and that's one of the things that you have to be conscious about, even in your everyday setting, even among your friends, [that] you're a beautiful black woman.

Internalizing her perceived role as the "Ugly Betty,"[13] Stacey believed that she was only part of her peer group because her friends did not view her dark skin and short hair as intimidating. She later confided that she felt that she had to engage in compensatory practices—such as getting a hair weave or wearing a new outfit—in order to feel on the same level with her lighter-skinned friends. Stacey recognized the irony in doing these things because she noted that it typically results in even more scrutiny from her friends. Hearing her girlfriends react with comments like, "Wow, you look so nice today," further reinforces the ideas of colorism; there is no expectation for a dark-skinned girl to look nice and be attractive. Being in this circle of friends and going through these varied experiences provided Stacey with transformative moments that altered her thinking about colorism. At the end of the focus group experience, Stacey acknowledged that she is more enlightened and determined to challenge many things in her friendships that she previously left unquestioned. Her language, internal scripts, and external practices shifted to an oppositional understanding of colorism. Stacey changed from seeing herself as the unattractive friend to waking up every day and affirming that she indeed is a beautiful woman.

Finding herself in the same situation as Stacey, 20-year-old Rosetta also revealed how colorism unveiled itself in the context of her peer group. The light-brown-skinned young woman described that she has a "diverse group of friends," and when all the women come together,

[colorism] comes out and [. . .] some people will say, "Well you know, dark-skinned people don't need to wear that color," or "Dark-skinned people don't need to wear that type of make up," or "Dark-skinned people don't need to have this type of make up on," and "light-skinned people, they can wear any color because you can see any color on lighter people."

Rosetta mentioned that she doesn't believe her friends' actions to be malicious or intentional. Yet, they do serve to perpetuate difference by privileging light skin.

To be sure, experiences in dating provided focus group participants with even more recollections of how colorism impacts their intimate relationships and everyday experiences with black men. Color stories surrounding dating and marriage surfaced during each focus group, and many of the narratives shared reflect the normative ideology of colorism.

As the conversations in each focus group revealed, young women consider the decisions black men make in dating or marriage to be more about status and less about love. In fact, second only to beauty, the majority of participants saw how men perceive or approach other women as revolving around colorism. Not surprisingly, common responses from women of all skin tones were that light-skinned women carried the most advantage and privilege in relationships. Lighter-toned women are seen as more attractive, and thus are better choices in the areas of dating and marriage. For many, light skin is synonymous with freedom and options; it is believed that fairer women have carte blanche over other women. The exception, of course, is white women, who are seen to be the largest competition for black men beyond the fairest black girl. One downside for light-skinned women is perhaps best described by Mary, a brown-skinned participant who admits that she harbors no feelings of jealousy or resentment toward her lighter friends because, in her mind, they are the ones who have a more difficult time separating serious suitors from the "crazy guys" who are only after them for their looks. Another disadvantage noted by lighter-skinned women is the frequent assumption by women of other skin tones that they get all the guys and are always the center of attention. As one light-skinned participant added, "I have a problem with dating because I don't want to be seen just for the way I look." Undoubtedly, it is this popular notion of normative colorism that fuels competition and division among black women.

Consider the riveting narrative of Nia, a 21-year-old woman who struggles with the fact that black people typically devalue darker skin tones. Sharing a dating story with her focus group, Nia spoke about being turned down for a second date with a young man because he "usually" doesn't "date dark girls." Talking about this experience led Nia into a shocking yet frank disclosure about her feelings:

Nia: I used to hate light-skinned girls. I used to truly, truly hate them. And I don't mean like, "Oh, you're lighter than me." No, I mean like, if I look at you, you look high yellow, but you're still black. And you will still claim black, like, that used to get on my damn nerves, because I got the impression that most will walk around all high and mighty because they are preferred. [. . .] And whenever someone says to me, "Oh you're pretty for a dark girl," like, it just, it gets me really pissed off 'cause it's, that's not a complement. [. . .]

JeffriAnne: You mentioned that you hated light-skinned women. You mentioned that earlier. . . . I wanted to ask you . . .

Nia: Used to . . .

JeffriAnne: Used to, exactly, I want to know if you can understand this issue from their perspective, what it's like to experience the same things that you experience, but on the other side of the spectrum?

Nia: Yeah, I can definitely see how the shoe would be on the other foot with them because I mean, I'm not, the thing that I can't wrap my [head around], I mean I've spoken to one, to one [laughs] but, I mean 'cause I don't really care to hear your pain, you know what I mean [uhuh]? Like I hate it when it sounds like, it sounds like the [. . .] the mulatto and . . .

JeffriAnne: tragic mulatto?

Nia: Yeah, you know what I mean? [mocking light-skinned women] *"Oh, life is just so hard for me. I'm just so light-skinned. Oh my goodness. It's just so hard with all these men hitting on me all the time."* Shut up! You know what I mean? Come on now. I can't fathom being in your shoes, but at the same time, can we not play the "Oh I'm just the victim" because, and I'm not bitching as the victim, but don't play the victim knowing good and well that you are at an advantage. I mean when it comes down to it, you really are.

Nia's honest and raw emotion dominated the focus group (composed of women with varying skin tones) conversation for several minutes. At the end of this young woman's diatribe on lighter black women, Nia ended her comments on a somewhat happier note, convincing the group that she had progressed beyond those negative feelings and remained committed to moving toward a place of education and agency. Yet it is Nia's final comments that resonated with me as a fellow black woman and a researcher: "It's like a slap in the face though, because it wasn't until I got here that I realized how sad it is, like, where does this all come from?" The answer to Nia's question escaped me. On the surface, the knee-jerk response is colonialism and white racism. But this young woman, who is college educated and has a keen sense of agency and a critical consciousness of colorism, simultaneously has a strong sense of conflict, bias, and discrimination. Where does Nia assess blame for her hatred? Where does her empowerment truly begin? Time and again, these devastating accounts—followed by even tougher questions—point to the complex and problematic struggle of colorism for young black women in contemporary society.

While lighter-skinned women are viewed as having free reign in which men they are able to date, some brown and dark-skinned women talk about considerable limitations in their dating choices and position. Returning to Margaret Hunter's notion of the beauty queue[14]—the idea that black women are placed in a hierarchical "pecking order" from light to dark skin— common responses elicited from darker-toned women in the focus groups indicate that they are less frequently sought after as potential dating and marriage partners. Supporting this widespread notion is the belief that "boys don't look at dark-skinned girls." This viewpoint is perhaps best illustrated by Becky, a young woman who related an incident involving her aunt and cousin:

> I have a cousin, and she has a very dark complexion but beautiful skin, and [. . .] she want[ed] a boyfriend, and her mom chuckled and said, "Oh sweetheart, you're just going to have to find a white man, because he's the only one who's going to find beauty in you. [. . .] You're going to have to go to Europe because [. . .] those are the only men who are going to appreciate the beauty in a black woman." And she was like, "You know, a black man will never ever date a darker-skinned woman."

This "rule" associated with normative colorism is echoed by many women participating in the focus groups. As Vivica explained, in fifth grade when she noticed all the boys "flocking to the Spanish-looking and light-skinned girls," she recognized that her brown skin tone only afforded her a certain number of dating choices. Vivica stated, "You could be the prettiest dark-skinned person . . . but society has already set limits for you." Likewise, Callea learned a hard lesson when she was heartbroken by a cheating boyfriend. Describing to the group that although this young man "was a lot darker than me, he was surrounded with people who had extremely light-skinned girlfriends." Confused about why her relationship was in trouble, Callea consulted a close friend for advice.

And she said something really interesting. She said that he had a rep-
utation to uphold. [. . .] It wasn't that I was a bad person, [it was] just
that all of his friends had light-skinned girlfriends, [. . .] and he kind
of wants to be a part of that. [. . .] That's how I interpreted what she
said [. . .] because I don't fit the bill, I'm not light-skinned and I don't
have long hair.

Frustrated with the rejection sometimes accompanying dark skin, there
are some women, however, like Tessa, who understand that their relationship choices are limited and therefore engage in compensatory practices by
dating partners who are not black.

Not surprisingly, the color perspectives shared by the group of young
black men I spoke to confirmed the suspicions of the women in this study.
Open and honest about their skin-tone preferences, the majority of the men
in the group admitted that they were more attracted to light-skinned women:

I find myself to be more tended toward a light-skin woman, I'm not
really sure why, but I've also found, like, darker skin more attractive
sometimes. . . . I work on myself, I wonder why, why am I always looking at lighter-skinned women. . . . I kind of want to find out why I do
that. (Donald, 19, medium)

I find myself to be, like, immediately attracted to someone who has
longer hair, lighter eyes, and a lighter skin tone. I feel like when I'm
walking on campus, and I see a light-skinned young lady, it's a quicker
head turn. . . . It doesn't mean that darker-skin women aren't attractive, but for me, as far as dating, I just think that lighter skin tone is
more attractive. (Stephen, 20, dark)

I prefer a girl that has her own hair. I prefer it to be longer, and I prefer
it to be straight. . . . I don't care for weave. . . . Sometimes when you see
the girls that have extensions all the way down to their knees and it's
too long. . . . I don't think that's attractive. (Alex, 20, light brown)

Although the women in this study blame dominant standards of beauty
for impacting their intimate relationships with black men, it is imperative to
highlight that in some instances, women play an equal part in colorism by
discriminating against lighter-skinned men. The literature on gendered colorism clearly indicates that black women are more affected by colorism
compared to black men. However, the literature also points to bias and discrimination against light-skinned men as it relates to issues of attractiveness
and desirability. The adulation often reserved for light-skinned women is

not extended to light-skinned men; as sociologist Mark Hill suggests, for men, dark-skin has stereotypically been associated with masculinity and sexual attractiveness.[15] Contemporary black male celebrities, including Denzel Washington, Morris Chestnut, Djimon Hounsou, and Idris Elba are all examples of dark-skinned men who are considered sex symbols partly because of their skin tone. There are respondents who openly expressed bias when making decisions in dating and relationships:

> Personally I'm more attracted to dark-skinned guys, [. . .] in my mind, [. . .] I'm kind of light so I guess he should be darker, so if we reproduce it will be, that's the way I think. I don't know if that might be good, but I try to overcompensate. [. . .] I haven't really seen two dark-skinned people together, and I know it's weird, but I've never seen it. And I've never seen two light-skinned people together either. It's usually either one is darker than the other, like just a little, or one is really darker than the other. You know, it's never the same thing. (Kira, 19, medium)

> I don't know if anyone has ever heard this [. . .] but older people in my family, and some people that I've talked to [tell me], "Don't bring home a light-skinned guy 'cause he's not going to work, or he's going to think he's too pretty to work," that kind of stuff. (Fuze, 20, medium)

> I actually prefer darker guys because lighter guys with curly hair, they're too pretty. I don't think that they would be strong, and I'm sure that there are [strong] light-skinned men, you know, I'm sure. But I prefer the dark skin, more chestnut. (Keesha, 20, dark)

Kira chooses to date dark-skinned men exclusively due to the common belief among black people that light- and dark-skinned people should date or marry their "color opposite." Citing the stereotype that light-skinned men are not as capable as dark-skinned men, Fuze avoids dating men who are lighter than her medium skin tone. Likewise, Keesha's preference for dark skin relates to their perceived strength over lighter men. The nature of gendered colorism has reverse effects for black men; lighter-skinned males are viewed as less attractive, intelligent, and desirable in many of the same ways that dark-skinned women are regarded. At times, there are some exceptions to the normative ideas about the perceived physical attractiveness and desirability of light-skinned men, as in the case of Jeremy Meeks, the light-skinned felon who in 2014 was dubbed the "world's sexiest criminal." These normative ideas about light- and dark-skinned men became the focus of one group conversation when I asked participants to describe the characteristics of their ideal mates:

JeffriAnne: If you could choose the skin tone of your significant other, what color would that be and why?

Luann: And I know it would be light, because I know for some reason, I love red men. I'm not sure why, and I feel terrible about it. I know it's, I know it's like this is like a stereotype that I have, but I love red men. I don't know why. I do, and I'm not sure why. And my dad was darker, my grandpa was darker, my uncle is dark. I just don't know why.

Kelly: Mine would be brown, because [. . .] there are a lot of light-skinned people in my family, and I would never date a light-skinned person. And I don't know why. It's just weird, like, I'm not attracted to, like, red people, I don't know. [. . .] It's just interesting that I've never dated someone red; it's always dark or brown skinned.

Patricia: I mean, I don't think I would like guys darker than me. I don't know why, it just seems like, I don't like a lot of light men and, honestly, [. . .] they're just not attractive to me. They gotta be either brown or a darker complexion. But there's a reason. [. . .] Light-skinned men [. . .] they are possessive, they are controlling, they don't want you to . . . I've heard they're controlling and everything, and so the red men [I know] are like that, conceited and [. . .] my personality is totally different from them, so I'm just attracted to brown-skinned men.

Colleen: Um, so I have [had] two boyfriends. And one was red. [. . .] One was darker, and you're right about the red one, he was crazy, he was possessive. He would check [my] phone and everything, he wasn't that smart, [. . .] he really had security issues, and it was [the] dark-skinned [boyfriend] I had more fun with. I think I loved [him] more, and he was very clever though. He would keep secrets, he wouldn't tell me stuff, like he was very, very smart. [. . .] But I don't really have a preference, I like[d] both of them [. . .] but the dark-skinned men, there's just something so sexy about the skin tone.

Luann: [. . .] Okay, like we all said [about] red men, [. . .] I think because they're red they're not as black, so they are men constantly trying to prove how black they are, they have to prove how much of a man they are, let alone a black man. [. . .]

Stacey: I just think light-skinned men [. . .] are douchebags. Because they are closer to white. [. . .] Give me a fine black brother.

This particular discussion made me aware of the paradoxical and multi-dimensional nature of colorism. All of the women featured in this excerpt mentioned at other points how their lives have been impacted—for some quite negatively—by colorism. In spite of that, they openly discriminate and stereotype light- and dark-skinned men. Furthermore, the internalized scripts and external practices of colorism (i.e., thinking that lighter or darker skin is better, and acting—discriminating—accordingly) are at times shared by black men and women. This is an excellent example of how both the normative and oppositional forces of colorism compete within the lives of the study participants, illustrating just how challenging and complex they can be. These color stories reveal the ever-continuing significance of skin tone in the 21st century.

Sidebar 4. A Note on the Media

Although family, school, and relationships are cited by the women in this study as the most central agents in shaping their ideas and experiences with colorism, there was, to some extent, a smaller reference to the media. As a researcher, my initial assumption was that respondents would talk much more about the media shaping their lives, as this particular generation has been more affected by various media and technological advances compared to previous generations of black Americans. Yet, as social researcher Rana Emerson explains, "although surrounded by distorted and disparaging images of themselves, many young Black women seem to find the ability to avoid internalizing and accepting these representations as reflections of their own lives and experiences."[16] Although the data from the focus groups suggest that young black women *are* in fact impacted by colorism, part of what Emerson is hinting at is the idea that young black women are not heavily influenced by the media. This, of course, *is* reflected within the data, as influences from family, school, and relationships outweigh media representations. To be sure, many focus group participants have a clear understanding that the most popular and celebrated images of black women in the media embody Eurocentric standards of beauty. For example, Denise's remarks about the members of singing group *Destiny's Child* reflect this awareness:

> Kelly [is] not even looked at, in Destiny's Child she doesn't really get the focus, but Beyoncé gets all the focus because she's [. . .] more appealing to the white and the black, the whole entire United States, all the cultures, 'cause she's fair skinned and [. . .] more appealing to both cultures, but Kelly [. . .] a lot of people

find Kelly to be really, really attractive 'cause she's dark skinned [. . .] but she doesn't get all the limelight.

Similar to Denise's comments about megastar Beyoncé Knowles, other entertainers—including Alicia Keyes, Halle Berry, Tyra Banks, and the cast of the popular television show *Girlfriends*—were discussed as the most beautiful black women in popular culture. Yet respondents were equally critical of these images, suggesting that light-skinned and biracial women have always been viewed as the standard. It is common knowledge for many of the women interviewed that the media embraces colorism through the proliferation of light-skinned women in movie, singing, and television roles.

Similar to Meeko, Jessica—a 19-year-old participant who describes her complexion as "medium"—reveals that the media was also her introduction to colorism. For this young woman, however, hip-hop music videos made her conscious of the dominant and prevailing standards of beauty. As bell hooks articulates, rap music is indeed responsible for promoting the value of light-skinned beauty over dark skin.

It is quite rare to see darker-skinned black females among the groups of women that are seen as sexually viable and desirable. In most music videos, whether rap or otherwise, [. . .] it is the light-skinned, preferably long-haired, preferably straightened-haired female who becomes once again re-inscribed as the desirable object. This again is one of the tragic dimensions right now of race in America because more than ever before, color caste systems are being overtly affirmed.[17]

It is the overt placement of light skin and long hair as the beauty standard in videos that prompted focus-group member Jessica into a color consciousness. She described, "When I was younger, I watched music videos and I'd always see the light-skinned girls with long hair, so I used to want to be light skinned [too]." This young woman, who openly admits comparing her medium skin tone to the women she saw in the videos, illustrates how this has shaped her experience:

I was never really color conscious until I really started watching "106 and Park" in school. All the girls were light skinned in the video, and like I said, coming, and after a couple of videos I was starting to notice and [it] really started bothering me because I, soon I started looking for dark-skinned women in videos. [. . .]

So I'm not really that color conscious any more, 'cuz I'm starting to love myself more and more every day.

Jessica is able to be critical of the colorism in music videos because, as she noted, she began to love herself more. Self-love cannot be underestimated as a key strategy in battling the normative forces of colorism. What is mentioned within the context of these focus groups only scratches the surface of the context of colorism and the media—especially hip-hop lyrics. More research is needed to understand how today's hip-hop shapes and or challenges colorist ideology.

Sidebar 5. Colorism Has No Gender

I have spent this entire book addressing the issue of colorism among black women. While the literature and the color stories in this book show that notions of colorism are typically gendered and more impactful for women and girls, black men and boys contend with color bias and discrimination as well. As a point of illustration, I am sharing the story of a mother—a light-skinned woman who refers to herself as Kathy—who struggles with teaching her adolescent son, Jacob, how to love his skin. In a letter she titled "Colorism Has No Gender," she writes:

(April 2014)
My son Jacob is an energetic, intelligent, outgoing, gifted, and talented young man. He is 12 years old. We have just relocated to the state of Georgia from our home state of Florida. In my family, my son and I have the lightest skin complexions in our family. When I was growing up, I had to face colorism within my family and with close friends. Yet, it has been more difficult for me to face colorism through my son's own agonizing experience.

About two years ago, my son spent his summer break with family in Florida while I stayed in Georgia. This was the first time that we were separated by distance. This was not only a traumatizing experience as a mother, but also an experience my son would never forget. Jacob left a happy, free spirited and loving child. When he returned, Jacob was a broken and confused child who questioned his identity, and was angry at his new skin complexion.

Jacob spent a lot of time in the Florida sun, and he came home a few shades darker than his normal complexion. He clearly was not comfortable in his new skin. When Jacob first saw me, he ran into my arms and held me tight. I immediately took note that he glared at his hands as he held me tight around my waist. I asked Jacob what was wrong, and he said with tears, "I'm dark. It won't wash off. How do I get light again? I don't like being dark." As a mother, the lump in my throat had to be absorbed with a deep sighing exhale. As I felt my heart break, I had to hide the pain in my chest with a smile for my son. I smiled with a hesitant laugh and said, "Jacob, I love you. It will be okay, you will be fine. It's just skin, baby." He was visibly displeased. To follow up, I slightly laughed and said, "Didn't you have fun playing outside in the sun every day? That's what summer is all about."

You would think that the experience ended there. My child continued to monitor his skin as the seasons changed. As the fall season blended into winter season, Jacob expected his color to lighten and go back to normal. The pain of my child's lost identity was only worsened by family members who teased Jacob with statements like, "Jacob's gotten so dark, you can barely recognize him," or "Are you sure you have the same child?" or " Jacob, you're one of us now." Another family member commented, "Well, I guess your mom is the only light bright now." Of course these comments came from several family members who thought that this kind of behavior was ok.

Jacob still monitored the tone of his skin, and as his skin began to lighten, his smile began to get bigger.

It is my job to protect my child, to encourage, and instill a sense of self-love into him. I'm the one who needs to validate my son and get him to look into the mirror and love the essence of himself. This experience gave me the moment to teach him about the ugly words of jokes from those we love and consider safe and trusting people. This painful and emotionally scarring life lesson of colorism shows how much self-hating we do in our own community. This issue is more than just the girls—it's bigger than us.

CHAPTER 5

Place Matters: The Counter-Narratives of Everyday Colorism

People arrive at an understanding of themselves and the world through narratives—purveyed by schoolteachers, newscasters, "authorities," and all the other authors of our common sense. Counter-narratives are, in turn, the means by which groups contest that dominant reality and fretwork of assumptions that supports it. Sometimes delusions lie that way, sometimes not.

—Henry Louis Gates[1]

Speaking to the divergent perspectives of Black Americans that run counter to mainstream (white) society, African American intellectual Henry Louis Gates Jr. defines *counter-narratives* in the above excerpt as stories or beliefs that challenge dominant ideology and narratives. Cultural theorist Martin McQuillan further explains that narratives and counter-narratives exist together, and that both are equally valid and legitimate as forms of the truth.[2] The previous chapters show that for the women in this study, colorism is very much alive and well in their everyday lives. This is perhaps the dominant narrative overlapping throughout many of the color stories shared in this project; albeit in various ways, colorism impacts everyday experiences in many areas from family to relationships. Further, some young women

understand colorism through a *normative framework*, embracing dominant ideals about skin tone inherent throughout mainstream black culture;
others have developed an *oppositional knowledge* to these conventional ideals. Yet, it is interesting to note that despite the dominant narrative speaking
to the sustained presence of colorism, three counter-narratives—all centering on "place"—emerged throughout the course of this study: 1) the absence of colorism in the North and Midwest sections of the United States
(place as a region); 2) an increased emphasis on colorism in the Caribbean
(the American "place" compared to the Caribbean); and 3) "post-colorist"
attitudes of younger generations of black Americans (age or generation as a
distinctive ideological "place"). This chapter is devoted to a discussion of
these three place counter-narratives. While these ideas are not generalizable to broader populations of black women, they are nonetheless useful in
understanding the complex and often contradictory nature of colorism.

COUNTER-NARRATIVE #1: THE REGIONAL COLOR HYPOTHESIS

The history of black America points to palpable differences in the lives
of African Americans residing in the North compared to those living in the
South. From the escape of slaves prior to the emancipation of slavery to the
Great Migration, many African Americans sought better opportunity and
overall quality of life outside of Southern states that were rife with segregation and racism.[3] Of course, many black Americans fleeing to the northern
half of the United States still had to contend with prejudice and racism. Yet
the anti-racist ideology accompanying perceptions of life in the North becomes apparent in this project as many participants quickly made distinctions between the North and the South. These ideals developed into the
first counter-narrative I am terming the *regional color hypothesis*, which
suggests that colorism is an obscure, insignificant matter in the lives of
many black Americans residing in the North and Midwest. As a researcher,
I did not anticipate that region would come up during the focus group sessions. However, it was first mentioned by participants involved in the pilot
study. Since that initial discussion, differences about the North and the
South re-surfaced during subsequent focus groups. The consideration of
geographic placement of black Americans is key as it relates to African
Americans' perceptions of quality of life, particularly as it relates to
race(ism) and color(ism). Today, the majority of blacks have (re) migrated
back "down South."[4] According to Monique Morris, author of *Black Stats*,
the American South is currently home to more than half of the African
American population.[5] This is in large part due to the influx of many

college-educated and retired blacks to the South (to places including Atlanta, Dallas, Houston, and Raleigh).[6]

All of the women in this study were living in the state of Florida at the
time of data collection; the majority of respondents (63 percent) cited Florida as their home state. Of the women born in the United States (but not
native Floridians), the remainder of those respondents reported growing
up in the North and/or Midwest (New York City, Chicago, and Washington
D.C., for example). Among all participants, however, there is an overwhelming sense that the Northern United States is much more diverse and
progressive than the South. As one young woman explained, "There's just
something about that down South mentality, [. . .] residue leftover from
you know, the Civil War, it's kind of just lingering, [. . .] I didn't think that
[colorism] was a big deal [. . .] up North, people seem pretty comfortable
about their skin color, skin tone, but I think that when it comes down here,
people are much more conscious and they are made to be aware." This is
precisely the same sentiments shared by Nicole, a very light-skinned respondent who was 41 years old at the time she participated in a focus group
discussion. Nicole grew up in D.C. and moved to the South as a young
adult. She described her experience living in Northern Florida as much
more difficult compared to being in D.C.; for Nicole, this difference is most
noticeable in raising her two daughters:

> I spent my teenage years in the D.C. area, which was probably one of
> the few places in the country where blacks outnumber whites, so
> there was such a wide array of skin tones and colorism really wasn't
> [an issue] . . . and to see somebody my complexion is not a rarity as it
> is [here] in the South. So it wasn't a big to do for me . . . but then . . .
> when I came here to [Cityville[7]] I think I had the most impact. I have
> two daughters who are fair skinned, and their experience in [City-
> ville] has been much harsher than mine was growing up . . . girls
> wanting to jump them and . . . and my kids were called white. [. . .] I've
> never had as many questions about my ethnicity, both of my parents
> are black. . . . And so here in [Cityville], I've noticed that even the
> blacks that are from here are still very much stuck way behind as op-
> posed to maybe up North.

Nicole's comments regarding the absence of a color complex in D.C. are
quite interesting, given the historical evidence offered by Audrey Elisa Kerr,
Marita Golden, Lawrence Otis Graham, and others who present empirical
and anecdotal evidence citing Washington, D.C., as a black metropolis that
has considerable issues with class and color.[8]

For Alicia, a light-brown respondent who is African American and Puerto Rican, growing up in various parts of the country due to her parents' military background enabled her to see the contrast of black life in the North compared to the South. The 22-year-old recounts her experiences:

> I grew up partly in the North and partly in the South, and I do notice there is a difference in behavior [between . . .] black people [. . .] in the South and in the North. You know, black women are loud [. . .] but confident and very, you know, the matriarch, I see that predominantly in the South. In the North I kind of see [. . .] both man and wife together.

Alicia's comments point to a belief that there are more black female-headed households existing in the southern parts of the United States, while there are more two-parent black families residing in the northern half of the country. Agreeing with Alicia's statement, Toni, a respondent from the same focus group, makes a similar connection:

> I've lived in the South and I've lived in the North and [. . .] I always wondered why there was such as difference, [. . .] The family was able to develop more along the lines of your typical Caucasian family where there [are] two parents in the home and they were able [. . .] to have wealth and to pass that wealth onto generations, which is why I think you find a lot more wealthy [black] people up North than you find in the South. [. . .] I do agree that there are differences in the North and the South [. . .] that directly relate to the differences in how women are perceived and how they act as well.

Because participants view the North as a place where black Americans are able to flourish, colorism is viewed as insignificant there, and therefore reflects more of the attitudes, perceptions, and beliefs of those blacks who are living in the South. One participant specifically ties this to its historical origins by explaining how it was that more fair-skinned blacks moved to the North during the Great Migration, and those that stayed in the South were often, "not always," those who had darker skin.[9] Others argue that the spectrum of skin tones is wider in the North. An interesting observation Nicole (whose story was referenced earlier) made is her impression that there are more light-skinned people living in the North. She stated, "my spectrum of what light skinned is and dark skinned is, is much wider" living in Florida. Nicole went on to explain that individuals who could "pass" for light skinned in the South would not have the same latitude elsewhere.

There is no census or demographic data available to support these participants' claims that there are more light-skinned blacks living in the North compared to the South—or, further, that there is more skin tone variation present among African Americans living above the Mason-Dixon Line.[10] However, what can be learned from these statements is how internalized scripts get "mapped" onto the broader color narratives of black culture. Present within these internalized scripts of color is the notion that black people in the South are darker, poorer, and less educated than their counterparts living in the North. These color myths also reinforce racial, gendered, and class-based stereotypes of black women (e.g., black women in the South tend to be loud, single women). Unfortunately, these participants do not recognize the problematic nature of their comments. Their remarks are incredibly ironic given that many of these same women talk about being discriminated against in their own lives due to their skin tone.

Another interesting consequence of this regional color hypothesis set forth by participants is the belief that people up North are more comfortable and thus more accepting of a variety of skin tones, even tones falling at the extremes. These perceptions go against the dominant ideology that colorism is an issue for blacks in all regions of the United States. The following accounts describe this counter-narrative further:

> I was born [. . .] in New York. I [spent] the majority of my younger years in New York, up North. [. . .] And to tell you the truth, in the nine years that I was there, it was never a problem. Nobody's ever come to me and said anything. I've never heard anything. And even my cousins who are up there [now], they don't have a problem dating a lighter-skinned, darker-skinned [woman]. It's just not a problem in the North. (Lela, 20, medium)

Lela's viewpoint indicates that similar to an antiracist ideology associated with northern states, there exists a parallel discourse of anticolorism. Chanel, a 21-year-old respondent who talks openly about the negative experiences she has as a dark-skinned woman, concurs that Southern black people are more colorstruck:

> I know growing up here, down South, [. . .] men have just been so conscious about skin tone where they don't even approach me, you know. And by the time they approach, it's more like, oh, you know, you kinda look good for a dark-skinned girl. And I'm just looking at them saying, "You fool." But when I go up North, it's very different. I

mean I'll walk down the street, and the men, they'll literally stop to look at me, and I feel so much better up there.

The idea that dark skin is more exalted in the North is echoed by many women participating in the focus groups. Consider, for instance, the comments of Mary, a 24-year-old woman who completed her undergraduate degree in the city of Philadelphia. Contrasting this time to her current experience attending graduate school in the South, Mary recognizes that her life is distinctly dissimilar:

I've been up North also where "the blacker the better, the sweeter the juice," you know, she's so beautiful, she's so strong, or the same thing, this man is so beautiful, he's strong because he's darker. The same thing with the [black] woman. I don't know if it's the whole Black Power thing, [but] you want to celebrate darkness. But [here] I think color is definitely an issue, and you tend to point it out in different situations, and sometimes [it is] the first thing that people look at.

Mary also mentions that as an undergraduate student, she formed friendships with first-generation black immigrants from Jamaica, Trinidad, and Nigeria, and that these friends were less concerned about her dark skin tone compared to African Americans. In addition to the belief Mary has about the North being more accepting of black people of all skin tones, she holds the same views about black people who are not from the United States.

These statements are both eye-opening and ironic. The ways in which participants characterize the experiences of black Americans in the North is quite nostalgic and a stark contrast to a number of contemporary events and books providing evidence that colorism is alive and well all over the United States, including the North. The 2007 controversy over a party exclusively for light-skinned black women occurred in Detroit, Michigan.[11] There is a proliferation of work documenting the existence of colorism across the nation. As an African American growing up in Cleveland, Ohio, I can personally attest to the presence of colorism during my childhood and adolescence. Although I acquired an oppositional knowledge about colorism from my mother, I was, however, made aware of skin color differences through my school experiences, personal relationships, and from members of my extended family. I will concede that since moving to the southern part of the United States, I *am* reminded more often in my daily life about skin tone differences. I hear black people regularly make distinctions between "red" girls and "black" girls; the language of color appears more pervasive in this region. However, colorism *does* exist in the North—but why do the women in this study maintain a different belief? This counter-narrative points to the need for further research comparing the viewpoints of black women living in various regions in the United States.

COUNTER-NARRATIVE #2: CARIBBEAN AND AMERICAN CONTEXTS OF COLORISM

In addition to perceiving colorism as less of an issue in the North, many participants discussed how their experiences of colorism are connected to their nationality and/or ethnic identity. Certainly, issues of skin color are present across the globe and throughout the African Diaspora; yet, the second counter-narrative emerging from the analysis points to the idea that the context of colorism in Caribbean societies (most notably Haiti and Jamaica in this project) is markedly different compared to the American context. To be sure, shared histories of slavery and European colonization—resulting in caste systems of phenotypic difference and the common desire for whiteness—are parallel for American blacks and those born in Caribbean nations. Yet there are nuanced differences and varied discourses of blackness, identity, and colorism based upon place. Given these intricate variances, coupled with the influx of the "other" African Americans migrating to the United States in the 21st century,[12] there is a need for more scholarly attention to the comparative experiences of African Americans and Afro-Carribeans. In this project, the study sample included 32 respondents who identified as Afro-Caribbean (primarily as first- or second-generation Haitians or Jamaicans); this represents 48 percent of the study sample. Although I would not classify this project as a comparative study in relation to ethnicity, respondents who were of Caribbean descent talked freely and often about their ethnic culture. For example, there was a tendency for some participants to qualify their comments with phrases such as, "Speaking for the Jamaican community," or "If you're Haitian, you know what I'm talking about." These references to ethnicity signify a differential representation of colorism experiences and its specific connection to the Caribbean.

In order to illustrate this idea, consider the story of Patricia, a 36-year-old Dominican woman who classifies her skin tone as "medium." When discussing her perspectives about colorism, she immediately interjected the situational context of the Dominican Republic:

> I would probably have to start with the Caribbean, the Dominican Republic where it's very different. [. . .] We don't have the same racial

categories that we have here, and people, we can use so many different ones, [. . .] I can use one label today and, you know, drive two hours and go to a place where I could just immediately be assumed as a different race, or even myself I can assert, you know, another racial identity. It's so flexible. And in the Dominican Republic as well as, where you [referring to another focus group participant] are from, Jamaica, you know more, I mean very similar. . . . I learned about skin tone at a very early age because my mom is very, very light skinned; her grandparents are from the Canary Islands in Spain, and then my father is very, very, very, very, dark and [. . .] so I learned about the importance of skin color at a very early age because of those family interactions. [. . .] But the thing is that in the Caribbean, it's so different because hair is also very important, as you say. You can have, you know, very dark skin, but if you have straight hair, or a specific feature in your face, then you can, you know, somewhat pass as white or something. And you see those dynamics. [. . .] That's very common in the Dominican Republic, you know, lighter skin . . . darkness, ugliness. It's changing a little bit now, but still many of the stereotypes are there and the assumptions about beauty based on how white you are, or how close to Spain, to the Spanish look you are. And of course when I came to the States, it was so difficult because even when there is so much racism in the Caribbean, especially the Dominican Republic. [. . .] It's just different, the dynamics are very different.

These "dynamics" that Patricia discussed are intricately tied to the history of the Dominican Republic. The only nation in the Caribbean to gain independence from black colonial rule (Haiti), the nation of the Dominican Republic has a long-standing history of colorism connected to an anti-Haitian sentiment and the widespread discourse of "black denial." Regardless of the lightness or darkness of any Dominican citizen's skin tone, they, by and large, refer to themselves as anything but black.[13] Another key difference within the context of colorism that Patricia mentions is the ability of Dominicans to "opt-into" whiteness (and out of blackness) through straight hair (and for many others, education and money.) As reporter Frances Robles explains, in the Dominican Republic, "the 'one-drop rule' works in reverse: One drop of white blood allows even very dark-skinned people to be considered white."[14] For this reason, as participant Patricia addresses, notions of skin tone (and racial categories) are ultimately more fluid on the island compared to the rigid "black–white" racial binary present within the United States.

Janice, a very light-skinned participant who grew up in the Caribbean island of the Bahamas, also recognized that being in the United States equates to a differential experience with race and class. In the excerpt below, she details this distinction:

> My experience growing up in the Bahamas was very different than what happens here. [. . .] And one of the things I try to explain to fellow Caribbean people when they don't understand racism in this country, because I think that there is a real difference, um, even though there is racism embedded throughout the Caribbean and it's linked with classism. So it's kind of difficult for me to talk about, but you know, I try to explain, like, listen, we grew up seeing black people in positions of power, and even if you're light skinned, the possibility of being, you know, a doctor or a politician or a lawyer or whatever [. . .] the possibility is real.

Janice immediately connects the fact that African Americans are a minority in the United States, making their historic and contemporary experiences with racism different compared to other places. As she clarified, there are black people who have access to larger amounts of privilege and power in the Caribbean, where the citizens of color are in the majority. On comparing colorism in the Bahamas to the United States, Janice stated, "That one-drop rule thing is still deeply entrenched, and I didn't understand that until, you know, I moved here." She goes on to say:

> When I came to the States, it was very different because, you know, the, even though the, I think the "lighter is better" is pretty much across the board, I think that that's, you know, through the colonization process. But in the Caribbean, it's much more specific to Islands, it's specific to demographics on that particular Island. But in the United States, I very much became aware of how much race and class intersected and played a factor with sort of these everyday interactions. [. . .] I had to face figuring out who I was before I could be comfortable with being around black women and not feeling like, oh they're going to be offended by me, or they're not going to like me because I'm light skinned. And that was a fear, it sort of sometimes still is a fear. . . .

For Janice, her difficulties in developing relationships with other black women diminished as she grew to understand the American context of colorism.

Haitian Colorism

The republic of Haiti is a majority-black society located in the Caribbean that gained independence from French colonization in 1804. As scholar John Lobb describes, Haiti has maintained an anti-black ideology in spite of attaining its freedom so long ago. He writes: "The prestige of lightness of skin color, along with other white physical characteristics, was so deeply impressed upon Haitian society in pre-revolutionary days, that it has unfortunately survived [. . .] and carries great weight today."[15] Although Lobb articulates the presence of colorism in Haiti over 60 years ago, the young women in this study confirmed the survival of this scholar's report. There were 11 Haitian respondents participating in the focus groups, making up 19 percent of the total study population. Many of these women are second-generation, with their parents migrating to the United States from Haiti. Furthermore, these respondents identified with Haitian tradition and culture; colorism becomes an extension of that understanding. This was the case for Beyoncé, who discussed her mother's experience, particularly the interconnectedness of color and class:

> I'm Haitian, and um, my mother came over to this country when she was five years old, and like I said, she's very light skinned. Well first of all, people don't, don't think. [. . .] I'm Haitian, don't think my mother's Haitian because she's light skinned. They don't associate that with being light skinned, and also, well, what happened was she went to a school and um, none of the black kids really accepted any of the Haitian kids. [. . .] They use to call them Frenchies, they thought they were uppity and all that, all the stereotypes we talked about, light-skinned people, and she was just harassed to no end because she was Haitian, because she was light skinned.

In relating their experiences of colorism to their Haitian ancestry, the majority of these women made two specific connections: bleaching and class differences. More than any other group of respondents, young women of Haitian descent talked more about using bleaching products themselves or knowing family members who bleach their skin on a regular basis. Recall from an earlier chapter the narratives of Stacey, Vivica, and Chanel, young women who linked their ritualistic bleaching habits to a specific part of their Haitian culture. A similar story was shared by Amy, an 18-year-old Haitian woman who noted that her mother regularly encourages her to bleach her skin:

I know that my mom is always trying to get me to use products to lighten my skin color because my mother is pretty light, and she wants me to be more like that. [. . .] She sees the other people look at being darker as a bad thing, so she doesn't really want me to go through that stereotype.

Likewise, Stacey mentioned that the pressure she received from her mother to bleach her skin was due to her dark complexion but, also, to the relationship between class and color often highlighted within the Haitian culture. This young woman even noted that extended family members were shocked to find out that she was attending a respected four-year university, as many reacted with comments such as, "Oh she's black. [. . .] She's going to have to go to a community college." Stacey explained about Haitian culture, "These things are associated with being dark skinned." Other respondents made parallel connections about their Haitian ancestry:

You kind of know that in Haiti there is a class division, and the lighter you are, the better you are. Haiti and the mass of the people in Haiti are poor, whatever, and they're dark. [. . .] You already understand it's a systematic thing that's been going on since you know, you great gran. . . . I mean, it's been going on. [. . .] The elite are light, they don't work with their hands, they know how to read. The black work with the soil, whatever, they work with agriculture, and they don't know how to read. (Vivica, 21, medium)

I think I mentioned this before, but in Haiti there's a class issue, and it's associated with the color of your skin. And in my family, a lot of them that are [still] in Haiti, they're really light skinned, and they have servants and things like that. And they're considered upper class in Haiti. [. . .] I don't really know too much about slavery here,[. . .] but [in Haiti] people were treated differently because of their darker skin. (Karina, 21, medium)

Both of these statements are evidence that skin tone and class are two interconnected and immutable categories within Haitian society. While focus group member Charlie did not offer an experience that paralleled the stories of Karina and Vivica, she did, however, discuss her perception that Haitians are more influenced by skin color. The 18-year-old participant related to her focus group the following story about her light-skinned cousin, whom she noted to receive more attention:

Lighter-skinned people get treated really differently in Haiti. Because whenever my cousin goes back, she says people [. . .] treat her really differently [. . .] because she's lighter. I guess being light is valued there a lot like it is here. Light-skinned people are special and prettier.

While we cannot draw conclusions that apply to the entire Haitian culture, it is evident from the young Haitian women in this study that bleaching and class stratification are believed to be common features of their culture, supporting the notion that colorism is more prevalent in that nation.

Jamaican Colorism

Similar to Haiti, Jamaica is a predominately black nation that was once dominated by (English) colonial rule; the country received independence from Britain in 1962. While race tensions are virtually nonexistent within this nation, Jamaica does, however, have significant issues related to class and color distinctions. Also present within this Caribbean society is the elevation of light skin; in fact, colorism scholar Christopher Charles notes a widespread bleaching phenomenon among many Jamaican girls and young women.[16] While there was far less mention of bleaching among the 13 Jamaican respondents in this study, the young women *do* believe that colorism is more blatant on the island compared to the United States. They articulated this difference in the areas of class and beauty. Similar to the racial structure in Haiti, skin color structures class status and overall opportunity. In writing about her research on colorism in Jamaica, author Obiagele Lake observes,

My field work in Jamaica and other parts of the Caribbean [. . .] indicates that the positive value placed on "whiteness" persists. If one is not actually white, then one's education, speech patterns, place of residence, and close associates combine to codify one's proximity to the white ideal.[17]

This is the same pattern noted by the women I interviewed. Many of the Jamaican respondents commented on spending time both in the U.S. and in Jamaica and, thus, are able to pinpoint specific features of Jamaican culture. The following comments demonstrate these noteworthy differences:

I think [colorism] almost depends in a way where you are. Because if you're in Jamaica and you're dark skinned, it's not good. Because you will be looked over for jobs. You won't be considered in the upper-classes of society. You are basically looked down upon if you're dark skinned. And the funny thing is, you can be the smartest person in your class and a light-skinned kid could be the dumbest person. [. . .] If you are compared to them, they might just win because of their light skin. (Callea, 21, dark)

I don't know if it's a Jamaican thing, but most people teach their young kids that when you're lighter, you get more opportunities, and you get to do more things than when you're darker. Even when we used to go to the beach in Jamaica, we weren't allowed to stay out [in the sun] too long [we were told], "You need to stay out of the sun," things like that. It's going to affect how pretty I am. (Natasha, 18, medium)

Outside of being more aware of skin color differences in Jamaica, some participants also talked about differential treatment in Jamaica compared to the States. Indeed, this is the case for Callea, a young woman who identifies her skin tone as "dark." She explained that because she has extended family still living in Jamaica, she spends a considerable amount of time there during the summers. This young woman also stated that because there is a strong Jamaican community at her university, she often runs into her college mates while visiting the island. Yet, as Callea told the members of her focus group, skin color becomes much more of an issue once she gets to Jamaica:

But the fact is that when I was in Jamaica when I use to go home and visit, like [my friends from the States] wouldn't even spit on me, they wouldn't talk to me, nobody called me, nobody said anything. When I came back up to school, [my friends] would call [and ask], "Do you want to go out?" Because at school [. . .] you want to be with your kind, you don't want to stand out, but when you're in Jamaica and they're amongst their own, to hell with her, whatever. She's not, you know, Jamaican anymore.

As Callea recounted in this story, skin color takes a back seat to ethnicity while she's in the United States; identifying with other Jamaicans is much more important for those who wish to cling to their nationality rather than identifying with African Americans. However, going back to the island means reverting back to the color and class hierarchy that is so commonplace there.

Although it has been documented throughout this project that the majority of women (regardless of their ethnic identity) perceive light skin and

European features as the standard of beauty, Jamaican respondents shared a strong sense that these standards are much higher in Jamaica. When discussing the issue of beauty, Jasmine, a second-generation Jamaican, mused that, "there's never any dark-skinned flight attendants [in Jamaica]. They are always light skin with the long hair, the Jamaican accent and some pretty eyes." On a more serious note, Monica stated, "there's such a struggle to become like the red-skinned girls, the light-skinned uptown girls in Jamaica, that's the kind of status that you want to aspire to." Other participants recognized this pattern in Jamaica, and were quite critical of the way things are in Jamaican society. One such critique was given by Callea, who followed up her story about being snubbed by lighter-skinned Jamaicans with an interesting analysis of beauty pageants:

> [My friend] and I were talking about it the other day, about Miss Jamaica, how every single year, we send a light-skinned girl to the competition and ninety percent of the country is dark, is black. We sent a white Jewish girl a couple years ago, and I don't think we've sent a dark-skinned girl since 1978, and it's really sad because they say, "Out of many one people," but less than ten percent is Lebanese or Indian. [. . .] The majority of us, we're dark skinned. [. . .] And it's not like Jamaica is lacking in beautiful dark-skinned women. You can walk any road in Kingston, in the country, Montego Bay, Ocho Rios, or wherever and find dark-skinned women. Short hair, long hair, [. . .] but the thing is we don't want to send them to represent our country because [. . .] we can't get past that slave mentality. 1838, we abolished slavery, and we can't get over that, we can't get over the thought that white people or mixed people are better than us, the house slaves are better than the slaves out in the field.

From Callea's comments about beauty contests, it appears that similar to black American society, Jamaican society is still stuck in the "slave mentality." Overall, the majority of Jamaican and Haitian respondents constructed colorism as a more complex and exaggerated phenomenon in the Caribbean compared to the U.S. Their beliefs, of course, are connected to their social locations as first- and second-generation Afro-Caribbeans. What is ironic, though, is that these same women simultaneously report significant (and at times negative) experiences of colorism here. Despite these experiences of colorism, the Caribbean nations of Haiti and Jamaica are believed to have a greater color complex. Undoubtedly, more research is needed to further illuminate this debate.

COUNTER-NARRATIVE #3: MILLENNIALS ARE ANTI-COLORIST AND POST-RACIAL

Talking to the young women in this study uncovered that colorism is indeed part of their everyday lives, yet it is important to note that this current generation views their experiences as radically different from previous generations of black Americans. While there has been a tendency to project narratives of color blindness and post-racialism upon the millennial generation (i.e., young people don't see race and, furthermore, do not experience racism), some data suggests otherwise. For instance, the work of the Applied Research Center concluded that millennials (the group of individuals born between 1980 and 1997) do, in fact, believe that race matters but have a hard time articulating the structural nature of racism in the 21st century.[18] This same pattern appears through the third counter-narrative surfacing in this project—that this cohort of black women is not as color conscious as earlier black women—and develops through three factors participants cite as reasons for the overall decline in colorism.

The first idea related to this counter-narrative is that colorism is gradually weakening in presence. This belief supports predictions made by scholars researching the issue of colorism shortly after the Civil Rights and Black Power movements. Several empirical studies examined the effect of the "Black Is Beautiful" ideology upon the generation coming of age during this era. These scholars observed a definite shift in the attitudes surrounding skin color and point to future generations of black Americans who will potentially be unscathed by colorism. As sociologist H. Edward Ransford suggested in 1970,

> Indeed, one meaning of "black is beautiful" is that color no longer makes a difference. In fact, for some segments of the black community (i.e., young college students), the traditional evaluations appear to be reversed—dark skin is now admired and light skin is not. A provocative question is whether the black pride movement has been powerful enough to override completely the traditional stigma of dark color. One can speculate that dark color will not lose its negative evaluation until a new generation of black children has been exposed to "black is beautiful" values and has replaced the current generation in power and status.[19]

As postulated, these forecasts are supported by some of the respondents, typically toward the end of focus group sessions, when I asked how participants viewed skin tone bias in relation to their parents' or grandparents' generations. Twenty-one-year-old Fiona observed,

> Definitely, definitely, it's different. [. . .] It's pretty much one hundred percent that if I talk to somebody in my mother's generation about this issue, I'm going to hear the very same thing [. . .] that light is right, and dark is not. But I feel like in this generation [. . .] it's a lot more common to hear opinions like the ones we're hearing today. [. . .] You understand that it's present in our society, but we don't agree with it and we're not going to really go along with it. It's fading out, I think.

Fiona's comments are particularly interesting. At several points during the focus group, Fiona talked about areas in her life where colorism is insignificant yet also offered clues to the contrary. Fiona began the focus group by indicating that because she falls within the middle of the spectrum, she has "escaped" the negativity attached to being too light or too dark. However, when the subject of family came up, she noted,

> I guess my family has had a huge impact on what I think about color. And you know, my mom uses bleach cream, I've used it at one point in the past, and, you know, you'll just hear them make certain comments. My brother, he's pretty light skinned, but his father's very dark, so my mom [would say] "Oh, you know, thank God he didn't come out like his father," things like that.

This remark runs counter to Fiona's overall perception that colorism is "fading out." Yet her previous comments about her own experiences speak to the contrary.

Similar to Fiona, Maxine—a participant from a different focus group—understands colorism to be an issue plaguing previous generations, but not hers. On the question of where the current generation of black Americans stands, Maxine answered, "My grandmother [. . .] was very prejudice[d]. My mother isn't, and I turned out not to be." Maxine further explained that her lack of colorist beliefs stems from how and where she grew up:

> It depends on how you raise your children and where you raise your children. That's exactly where the division came from, where in the North, you don't really see that; in the South you do.

Present within this young woman's narratives are counter-beliefs that she is not affected by colorism because of both her age and because of her upbringing. A particularly quiet participant, Maxine openly admitted to having limited knowledge on colorism and asked for clarification from other focus group members when the brown paper bag test was brought up in conversation. Rather than developing a normative or oppositional knowledge about colorism, Maxine's understanding of skin tone bias represents a counter-narrative that speaks to the absence of colorism in her everyday life.

The second reason given for the decline in colorism is that the current generation is more color conscious and aware compared to their older counterparts. This idea was reinforced by several participants who noted that younger black Americans are more critical of colorism and are therefore more willing to discuss and confront the issue:

> [. . .] the new generation now is definitely more open to everyone. However, we all have that underlying thing in the back of our heads. [. . .] I just think that everyone's idea is maybe the same; however, it's just more spoken in our generation. (Amy)

> I also believe [colorism is] changing, simply because of discussions like this. They didn't talk about colorism in my mom's generation, and she didn't talk about this and they didn't gather to say, "You know that this is an issue," because to them it wasn't an issue, it just made sense, that's just how it was. If you were lighter then you were good, if you were darker, you're bad. [. . .] So because of discussions like this and [. . .] because you're able to talk about it more now, I guess it's better. (Michelle)

These statements illustrate that younger generations have learned to openly challenge colorism, indicating a belief that there has been a large-scale shift to an oppositional color consciousness.

During one particular session, Toni—a 22-year-old participant—described in great detail exactly how she thinks the current generation compares to older African Americans. Telling the story of how colorism devolved within her own family, Toni explained how history had shaped this progression:

> [My parents] were in college in the late sixties, early seventies, and it was great to be black. It was great to have an afro and it was great to, you know, wear dashikis and kari beads, and things like that. And both of my parents are [. . .] my dad is darker than I am, my mom is probably about my complexion, and so I think that because of the times, I think a lot of perceptions are shaped by the times, and during

that time, it was acceptable, it was beautiful, it was great, it was a re-
surgence of appreciation of Africa and African culture, [. . .] during
my grandparents' era. I know that my grandmother is very [. . .] light,
her mother was mixed, [. . .] my grandfather was very dark. And it
was a whole ordeal that they were getting married. Her parents did
not want her to marry him, under any circumstances, [because he]
was so dark. And her parents said to her, "What about your children?
What are your children going to do? [. . .] They're going to be dark.
[. . .] They're going to have more obstacles."

From Toni's narrative, it is apparent that her grandmother's decision to
marry across color lines, combined with the widespread celebration of
blackness during her parents' generation, resulted in a better experience for
her own generation. She noted,

When my grandparents were getting married, it was Jim Crow South,
you know, it was a very different time than it is now, and so I definitely
think that our generation has more awareness, more ways to gain
awareness, more venues for talking about the issue, like this one.

The mere fact that this research project is being conducted is a signal for
Toni that the nature of colorism has improved since her grandmother's
generation. Nevertheless, this idea remains a counter-narrative in that it
contradicts the majority of the other stories Toni shared during her group
session. The following statement is illustrative of this point:

I definitely think that [colorism] exists. I think that it is perpetuated
on a day-to-day basis by the media and in our communities and in
businesses. People that you see that are very wealthy and successful—
majority of the time, they are light, unless they're maybe a basketball
player or something. [. . .] The only way to, I guess, deal with the issue
is for people to first realize that the issue exists, and no one wants to
believe [it], no one wants to think that we're still back in that house
slave–field slave kind of mentality.

Toni's beliefs, along with the viewpoints expressed by many other women in
this study, undeniably show that colorism is at times inconsistent and paradoxical in the everyday lives of these women. While in one breath respondents are confident that today's young women have transcended colorism,
another moment quickly reflects that there in fact has been no change. Although these young women were not comparing their experiences with older

black women, it was quite apparent that the idea of colorism being different today than it was in previous decades is a counter-narrative that is symptomatic of the denial that characterizes the contemporary nature of colorism.

The last factor associated with this counter-narrative deals with the perception that colorism is better *now* because African Americans today are no longer deliberate and obvious in their intentions; colorism is much more muted in contemporary society. Consider the parallel statements of Vivica and Chanel, young women who illustrated in a previous section of this chapter the presence of colorism in Haiti. They also share a belief that colorism operates on a more subtle basis for their generation:

> [. . .] at least we're not doing the brown bag test any longer and we have moved from that. You know, [. . .] we might be doing it, might, [but] it's not as prominent. [. . .] I will say that for my generation. (Vivica)

> [. . .] in terms of generational differences, [. . .] I would say [that] people just aren't as blatant as they used to be and say, "You are ugly because. . . . I think you are ugly because you're dark skinned." You know, they do it in different ways. (Chanel)

This commonly held idea appeared across focus group sessions. In comparing old and new generations of black Americans, the majority of women in this project agreed that colorism has reached a point of progression. Of course, what makes this idea a counter-narrative is that, similar to the other beliefs expressed in this chapter, they prove to be quite contradictory to the majority of the narratives shared.

In this chapter we saw respondents talk about colorism as a phenomenon that is worse in the South, stronger in the Caribbean, and improved compared to earlier generations. However, their larger narratives, stories, and experiences show that colorism is a vital force in their daily lives. In the previous chapters, we learned that the ideas offered by the young women interviewed are shockingly similar to the ways in which black Americans talked about colorism *before* the Civil Rights Movement. Yet simultaneously, these counter-narratives represent ideas that are distinctly different from previous points in history. To be sure, these young women's experiences speaking for and against colorism are equally legitimate and valid. Perhaps this underscores that this generation of young black women battle more with the two competing ideologies of colorism. In this day and age, marked with a "color blind" racist ideology—a discourse of attitudes that minimize and downplay discrimination and racism—colorism, too, has become minimized and downplayed. The matter of skin tone bias and hierarchy then becomes abstracted as something that fluctuates depending upon where you live and how old you are. This leads to the greater inquiry of this research: Has colorism improved or degraded? Do modern-day forms of colorism look like the colorism of yesterday? The concluding chapter attempts to shed light on this discussion.

CONCLUSION

If the Present Looks Like the Past, What Does the Future Look Like?

I would say that the problem of the twenty-first century will still be the problem of the color line, not only "the relation of the darker to the lighter races of men in Asia and Africa, in America and the islands of the sea," but the relations between the darker and the lighter people of the same races, and of the women who represent both dark and light within each race.

—Alice Walker[1]

In Alice Walker's 1983 book, *In Search of Our Mothers' Gardens*, she devotes a chapter to the topic of colorism that is so aptly titled, "If the Present Looks like the Past, What Does the Future Look Like?" In many ways, Walker reminds us of the survival of the color hierarchy within black society and challenges black women to recognize the limitations of a (future) black sisterhood that continually pits the "light- and white-skinned black women" against the "black black women."[2] The focus group narratives of the women participating in this study provide interesting and enlightening answers to the inquiry Alice Walker posed over 30 years ago. Although the findings from this research project are not generalizable to an entire generation of young black women, they are, nonetheless, quite useful in understanding where black women today stand on the issue of colorism.

DOES THE PRESENT LOOK LIKE THE PAST? WHAT WE LEARN FROM COLOR STORIES

The analyses of scholars studying colorism in the 1960s and 1970s show an overwhelming optimism about future generations of black Americans. Referring to the shifting skin tone preferences of black youth in the 1970s toward medium and dark skin tones, Goering predicted that this change in attitudes among young people would continue to pervade black American society, stating that "there is a new joy in blackness which did not exist twenty years ago."[3] While he and other scholars were not implying that racism and colorism would magically disappear (given the history and context of race and color for blacks in American society, they knew better), there was, however, a more hopeful forecast of a "shifting" of attitudes about skin color—that people born in the post–Civil Rights era would no longer embrace the antiblack attitudes and ideals of generations past. Researchers envisioned that for future cohorts of African Americans, skin color would lessen in importance and no longer function to structure experience and opportunity. (This, of course, is the same type of assertions that many folks make about today's millennial generation: that they are color blind and post-racial.) What we learn from these narratives is that in spite of these predictions, in the face of the 21st century, *beyond* race, class, and gender, color plays an integral role in shaping the life experiences of today's black women. This finding may not appear that remarkable considering the growing body of literature examining the endurance of colorism in the post–Civil Rights era. Yet, what is noteworthy is how this form of internalized racism impacts the attitudes, beliefs, and behavior of young black women in much the same way that studies illustrated colorism *before* the Civil Rights movement. This is rather significant considering the large-scale disappearance of blatant colorist practices, such as the brown paper bag test and the apparent integration of black organizations and institutions that once excluded members based upon their phenotypic features.

Based upon the focus groups, black women in this project articulated their everyday experiences of colorism through *language, internal scripts,* and *external practices.* Although respondents talked mainly about their daily interactions, there is a broader, macro-level connection to these occurrences, as these individual experiences are oftentimes embedded, created, and reproduced via such institutions as the family, school, and the media. Given this, I am positing the term *everyday colorism* to capture how these women understand and acquire knowledge about colorism in their lives. In employing this framework, I borrow from race and gender scholar Philomena Essed's groundbreaking theory of *everyday racism*. In Essed's 1991 book of the same name, she shows how black women's daily experiences with racism are connected to the broader patterns of racist practice at the structural level. Similar to Essed, I highlight the everyday as a way to discuss the interconnected nature of micro- (individual) and macro-level (institutional) processes. Everyday colorism, then, is a starting point for a theoretical foundation of the daily occurrences of colorism operating through structural and interpersonal domains of oppression and domination.

Recall from Chapter 2 that everyday colorism is comprised of three elements. The first element, *language*, refers to the color names that participants hear and/or use on a regular basis relating to the various categories of skin tones. Pointing to a somewhat seamless transmission of color terms across generations, the analysis in Chapter 3 reveals that there is an extensive vocabulary of color present in the lives of these women. In keeping with the traditional language of light skin, the majority of respondents recognize that the labels used to refer to light skin are rather positive, while the majority of the terms for dark skin are loaded with negative and derogatory connotations. There are fewer names for medium skin tones, and these terms appear to be rather neutral. The persistence of such terms as *yellow, caramel,* and *tar baby* (originally documented in the 1946 work of Charles Parrish) indicates a survival of a color terminology originating in the 19th century.

In addition, we learn that the language of skin color influences the second component of everyday colorism, *internal scripts*. Similar to Pierre Bordieu's concept of *habitus*,[4] or even Eduardo Bonilla-Silva's interpretation of *white habitus*,[5] the internalized scripts constitute the socially constructed ideas and expectations of various skin tones. Based upon the common color names, young women develop a "mental sky" about what it means to be light, dark, or brown-skinned, regardless of their own skin tone. While the participants in this study represent a variety of skin tones and experiences, they do share a somewhat collective *color habitus* about certain skin tones. Many of the color stories shared suggest that the predominant stereotypes and perceptions about light and dark skin (i.e., all light-skinned girls are pretty; all dark-skinned girls are "ghetto") signify an inheritance of similar attitudes documented in earlier generations of black Americans. A cursory glance at classic studies such as *Black Metropolis* and *Black Bourgeoisie* show parallel internalized scripts held by black Americans prior to the "Black Is Beautiful" movement. What I argue is new, however, is the construction of brown-skinned(ness) as a separate space and identity apart from light or dark skin. Many of the women in this study articulate the experiences of being brown skinned distinctly different from the experiences of women who are light and dark skinned. Previous literature suggests that future cohorts of African Americans would embrace brown skin over light and dark complexions. Although this is not proven within the analysis, it does appear that the current generation talks differently (and in a neutral manner) about medium skin tones.

The findings from my analysis also highlight how the internalization of color scripts influence behavior. The final component of everyday colorism—*external practices*—appears in several forms: *ritualistic, compensatory*, and *discriminatory practices*. Young women learn to execute certain rules of colorism, from avoiding the sun to bleaching their skin. At times respondents noted engaging in certain practices (such as getting a hair weave or dating outside the race) in order to "level the playing field" in the color hierarchy. Further, respondents more commonly noted that their inner viewpoints about skin color limit and prevent their interaction with other black women. Some mentioned avoiding friendships with certain women based on ideas that they will either not relate to women with differing skin tones or that friendships across color lines could potentially bring them down. Oftentimes, the practices of everyday colorism are carried out with very little thought, while other actions are quite deliberate and planned.

In addition to the three elements of everyday colorism, we also gain knowledge about the distinctive features of colorism. Although it can be argued that these characteristics have typified the nature of colorism throughout history, based on how these young women talk about their experiences, I am offering the following critical lessons learned from the color stories shared by the women in this research:

First, it is important to underscore that colorism is a byproduct of racism. As stated earlier, colorism is a form of internalized racism, and, as such, colorism mirrors many of the same qualities of racism. The analysis shows the reification of racism through various aspects of the language, internal scripts, and external practices of colorism. To that end, it remains crucial to situate colorism within the larger context and discussion of racism.

Second, it is imperative to note that although colorism is a derivative of racism, colorism exists as its own (sub)structure operating at the individual and institutional levels. The women in this study understand and experience colorism apart from racism. Yet colorism functions as a structure that interacts and co-exists with the larger structures of race, gender, and class; colorism therefore must be understood within the context of these other societal structures.

Within the structure of everyday colorism there exist two competing ideologies: *normative* and *oppositional.* This aspect represents the third feature of contemporary colorism. The normative ideology characterizes the dominant discourse of colorism that privileges light skin over dark skin. Alternatively, the oppositional discourse of colorism represents an ideology of skin color that equalizes all the various shades and hues of blackness. Many of the women interviewed noted shifting back and forth between both ideologies, causing on numerous occasions an inner conflict and struggle. A recurring point of contention lies in the reality that while many participants have acquired the knowledge to challenge colorism, they still find themselves in positions of prejudice and discrimination. As illustrated in Chapter 4, *points of origin, stabilizing agents,* and *transformative agents* function to mediate movement between the normative and oppositional forms of colorism. We also see this displayed through the counter-narratives of colorism highlighted in Chapter 5.

Fourth, colorism operates as a three-tiered structure rather than a binary one. The vast majority of scholarly research (past and present) has situated colorism within an opposing two-fold hierarchy: light girls versus dark girls, "good" hair versus "bad" hair, etc. Correspondingly, our knowledge of colorism has been informed by those women who fall into either one of these categories; oftentimes light and brown skin gets conflated into one category (light). Yet what we discover from this project is that placing colorism within a binary frame leaves out the unique experiences of women who are neither light nor dark. The analysis shows three groups of women: those who readily identify as red (light-skinned), brown, and black. As we learned in Chapter 3, while the majority of language and internal scripts relate to light and dark skin, there is a separate experience offered by women who fall in the middle of the color spectrum.

The next feature of colorism is concerned with the classification of the structure as a one-dimensional hierarchy. The framing of colorism as a hierarchy assumes that the interactions and experiences of colorism are one directional. In clarification, oftentimes the literature on colorism suggests that although light-skinned women occupy the highest rung of the color ladder, they are simultaneously victimized for their position. Dark-skinned women are oftentimes noted as the victimizers, partly because of their lower place in the color hierarchy. The results of this research point to a different pattern of colorism where victimization occurs at all levels (we even see brown-skinned women talk of victimization, too). Although the young women concur that the ability to "move" within the hierarchy is fixed, the experiences, however, of light- and dark-skinned women are quite similar. The findings in this project illustrate that light- and dark-skinned women find themselves in the position of proving, disproving, legitimizing, and de-legitimizing the socially constructed perceptions of who and what they should (or should not) be because of their skin tone. This points to *variable relations of control* within the system of colorism. At the structural level, the language and scripts of colorism are institutionalized, and *all* women become casualties of bias and discrimination. However, we also learn from this study that women have dual roles of victims and victimizers. There are many narratives that show women of various skin tones perpetuating and reinforcing colorism at the individual level. As bell hooks points out, "Women can and do participate in politics of domination, as perpetuators as well as victims—that we dominate, that we are dominated."[6] To that end, colorism is a multidirectional (and, perhaps, multipositional) hierarchy that exhibits unsteady relations of domination.

Finally, the analysis shows that colorism is a strong yet covert phenomenon. Throughout the process of conducting the focus groups, it was surprising to learn that many young women do not even recognize the term *colorism* or initially believe that this issue shapes their daily experiences. But as the group discussions progressed, participants realized just how much they are, in fact, impacted by the various forces of colorism. Overall, the women in this study noted that colorism—like racism—is much better in their generation because overt expressions of skin tone bias are now just a piece of black history. This was also consistent with the findings from a more recent statewide poll. In October of 2013, the University of North Florida's Public Opinion Research Lab conducted a statewide survey of various political, social, and cultural issues related to the state of Florida. When respondents were asked specifically about colorism ("Are you familiar with the term *colorism*?"), 80 percent of the participants had never heard of the term. The black participants in the survey were queried about the persistence of colorism in the black community, and the overwhelming majority (80 percent) agreed that skin tone discrimination impacts the black community. Yet 68 percent of these same respondents noted that this impact was better today compared to 50 years ago.[7] Both the qualitative analysis in this project and the short quantitative assessment suggest that while colorism is perhaps better in the 21st century, in many ways, the present bears a strong semblance to the past.

WHAT DOES THE FUTURE LOOK LIKE?

On July 9, 2007, the National Association for the Advancement of Colored People (NAACP) held a public burial in Detroit, Michigan, for the controversial and politically charged term *nigger*. A formal and public funeral for the N-word was deemed necessary as a first step in challenging the racism, hatred, and internalized oppression accompanying the usage of the term. As former Detroit Mayor Kwame Kilpatrick stated on the day of the ceremony, "Today we're not just burying the N-word, we're taking it out of our spirit. We gather, burying all the things that go with the N-word."[8] According to an article written on the topic for the *Washington Post*, there was a similar funeral held in 1944 to symbolize the death of Jim Crow segregation and discrimination. To be sure, this recent event marks a sign of the times; although there are many black and non-black people alike who will no doubt continue to use the N-word in their day-to-day lives, there are similarly many people who will openly challenge and resist the use of such language. To a certain extent, it appears that a growing population of everyday citizens is beginning to develop a level of critical consciousness and awareness that interrogates the traditionally held structures of racial inequality and injustice in our society.

In many ways, colorism mirrors some of the same qualities as the N-word. Skin-tone bias and discrimination are also rooted in racism and colonialist ideology. Despite having a much broader language base, like the N-word, colorism has survived in the black community for generations, being internalized in the mind and externalized through practice. Given this, what does the future of colorism look like? According to the women interviewed for this study, does colorism share the same fate as the N-word?

As the participants in this project candidly revealed, there is unfortunately no end in sight. When asked about whether there will ever be an end to colorism, the majority of women were overwhelmingly pessimistic about the future. As one woman pointed out, "As long as racism is around, I think colorism will be around." Participants provided concrete reasons for the continuing significance of colorism. One such explanation was provided by Monica, who considers colorism an inherent part of human nature:

I don't think [colorism is] something that can be fixed because, as far as human beings are concerned, we always look at a way to differentiate ourselves. Whether it [is . . .] where we live or neighborhoods or the schools we go to [. . .] we find a way to separate ourselves, and I don't see why skin tone is going to be something different. I'm always going to look, like, at somebody and [. . .] form opinions [. . .] based on their skin tone. [. . .] I think that's something that can't be fixed. [. . .] I don't think that's something that people are going to easily let go.

For this young woman, a core feature of society includes division and separation. A similar reason is given by Yolanda, a 19-year-old respondent who adopts a functionalist perspective of society:

Even if [colorism] stops being an issue, there will be another issue to separate us. Because in the wonderful world of America and everywhere across the world, we base ourselves on capitalism, and you have to have somebody on top and someone on the bottom. So that means you have to put somebody on the bottom; that's how it works.

Yolanda blames the political and economic structures present within our society for the survival of colorism. This perspective was shared by many focus group participants.

There were several women interviewed who cited the common presence of colorism for all minority groups as another reason for maintaining a presence in the future. Tessa explained,

I'm really not optimistic on colorism not being an issue. [. . .] It's just so engrained in not just our society, but [. . .] trans-nationally [. . .] Latinos, Asians, Indians, blacks, it's everywhere. Because there's always going to be a way to segregate people, and I think the easiest way to do that is color. It's just the easiest way to hurt people. And I just don't think it will stop being an issue. There might be a day when dark-skinned people are on top and light-skinned people are on bottom, but I don't see that happening.

This young woman is alluding to the notion that skin color may one day hold a more important social value compared to race. She of course points to the various racial and ethnic minority groups who internalize the privilege of light skin and the stigma of dark skin. More importantly, Tessa's argument about the continued (and perhaps, more significant) existence of skin color reflects race scholar Eduardo Bonilla-Silva's framework for the "Latin Americanization" of the United States.[9] A paradigm based on this scholar's projection of race in the future, Bonilla-Silva asserts that racial classification in the United States will move from a binary system to a three-tiered one: inclusive of whites, honorary whites, and collective blacks. What is interesting to note in Bonilla-Silva's model is that classification into one of these three groups will not be based on race but, rather, skin tone. The group at the bottom includes dark-skinned Asian Americans, Latinos, blacks, and Native Americans. Those minority group members with lighter skin tones are predicted to fill the middle category of honorary whites. Bonilla-Silva's model, in conjunction with the work of other race scholars, and the voices of the women interviewed in this project, point out that colorism will endure and could ultimately edge out the prevalence of racism.

To that end, holding a funeral for colorism would mean doing away with the *structure* of a color hierarchy, in addition to eradicating the interconnected structures of race, class, and gender hierarchies. Further, abolishing colorism is particularly challenging given that many of the women in this study have never heard of, used, or have a firm grasp of the term's meaning. The N-word—and its meaning—are both infamous and undeniable in American culture. What we see from the analysis is that colorism is at times unwitting and elusive. And this makes it much more difficult to bury.

RECOMMENDATIONS FOR CHANGE: TOWARD A COLLECTIVE OPPOSITIONAL KNOWLEDGE

Given the recent events surrounding race and justice taking place in the early part of the new millennium (tragedies ranging from Oscar Grant to Freddie Gray), it is clear that race still matters for many people in our nation. We are at a time in which we are desperately searching for ways to build bridges—not fences—as we aim to heal the deepest cuts of racism in our society. Issues of racial equality and justice are vitally important to many black Americans today. We should be earnestly engaged in simultaneously combating the social problem of colorism. Just like racism, the end to colorism may be farther away than we would like.

The major finding of this study reveals that colorism is a mainstay in the lives of young black women; the broader finding suggests that despite the exterior hegemonic structures that work to cripple black women as a whole, the divisions between black women are just as great. In 1983, black feminist scholar Barbara Smith wrote, "The gulfs between us hurt and they are deeply rooted in the facts of difference. Class and color differences between black women have divided us since slavery. We have yet to explore how riddled we are by this pain."[10] Contemporary black feminist scholars are continually looking for ways to bridge the gaps that prevent black women from attaining a universal sisterhood in the 21st century. Diversity scholar and community activist Sheila Radford-Hill writes about the crisis of black womanhood, blaming divisions from within (particularly class) and a lack of activism for this crisis.[11] Similarly, sociologist Katrina Bell McDonald highlights the contemporary state of black women through black sister-hood and step-sisterhood.[12] Through McDonald's in-depth conversations with black women, she uncovers how differences in social class impact the potential for unity and detachment among an ever-increasing diverse pop-ulation of black women. While a large emphasis (and rightly so) has been placed on class divisions, it remains important to address how color differ-ences between black women can be effectively challenged and transformed. Failing to challenge this particular gap also threatens the strength and po-tential of a universal black sisterhood in the 21st century.

In searching for concrete solutions, I suggest that we look to the core features of black feminist theory. As earlier noted, standing at the founda-tion of this theoretical framework are knowledge, empowerment, and rec-lamation. More importantly, black feminist theory looks to the everyday lives and experiences of black women for the production of such knowl-edge and empowerment. Many women in this study admit struggling be-tween the normative and oppositional forms of colorism. I argue that in order to conquer this struggle, a *collective oppositional knowledge* of color-ism needs to be created. The normative language, scripts, and practices that function to divide black women need to be permanently replaced with lan-guage, scripts, and practices that function to unite. The women involved in this study proved to be a wealth of knowledge about the everyday, lived experiences of colorism. Included in this knowledge are concrete strategies for change and empowerment. Their suggestions, combined with my own recommendations for change, have guided the following strategies for dis-empowering the dominant discourse of colorism. I recognize that we may not see the complete end to skin tone bias and discrimination in the 21st century, but I believe that these concrete solutions place all of us firmly within reach.

The first step begins with acknowledging that colorism is real, and we should not deny its presence. Just because some people have transcended (or have never had any significant issues with) colorism in their life does not mean that all black women have been as fortunate. Additionally, it is critical to understand that colorism is about much more than just standards of beauty. While much of the discussion of colorism centers on perceptions of attractiveness, this issue extends far beyond being pretty. (Just consider the scores of empirical data suggesting that dark-skinned people are subject to lower incomes, higher blood pressure, and longer prison sentences.) As the findings of this project highlight, colorism is a quality-of-life issue for many women of color. We should be mindful not to minimize the experiences of other adults in particular who still struggle with this issue. As people of color, we can readily relate to the frustration in hearing a white person say,

"Just grow up," or "Get over it" when black people discuss racism. Colorism matters. Period. We do not live in a post-colorist society any more than we live in a post-racial one. Therefore, it remains vitally important to debunk and de-institutionalize the falsehoods and fallacies about light, dark, and brown skin. Although this may appear to be a step that individuals alone are unable to accomplish, feminist scholars suggest that individuals hold the key to changing institutions. This can be achieved through personal politicization and activism. For many women, the road to change is reached through collectively strategizing via their own everyday transformative feminism. So many of the focus group respondents in this study mention a variety of people and events that served to re-direct their ideas and behavior about colorism—in both positive and negative directions. In order to challenge colorism at all levels, it is necessary for individual black women to work as everyday activists, becoming agents of our own transformations.

What does everyday activism look like? One key strategy could include engaging with social media tools to bring more awareness to the issue of colorism. Black Twitter, for instance, has been very successful in bringing voice to racial inequality in the cases of George Zimmerman, Michael Dunn, and Marissa Alexander. This platform, however, has been integral in reinforcing colorism. Consider starting a viral colorism movement with the use of creative hashtags like #colorstories, #endcolorism, and #allblackisbeautiful. One such example is the digital media campaign launched by colorism scholar Yaba Blay entitled #PrettyPeriod. Other blogger activists have been successful in launching blogs centrally focused on colorism—such as Sarah Webb's colorismhealing.org.

Earlier in this book, I wrote about the importance of naming colorism. Talking and naming go hand in hand; thus, the next strategy for change lies in talking about colorism. In her classic work *Talking Back*, bell hooks reminds us that "true speaking is not solely an expression of creative power; it is an act of resistance, a political gesture that challenges politics of domination that would render us nameless and voiceless."[13] My next suggestion, then, is that black women not be afraid about openly confronting colorism "in the moment." I have personally found this task to be difficult and, at times, very uncomfortable.

Several years ago, I was invited to a cookout hosted by John, a male member of my family, and his wife, Sharon.[14] This particular family gathering consisted of a predominately black roster of close friends and family members in attendance. The first group of partygoers to arrive was a family of four—James, Gina, and their two young children. James, a dark-skinned man, walked into the house first with his four-year-old son. His light-skinned wife, Gina, followed behind him, carrying their three-month-old daughter. Sharon quickly ran over to greet Gina and to pick up the new baby.

Lifting the baby out of her car seat carrier, Sharon exclaimed, "Whose baby is this? This is not the same baby I saw in the hospital! She's so *black*! What happened to this baby?"

Sharon was referring to the drastic change in the child's skin tone since she was born. The baby, according to Sharon, was the same light color as her mother and big brother the last time she saw her, but she had now somehow morphed into a "new" baby with a skin tone resembling her father's dark complexion.

"Good thing you are a pretty chocolate baby," remarked Sharon as she played with the newborn girl.

As Sharon continued to draw attention to the baby's dark skin, Gina shook her head in disbelief and remarked, "I don't know what happened to my baby either. The moment I took her home from the hospital, she changed."

The cookout lasted for several hours, and so did the comments about this dark-skinned baby. At one point, Sharon attempted to engage James in a conversation about his daughter's skin tone, but he was more interested in a card game. The only people who seemed to be paying attention to Sharon's comments were the women. I sat there the entire time, debating on how to call attention to the problematic nature of the discussion. I was angry at Sharon for being so ignorant. I was mortified that the child's mother did not come to the defense of her baby. And I felt sad for this three-month-old baby girl, who would undoubtedly be made to feel insecure about having her "daddy's color" for the rest of her life. I was even more frustrated at the mental warfare taking place in my mind. Ultimately, though, I sat in silence and did nothing because I did not want to disrupt the mood of the party, nor did I want my comments about colorism to be dismissed.

Although I have been academically enthralled in this issue for almost two decades, I still find myself in positions where I miss the opportunity to challenge colorism in my own daily life. I have even allowed colorism to impact my own friendships with black women. How could I have treated that situation differently? Having the courage to broach the topic right then could have turned into a teaching and learning moment for everyone at the party. As one participant in this project suggested, talking is of chief importance in the fight against colorism:

I think it all comes down to talking about it. I mean, when you don't talk about something, [. . .] it, and then it turns into a big boil, and it's a lot more dramatic. So I think if you, as a community, or as a race, if you voice these issues, and you say, "Well, you know, this is what's going on," and you ask yourself why is this, rather than just accepting it for [. . .] the situation that it's always been. I think things can get a lot better. (Sandra, 21, medium)

At the end of many focus groups, participants later told me that the dialogue and conversation about colorism changed their perspectives and level of consciousness. This, of course, was my initial motivation in developing a method for this project. Given the importance of talking, dialoguing about colorism in small groups can function as a transformative moment in creating a collective, oppositional knowledge. Focus group member Natasha described,

These focus groups are very good if light-skinned people, or medium, dark-skinned people [can] talk and share their views because [. . .] people always thought that [light-skinned people] had it easier, but if you let people know that you [. . .] still have struggles and you still go through stuff, if we share our views and put everything on the table, I think it would help.

Continuing to cultivate small group discussions within everyday settings—and not just the formal ones used to conduct academic research—can serve as the starting point for a critical consciousness that dispels the divisive myths of colorism.

Several participants suggested a more formalized strategy of education to combat the normative discourse of colorism. Many of these women noted that their exposure to black studies and women's studies courses in college exposed them to an oppositional knowledge that counters their initial socialization and mentality. To that end, focus group members called for the education of children and the education of self as a third strategy for change. It's never too early to start these life lessons. Finding ways to make black children feel good about the "skin they're in" (and the hair that grows out of their heads) is an important step in ending the bullying, teasing, and false elevation of light skin over dark skin and certain hair textures over others. The following remarks illustrate this idea:

I think that it's just important to educate [and] teach kids and young people that we all come from different backgrounds, and therefore we're all going to be different, and one of the most beautiful things about being black is that we do have so many different complexions, we have such a range of colors and features and hair texture, and that's one of the things that makes being black so beautiful. And I think that's just something that needs to be ingrained in the minds of young people. (Toni, 23, dark)

You [should] try to prevent the stereotypes of those names [like] midnight; you cannot allow children to use that name and [. . .] let them know that there's not a difference between skin tones. [. . .] So, like, I think that if you teach children from a young age—like I was taught—that there really is no difference between anyone's skin color, it would help. (Kira, 19, medium)

We need to reprioritize what's important to us, so that we can educate ourselves, so that we can know our history, so that we can know we're worth something, and so that we can realize that what's your problem is my problem because we are all black. [. . .] You can be whatever you want to be, but at the end of the day, you are still a black woman. [. . .] Use all of your tools that you have for the betterment of your people and to teach each and every person that you come across [about colorism] because knowledge is power, and that's the only [way] we're gonna ever dismantle racism and colorism at the systemic level. (Trina, 20, very light)

I would extend these suggestions by placing a formal emphasis on the education of young black women. Of course, colorism impacts black women in a different manner compared to black men; therefore, the public awareness and resistance of colorism must include this special focus on young girls. In dealing with the issue of colorism, I argue that while all black Americans should gain awareness—in light of this study's findings, young black females deserve attention.

Lastly, the final strategy for change requires true coalition building among black women. Individual empowerment, naming, talking, and education can only go so far if there is not a concerted effort to unify black women across color lines. As focus group member Keesha so rightly observed,

We are all African American. I think that's the problem, because you assume that because you are light skinned you are different, but from society's point of view, if you are dark then you are black, so regardless of your color, we still need to work together to get to where we need to be despite what shade we are.

In the new millennium, this is an immediate need. It is imperative for young black women to first recognize colorism, admit that they actively participate in this form of discrimination, and find ways to eradicate this issue in the 21st century. bell hooks writes,

> Black women must identify ways feminist thought and practice can aid in our process of self-recovery and share that knowledge with our sisters. This is the base on which to build political solidarity. When that grounding exists, black women will be fully engaged in feminist movement that transforms self, community, and society.[15]

In order to recover from the past and to protect the future, building an oppositional knowledge through individual politicization and collective action is essential.

A less discussed but equally vital strategy includes educating white Americans about colorism, too. White privilege and domination can make racist practice very difficult for white individuals to recognize, let alone address. The same can be said about white colorism, which sociologist Lance Hannon describes as the ways in which white folks privilege light skin over dark skin.[16] While the women in this study could not precisely name white colorism as such, they were still nonetheless able to recognize the ways in which white folk place a premium over lighter skin tones in the same manner people of color make distinctions based upon skin tone. Consider Patricia, who was in an interracial marriage and describes her experiences with her relationship with her white in-laws:

> I was married to a white man from Ohio . . . and I do think that my skin tone. . . . I don't know how to put it, but I don't think they [his family] would have felt as comfortable as they did with me if I would have been like really, really dark skinned. I mean these people are the whitest people I've ever seen, and, um, you know, I would go places and my mother-in-law would be, you know, just walking with me, showing me like I was this little thing. And I think the fact that I was kind of small too, like, it was, I don't know, important to them, like, you know, it was kind of weird, but that's how, you know, like, my mother-in-law treated me, like showing me around and . . . I don't think she would have been showing me around if I would have been darker skinned. . . . They thought I was more attractive because of having light skin, uh, medium skin, and being tiny. . . . It made fitting in a lot easier I guess, because I didn't feel threatened. I mean, I didn't feel like they were uncomfortable. . . . I think they felt comfortable with me, in ways that they would have not with a darker person.

Given this reality that all people—regardless of race or ethnicity and knowledge of colorism—reinforce color bias and discrimination, it is imperative that we do not omit and disregard how valuable white Americans can be in effectively combating colorism at the structural level (institutions and policy) and in our everyday lives.

Building multiracial coalitions to eradicate colorism is an important lesson I learned early on in my research process. At the onset of this project, I collaborated with a white female colleague, Dr. Colleen Cain. Colleen was just as passionate about understanding the manifestations of colorism in the black American community, and I believe that she learned a great deal in the process of our joint endeavors. As an instructor, I learned in my classes that my white female students were just as curious and impassioned about colorism work as my black female students. (See Sidebar 6.)

SAMPLE LIMITATIONS AND DIRECTIONS FOR FUTURE RESEARCH

This research contributes to the existing body of literature because it focuses specifically on the voices of young black women, addresses micro–macro linkages, and concentrates on whether colorism has changed or remained the same. Despite these contributions, I would like to attend to the limitations of this study.

The focus group participants were drawn from a convenience sample of black women working at or enrolled at a large university in Florida; this is perhaps the largest limitation of this project. Although the university community itself has a diverse student and staff population with a fair amount of black women, I did not extend the scope of recruitment beyond women who had an affiliation with the university. This, of course, creates in many ways a one-dimensional sample. Additionally, the majority of women interviewed fell into the middle three skin tone categories—light brown, medium, and dark—while there were only five respondents who reported their skin tone in the very light and very dark categories. This unequal distribution of skin tone categories presents another limitation to the study. Further, it was assumed that the sexual identity of all participants was heterosexual. There were no questions directed toward same-sex relationships, nor did any respondents share stories related to their intimate-partner relationships with other women. This points to a gap, not only in this research project, but also in the broader realm of research on colorism. Further studies should consider the experiences of the black lesbian, gay, and/or transgender community, as those voices would surely illuminate how colorism is similar or different for this subgroup of black Americans. Ultimately, there is a definite need for more empirical studies on the continuing significance of colorism among more diverse groups of black women.

I envision a number of directions for future research that builds upon the foundation of this current project. Many of the women interviewed shared a strong belief that colorism is not as prevalent in the northern portion of the United States; impending studies could benefit from a regional analysis of colorism. Further, the black Caribbean women in this study indicate that experiences of colorism are more significant in places like Jamaica and Haiti. Given the growing literature on the comparative experiences of African Americans and blacks living in the United States with Caribbean heritage, there is a demonstrated need for future research to address this other regional difference in colorism.

The core of this research relies on the views and perspectives of young black women between the ages of 18 and 25. Although I am careful to point out that my goal is to contextualize the current-day experience of young women, I am aware that this project could have been strengthened by the inclusion of more voices of older black women. This idea also becomes apparent in the stories of some women who note a clear presence of colorism in their own lives and consider their experiences to be not only better, but vastly different from their mother's or grandmother's generation. In order to draw more concrete conclusions on whether or not there has been a definite shift in attitudes and beliefs, soliciting the perspectives of black women who came of age, for instance, at the height of the Civil Rights movement would undoubtedly fill a gap in the current study, better informing our knowledge on this complex issue.

Although they are mentioned far less within this study, black men to some extent influence the ways in which young black women interact with each other. To that end, I recommend that more research is needed to illuminate the perspectives of young black men as they relate to colorism. As scholars Margaret Hunter and Mark Hill remind us, colorism affects black men as well. There is a need to address the nature of gendered colorism in the lives of black men.

Finally, it is imperative *not* to underestimate the value of this study as merely a one-dimensional project addressing the contemporary significance of colorism among young black women. Although this remains the focal point of this study, this research also contributes to the broader body of knowledge currently examining the continuing significance of skin color in the lives of *other* women of color. The recent work of many colorism scholars shows analogous patterns of colorism in Asian American and Hispanic communities. Further research comparing and contrasting the experiences of colorism across racial and ethnic lines could certainly help to explain the contemporary nature of colorism, as well as advance our theoretical understandings of this increasingly public and persistently complex social inequality.

Sidebar 6. The Importance of Building Multiracial Coalitions in Fighting Colorism: A White Woman's Color Story

An important step in building awareness about colorism requires people of color to talk openly and honestly with white folks about colorism. This is part of the reason why I have been teaching the course *Colorism in the United States* since 2009. When I taught the course most recently, it was a transformative experience for both my students and me. One contributing factor was the size of the class; there were nine students who attended class regularly. Another important dynamic was that there were several white women who took the course, and they were very open and honest about their biases and inexperience surrounding colorism. The following letter was sent to me by one of these students. It speaks volumes to the power of talking up—and loud—about colorism:

> When I first enrolled in this course, I honestly had no idea what the issue of colorism really was. I thought I was taking a class about African Americans and how the racial divide still exists in America. I thought maybe as a Caucasian woman, and a social worker, I could get a better understanding of how African Americans feel about being black and how their daily life experiences differ from mine. I had NO idea that not only is it a black/white issue for African Americans, but that there is actually another level of discrimination that they have to deal with every single day.
>
> The issue of dark versus light skin tone, and how prevalent the issue really is was an eye opening experience for me. I thought I had been around long enough to see it all, and because I love people, I thought I was really open and knowledgeable about lots of different races and what different people have to deal with. . . . Obviously, I came into this class very naive and clueless as I discovered I had a lot to learn about colorism and its horrific impact on people's lives.

Honestly, in the beginning, I was afraid to really speak up as a white woman for fear of coming across as racist, snobby, or insulting someone accidentally because of my ignorance about the subject. I had sooooooo many questions I WANTED to ask, but I didn't want the other African American students, or my professor, to judge me. I was fearful that they wouldn't see it as innocent ignorance, but as me looking down from a "white supremacist" viewpoint. I don't really know when or how it happened, but somehow our group was able to break down the racial walls, understand where each of us were in our understanding of the subject, and ultimately have amazing, open discussions about how all different people feel about the issues of race and colorism.

Frankly, I don't think the issue of colorism is going to go away until there are more people like us in this class that are willing to break down the walls of defense and understand that people of other races sometimes might just simply not be aware of another person's life experiences. Additionally, white people need to admit our ignorance because we don't know what we haven't lived . . . we can't judge based only on what we think we know based on our "white life experiences." Until we are all open to talking, listening, and trying to find common ground through respectful dialog, I'm afraid the issue of colorism is not going away anytime soon.

I am so glad that I took this class, and that I could be a part of this amazing group of people. It has been such a fulfilling experience to think that maybe our little group might be a small catalyst for getting more people talking about the issue of colorism. I would love to see that happen and have others experience the same feeling I have had of being able to talk freely about a touchy issue without worrying about being judged for asking the wrong question.

I feel like we need to keep talking about colorism and have more open forums for respectful discussion and educating people about this issue.

APPENDIX

Participant Characteristics by Skin Tone, Ethnicity/Home State, and Age

Name	Ethnicity/Home State	Age	Skin Tone
1. Berniece	Haitian	20	Medium
2. Keesha	African American	20	Dark
3. Mary	African American	24	Medium
4. Yolanda	Haitian	19	Dark
5. Tessa	African American	20	Very Dark
6. Maxine	Haitian	20	Light Brown
7. Alicia	African American & Puerto Rican	22	Light Brown
8. Toni	African American	23	Dark
9. Melissa	African American	19	Light Brown
10. Denise	African American	21	Medium
11. Desiree	African American	20	Medium
12. Vivica	Haitian	21	Medium
13. Chanel	Haitian	21	Dark
14. Trina	Bahamian	20	Very Light
15. Missy	African American	25	Medium

(*continued*)

Name	Ethnicity/Home State	Age	Skin Tone
16. Lela	Jamaican	20	Medium
17. Nia	Antiguan	21	Dark
18. Maria	Black & Cuban	20	Light Brown
19. Leah	African American	21	Medium
20. Karina	Haitian	21	Medium
21. Tatiana	Nigerian	19	Very Dark
22. Callea	Jamaican	21	Dark
23. Clarasol	African American	18	Medium
24. Jasmine	Jamaican	19	Light Brown
25. Shanta	Dominican Republic	20	Light Brown
26. Teresa	Jamaican	20	Dark
27. Regina	Haitian	21	Dark
28. Brenda	Jamaican	19	Medium
29. Shirelle	African American	18	Light Brown
30. Shanae	African American	18	Dark
31. Amy	Haitian	18	Medium
32. Monica	Jamaican	19	Medium
33. Asia	Jamaican	19	Medium
34. Kira	Panamanian	19	Medium
35. Keleechi	Black & Puerto Rican	18	Very Light
36. Sandra	Jamaican	21	Medium
37. Michelle	Jamaican	21	Medium
38. Natasha	Jamaican	18	Medium
39. Ashley	Hawaiian & African American	20	Light Brown
40. Fiona	Jamaican	21	Medium
41. Rachel	Jamaican	18	Light Brown
42. Rosetta	African American	20	Light Brown
43. Dr. Q	African American	20	Very Light

Name	Ethnicity/Home State	Age	Skin Tone
44. Charlie	Haitian	18	Medium
45. Star	No Answer	21	Light Brown
46. Lee	African American	19	Dark
47. U-neek	African American	21	Medium
48. Fuze	African American	20	Medium
49. Meeko	African American	20	Dark
50. Bo	African American	20	Medium
51. Beyoncé	Haitian	21	Medium
52. Becky	Jamaican	21	Light Brown
53. Pauline	African American & White	21	Light Brown
54. Jessica	African American	19	Medium
55. Luann	No Answer	21	Medium
56. Patricia	African American	18	Light Brown
57. Kelly	African American	21	Medium
58. Stacey	Haitian	24	Dark
59. Gloria	Jamaican	30	Medium
60. Selena	African American	40	Light Brown
61. Nicole	African American	41	Very Light
62. Janice	Bahamian	30	Very Light
63. Patricia	Dominican	36	Medium
64. Brenda	African American	36	Medium
65. Tanya	African American	43	Light Brown
66. Alia	African American	45	Medium
67. Stewart	African American	21	Light Brown
68. Bobby	Haitian	19	Dark
69. Donald	Jamaican	19	Medium
70. Pablo	Jamaican	18	Light Brown
71. Jason	African American	22	Medium
72. Alex	Haitian	20	Light Brown

There were a few participants who identified as black and not African American. This distinction indicates that they were racially black, but were not ethnically African American.

Notes

PREFACE

1. Kathy Russell, Midge Wilson, and Ronald Hall, *The Color Complex: The Politics of Skin Color among African Americans* (New York: Anchor Books, 1993).

2. Marita Golden, *Don't Play in the Sun: One Woman's Journey through the Color Complex* (New York: Doubleday, 2004).

3. Margaret Hunter, *Race, Gender, and the Politics of Skin Tone* (New York: Routledge, 2005).

4. Yaba Blay, *(1)ne Drop: Shifting the Lens of Race* (Philadelphia: BlackPRINT Press, 2013).

5. Nyong'o was awarded the Best Breakthrough Performance Award at the Essence Magazine Black Women in Hollywood Luncheon. The entire contents of her speech and video of her remarks can be accessed online, "Lupita Nyong'o Delivers Moving 'Black Women in Hollywood' Acceptance Speech," http://www.essence .com/2014/02/27/lupita-nyongo-delivers-moving-black-women-hollywood -acceptance-speech/.

6. The convicted felon was sentenced to two years in prison on a weapons charge, but signed a modeling contract to begin a modeling career upon his release. See Andy Campbell, "'Hot Convict' Jeremy Meeks Planning Modeling Career after Prison," *Huffington Post*, http://www.huffingtonpost.com/2015/03/03 /hot-convict-model_n_6789346.html.

7. William Edward Burghardt Du Bois, *The Souls of Black Folk* (New York: Vintage Books, 1903), 41.

INTRODUCTION

1. For the purpose of this research, the terms black and African American will be used interchangeably. In order to protect the identity of the research participants, pseudonyms will be used.

2. The terms "caramel," "dirty red," and "fried-chicken brown" are names that are commonly used in the African American community to refer to someone with light brown to medium brown skin tones. It is useful to point out that there is typically no consensus on what range of skin tones fall into certain categories. For more information on the various color names commonly used in black culture, please refer to Chapter 3.

3. In order to protect the identity of the people in this story, fictitious names will be used.

4. In order to protect the identity of the people in this story, fictitious names will be used.

5. M. Okazawa-Rey, T. Robinson, and J. Ward, "Black Women and the Politics of Skin Color and Hair," *Women and Therapy* 6 (1987): 89–102.

6. A. R. Hochschild, "The Cultural Spirit of Intimate Life and the Abduction of Feminism: Signs from Women's Advice Books," *Theory, Culture, & Society* 11 (1994): 1–24.

7. Among many scholars, the Willie Lynch Letter is considered to be nothing more than a modern-day myth. However, the contents of the speech are quite useful in structuring a discussion on the nature of colorism.

8. William Edward Burghardt Du Bois, *The Souls of Black Folk* (New York: Vintage Books, 1903).

9. St. Clair Drake and Horace Cayton, *Black Metropolis* (New York: Harcourt Brace, 1945).

10. Alice Walker, *In Search of Our Mothers' Gardens* (San Diego: Harcourt Brace Jovanovich, 1983).

11. Kathy Russell, Midge Wilson, and Ronald Hall, *The Color Complex: The Politics of Skin Color among African Americans* (New York: Anchor Books, 1993), 2.

12. Ellis P. Monk, "Skin Tone Stratification Among Black Americans, 2001–2003," *Social Forces* 92, no. 4 (2014): 1313–1337.

13. Vesla P. Weaver, "The Electoral Consequences of Skin Color: The 'Hidden' Side of Racial Politics," *Political Behavior* 34, no. 1 (2012): 159–192.

14. Lance Hannon, Robert DeFina, and Sarah Bruch, "The Relationship Between Skin Tone and School Suspension for African Americans," *Race and Social Problems* 5 (2013): 281–295.

15. Joe Feagin, *Racist America: Roots, Current Realities, and Future Reparations* (New York: Routledge, 2004), 70.

16. See Michael Omi and Howard Winant, *Racial Formation in the United States: From the 1960s to the 1980s* (New York: Routledge, 1986).

17. Omi and Winant, *Racial Formation in the United States.*

18. Verna M. Keith and Cedric Herring, "Skin Tone and Stratification in the Black Community," *American Journal of Sociology* 97, no. 3 (1991): 762.

19. See, for example, Russell, Wilson, and Hall, *The Color Complex*.

20. Beginning in 1850 and until 1920, the United States Census classified black Americans into four categories: *black, mulatto, quadroon,* and *octoroon.* An African American with ¾ or more African ancestry was classified as black; a mulatto was someone who had between 3/8 and 5/8 of African ancestry; a quadroon was someone with ¼ or less African ancestry; and an octoroon denoted an African American with 1/8 or less African ancestry. According to Melissa Nobles, these classifications were used to justify the principles of scientific racism and to "prove" true genetic differences between blacks and whites, in addition to exploring the perceived genetic shortcomings of those with "mixed" blood. Melissa Nobles, "Racial Categorization and Census," in *Census and Identity: The Politics of Race, Ethnicity, and Language in National Censuses,* ed. David Kertzer and Dominique Arel (Cambridge: Cambridge University Press, 2002), 43–70.

21. Lawrence Otis Graham, *Our Kind of People: Inside America's Black Upper Class* (New York: HarperCollins, 1999).

22. Tukufu Zuberi, "W.E.B. Du Bois's Sociology: The Philadelphia Negro and Social Science," *Annals of the American Academy* 595 (2004): 154.

23. See Audrey Elisa Kerr, *The Paper Bag Principle: Class, Colorism, and Rumor in the Case of Black Washington, D.C.* (Knoxville: University of Tennessee Press, 2006).

24. Graham, *Our Kind of People*.

25. In October 2007 twenty-seven-year-old Ulysses Barnes, a Detroit party promoter, was reproached by the black community and antiracism advocates for throwing a "Light-skin Bash," an event guaranteeing all light-skinned women free entry. Word of the party spread rapidly and black women across the country demanded the party be cancelled. When asked about his reasoning for throwing a gathering with such an offensive theme, Barnes quickly retorted that "it was a brilliant promotion at the time," and there were also future plans for similar events for "chocolate" and "caramel" black women, respectively. Retrieved November 28, 2007, from http://www.msnbc.msn.com/id/21367799.

26. Kiri Davis set out to reproduce the classic doll study originally employed by black psychologists Drs. Kenneth and Mamie Clark. For more information on the short film, refer to http://www.understandingrace.org/lived/video/.

27. CNN footage retrieved from https://www.youtube.com/watch?v=1Sfo32 rlkiE.

28. Season One, Episode Four of the ABC series *How to Get Away with Murder* originally aired on October 16, 2014. The final scenes of the show end with Viola Davis's character taking off her wig, exposing her natural hair.

29. "Projections Show a Slower Growing, Older, More Diverse Nation a Half Century from Now," *U.S. Census Bureau,* https://www.census.gov/newsroom /releases/archives/population/cb12-243.html.

30. Eduardo Bonilla-Silva, "From Bi-Racial to Tri-Racial: Towards a New System of Racial Stratification in the USA," *Ethnic and Racial Studies* 27, no. 6 (2004): 933.

31. Nina Jablonski, *Living Color: The Biological and Social Meaning of Skin Color* (Berkeley and Los Angeles: University of California Press, 2012), 168.

32. *Black Women in the United States, 2014: Progress and Challenges. 50 Years after the War on Poverty, 50 Years after the 1964 Civil Rights Act, 50 Years after Brown v. Board of Education.* Black Women's Roundtable Intergenerational Public Policy Network (2014).

33. *Black Women in the United States, 2014,* ix.

34. Johnnetta Betsch Cole and Beverly Guy-Sheftall, *Gender Talk: The Struggle for Women's Equality in African-American Communities* (New York: One World Ballantine Books, 2003), xxii.

35. For the purpose of this research, I focused explicitly on the experiences of black women and their everyday experiences with colorism. Although it is relevant to and important in the context of colorism, I excluded an in-depth discussion of identity development, issues of bi/multi-raciality, womanism, and the sociohistorical context of the French creoles in the state of Louisiana. These bodies of literature undoubtedly further our knowledge of colorism, race construction, identity, and racism in the United States.

36. The vast majority of women in my study were between the ages of 18 and 25. A smaller portion of my research sample included eight women over the age of 25, and even a pilot focus group of six black men aged 18–22. The study population was selected from a convenience sample of black women who were affiliated with (students, employees, etc.) a large public university in the state of Florida. At the time of data collection, 88 percent of the participants were between the ages of 18 and 25. The remaining 12 percent were between the ages of 30 and 45. Of the 66 participants, 88 percent of them (the same proportion of 18–25-year-olds) were enrolled as undergraduate students at the institution. Among the older respondents, four had completed undergraduate degrees and were currently enrolled in doctoral programs, two had already completed their doctorate degrees, one had earned a law degree, and the remaining three older women had completed high school and, at the time, had not furthered their education. At the onset of this project, I was interested in talking to black women of all age groups; however, my target population quickly shifted to young women between the ages of 18 and 25. I grew very interested in the attitudes, perspectives, stories, and experiences of college students—the Millennial Generation (also known as "Generation Y"), the group of individuals born between 1980 and 1997, which is routinely characterized as the generation that is the most diverse—both racial/ethnically and as it relates to ideological mindset. More detailed participant characteristics are located in the Appendix.

37. Patricia Hill Collins, *Black Feminist Thought* (New York: Routledge, 2000), 269.

38. Philomena Essed, *Understanding Everyday Racism: An Interdisciplinary Theory* (Newbury Park, CA: Sage, 1991).

39. See Margaret Hunter, *Race, Gender, and the Politics of Skin Tone* (New York: Routledge, 2005).

40. See Evelyn Nakano Glenn, ed., *Shades of Difference: Why Skin Color Matters* (Redwood City, CA: Stanford University Press, 2009).

41. A portion of this chapter was previously published: JeffriAnne Wilder, "Revisiting 'Color Names and Color Notions': A Contemporary Examination of the Language and Attitudes of Skin Color Among Young Black Women," *Journal of Black Studies* 41, no. 1 (2010): 184–206.

42. Lance Hannon, "White Colorism," *Social Currents* 2, no. 1 (2015): 13–21.

43. Sheryl Sandberg, *Lean In: Women, Work, and the Will to Lead* (New York: Knopf Doubleday, 2013), 11.

44. See David Oelberg, "WWBS: Fact or Fiction?" *Neonatal Intensive Care Magazine* 2, no. 2 (2014): 8, 29.

45. Melissa Harris-Perry, *Sister Citizen: Shame, Stereotypes, and Black Women in America* (New Haven: Yale University Press, 2011), 29.

CHAPTER 1

1. bell hooks, *Talking Back: Thinking Feminist, Thinking Black* (Boston: South End Press, 1989), 9.

2. Patricia Hill Collins, *Fighting Words: Black Women Fighting for Justice* (Minneapolis: University of Minnesota Press, 1998), 237.

3. Kim Lute, "The Problem with Black Women," *Huff Post Black Voices*, April 21, 2015, http://www.huffingtonpost.com/kim-lute/the-problem-with-black -women_b_7089452.html.

4. Joyce Ladner, *Tomorrow's Tomorrow: The Black Woman* (Garden City, NY: Doubleday, 1971), 7–8.

5. It is important to point out that during the first phase of data collection, I collaborated with a white female research partner and colleague, Dr. Colleen Cain. Although we shared equal tasks in the research process, I served as the primary moderator and facilitator for each focus group. Concerned about her identity as a white woman, my co-researcher served as a note-taker and participated in the discussion by following up with impromptu probes during each focus group. Ultimately, we found her presence during each focus group session to be negligible and it did not lessen participants' willingness to be open and forthcoming about their experiences of colorism. Dr. Cain developed her work in an unpublished master's thesis entitled "Sources, Manifestations, and Solutions: Exploring Colorism Among African American and Afro Caribbean Women."

6. Patricia Hill Collins, *Black Feminist Thought* (New York: Routledge, 2000), 221.

7. Lawrence Otis Graham, *Our Kind of People: Inside America's Black Upper Class* (New York: HarperCollins, 1999), ix–x.

8. Kathy Russell, Midge Wilson, and Ronald Hall, *The Color Complex: The Politics of Skin Color among African Americans* (New York: Anchor Books, 1993), 4.

9. Collins, *Black Feminist Thought*, 90.

10. Daphne Patai, "U.S. Academics and Third World Feminism: Is Ethical Research Possible?" in *Women's Words: The Feminist Practice of Oral History*, ed. Sharon Berger Gluck and Daphne Patai (New York: Routledge, 1991), 137–153.

11. See, for example, Namita Manohar, "'Yes You're Tamil, But Are You Tamil Enough?' An Indian Researcher Interrogates 'Shared Social Location' in Feminist Immigration Research," *International Journal of Multiple Research Approaches, Special Issue on Mixed Methods in Genders and Sexualities Research* 7, no. 2 (2013): 189–203.

12. Miriam Glucksmann, "The Work of Knowledge and the Knowledge of Women's Work," in *Researching Women's Lives from a Feminist Perspective,* ed. Mary Maynard and June Purvis (London: Taylor & Francis, 1994), 150.

13. Ibid.

14. For further information on the distinction between interpersonal and institutional racism, refer to Matthew Desmond and Mustafa Emirbayer, "What Is Racial Domination?" *Du Bois Review* 6, no. 2 (2009): 335–355.

15. Sojourner Truth, "Ain't I a Woman," Women's Convention, Akron, Ohio, 1851.

16. For further explanation of controlling images of black women, refer to Collins, *Black Feminist Thought* or Melissa Harris Perry, *Sister Citizen: Shame, Stereotypes, and Black Women in America* (New Haven: Yale University Press, 2011).

17. Tania Balan-Gaubert, "The Weight of Color: Black Women's Oppression and Resistance to Colorism," *The American Mosaic: The African American Experience.* ABC-CLIO, 2015. Web.

18. http://www.today.com/style/tamron-hall-wears-her-natural-hair-first-time -tv-1D79860450.

19. http://www.news.com.au/entertainment/celebrity-life/lupita-nyongo-deliv ers-an-incredible-speech-on-beauty-i-prayed-to-god-for-lighter-skin/story-fn90 7478-1226846866664.

20. http://www.oprah.com/oprahs-lifeclass/How-Colorism-Affects-People -Around-the-World-Video.

21. http://www.forharriet.com/p/about.html#axzz3ZgRsI9eM.

22. http://bougieblackgirl.com/declaration/.

23. JeffriAnne Wilder, Tamara Bertrand Jones, and La'Tara Osborne Lampkin, "A Profile of Black Women in the 21st Century Academy: Still Learning from the 'Outsider-Within,'" *Journal of Research Initiatives* 1, no. 1 (2013): 27–38.

24. "The War on Black Intellectuals: What Mostly White Men Keep Getting Wrong About Public Scholarship," *Salon* (March 11, 2014). http://www.salon .com/2014/03/11/the_war_on_black_intellectuals_what_mostly_white_men _keep_getting_wrong_about_public_scholarship/.

25. "Computer and Internet Usage in the United States: Population Characteristics," *United States Census Bureau*, P20-569, https://www.census.gov/prod/2013 pubs/p20-569.pdf.

26. Kathryn Zickuhr and Aaron Smith, "Digital Differences," *Pew Research Center's Internet and American Life Project* (April 13, 2012): 1–41, http://www.pewinternet.org/files/old-media//Files/Reports/2012/PIP_Digital_differences_041312.pdf.

27. Ibid.

28. Aaron Smith, "African Americans and Technology Use: A Demographic Portrait," *Pew Research Center Report* (January 4, 2014): 1–17, http://www.pewinternet.org/files/2014/01/African-Americans-and-Technology-Use.pdf.

29. Aaron Smith and Joanna Brenner, "Twitter Use 2012," *Pew Research Center's Internet and American Life Project* (May 31, 2012): 1–12, http://pewinternet.org/Reports/2012/Twitter-Use-2012.aspx.

30. Feminista Jones, "Is Twitter the Underground Railroad of Activism?" *Salon*, July 17, 2013, http://www.salon.com/2013/07/17/how_twitter_fuels_black_activism/.

31. Lizette Alvarez, "Zimmerman Case Has Race as a Backdrop, But You Won't Hear It in Court," *New York Times*, July 7, 2013, http://www.nytimes.com/2013/07/08/us/zimmerman-case-has-race-as-a-backdrop-but-you-wont-hear-it-in-court.html?pagewanted=all&_r=0.

32. Kimberlé Crenshaw, "Mapping the Margins: Intersectionality, Identity Politics, and Violence Against Women of Color," *Stanford Law Review* 43 (1991): 1241–1299.

33. Whitney Teal, "We Were All Supporting Trayvon Martin. Why Aren't We Supporting Rachel Jeantel?" *Clutch Magazine*, July 1, 2013, http://www.clutchmagonline.com/2013/07/we-were-all-trayvon-martin-why-arent-we-supporting-rachel-jeantel/.

34. Collins, *Fighting Words,* 35.

CHAPTER 2

1. William Edward Burghardt Du Bois, *The Souls of Black Folk* (New York: Vintage Books, 1903).

2. Jennifer Hochschild and Vesla M. Weaver, "The Skin Color Paradox and the American Racial Order," *Social Forces* 86, no. 2 (2007): 643–670.

3. Linda Burton, Eduardo Bonilla-Silva, Victor Ray, Rose Buckelew, and Elizabeth Hordge Freeman, "Critical Race Theories, Colorism, and the Decade's Research on Families of Color," *Journal of Marriage and Family* 72 (2010): 442.

4. Matthew Desmond and Mustafa Emirbayer, "What Is Racial Domination?," *Du Bois Review* 6, no. 2 (2009): 336.

5. See Michael Omi and Howard Winant, *Racial Formation in the United States: From the 1960s to the 1980s* (New York: Routledge, 1986).

6. Audrey Smedley, *Race in North America: Origin and Evolution of a Worldview* (Boulder: Perseus Books, 1993).

7. Omi and Winant, *Racial Formation in the United States.*

8. Desmond and Emirbayer, "What Is Racial Domination?," 336–355.

9. Nina Jablonski, *Living Color: The Biological and Social Meaning of Skin Color* (Berkeley and Los Angeles: University of California Press, 2012), 196.

10. Margaret Hunter, "Rethinking Epistemology, Methodology, and Racism: Or, Is White Sociology Really Dead?" *Race & Society* 5 (2002): 119–138.

11. Hunter, "Rethinking Epistemology, Methodology, and Racism," 120.

12. The majority of the interracial mixing between blacks and whites at this time was the result of the sexual exploitation of black women at the hands of white men.

13. Hunter, "Rethinking Epistemology, Methodology, and Racism," 123–124.

14. Sydney Kronus, *The Black Middle Class* (Columbus, OH: Merrill, 1971).

15. Hunter, "Rethinking Epistemology, Methodology, and Racism," 127.

16. Mark Hill, "Skin Color and the Perception of Attractiveness among African Americans: Does Gender Make a Difference?" *Social Psychology Quarterly* 65, no. 1 (2002): 85.

17. Hunter, "Rethinking Epistemology, Methodology, and Racism," 127.

18. Alice Walker, *In Search of Our Mothers' Gardens* (San Diego: Harcourt Brace Jovanovich, 1983), 290–291.

19. C. Wright Mills, *The Sociological Imagination* (London: Oxford University Press, 1959), 8.

20. E. C. Cuff, W. W. Sharrock, and D. W. Francis, *Perspectives in Sociology* (New York: Routledge, 2003), 322.

21. Pierre Bourdieu, "Vive La Crise!" *Theory and Society* 17 (1988): 782.

22. Pierre Bourdieu, *Distinction* (Cambridge: Harvard University Press, 1984), 466.

23. Patricia Hill Collins, *Black Feminist Thought* (New York: Routledge, 2000), 277.

24. Collins, *Black Feminist Thought*, 282.

25. Collins, *Black Feminist Thought*, 284.

26. Philomena Essed, *Understanding Everyday Racism: An Interdisciplinary Theory* (Newbury Park: Sage, 1991), 49.

27. Essed, *Understanding Everyday Racism*, 288.

28. Ibid.

29. Essed, *Understanding Everyday Racism*, 7–8.

30. Eduardo Bonilla-Silva, "Rethinking Racism: Toward a Structural Interpretation," *American Sociological Review* 62, no. 3 (1997): 474.

31. Barbara Risman, "Gender as a Social Structure: Theory Wrestling with Activism," *Gender & Society* 18, no. 4 (2004): 444.

CHAPTER 3

1. Virginia R. Harris, "Prisoner of Color," in *Racism in the Lives of Women: Testimony, Theory, and Guides to Antiracist Practice*, ed. Jeanne Adelman and Gloria Enguidanos (Binghamton: Haworth Press, 1995), 75.

2. Peter L. Berger and Thomas Luckmann, *The Social Construction of Reality: A Treatise in the Sociology of Knowledge* (New York: Anchor Books, 1966), 37.

3. Larry D. Crawford, *Negroes and Other Essays* (Atlanta: Ankoben House, 2000), 115.

4. Marita Golden, *Don't Play in the Sun: One Woman's Journey through the Color Complex* (New York: Doubleday, 2004), 7.

5. See Michael Omi and Howard Winant, *Racial Formation in the United States: From the 1960s to the 1980s* (New York: Routledge, 1986).

6. Charles Parrish, "Color Names and Color Notions," *Journal of Negro Education* 15, no. 1 (1946): 18.

7. K. Sue Jewell, *From Mammy to Miss America and Beyond* (New York: Routledge, 1993), 46.

8. Irving Lewis Allen, "Male Sex Roles and Epithets for Ethnic Women in American Slang," *Sex Roles* 11, no. 1–2 (1984): 43–50.

9. It is important to note that there is no universal consensus on what skin tone constitutes one being defined as red. At times, the terms yellow(bone) and red(bone) have been used interchangeably, but within the black community, some would argue that yellow is a term for a fair-skinned person, while red is a term denoting an individual with a reddish-brown skin tone.

10. A–Z Lyrics, "Right Above It," http://www.azlyrics.com/lyrics/lilwayne/rightaboveit.html.

11. St. Clair Drake and Horace Cayton, *Black Metropolis* (New York: Harcourt Brace, 1945), 496.

12. Angela M. Neal and Midge L. Wilson, "The Role of Skin Color and Features in the Black Community: Implications for Black Women and Therapy," *Clinical Psychology Review* 9 (1989): 327.

13. Pierre Bourdieu, *Distinction* (Cambridge: Harvard University Press, 1984).

14. Margaret Hunter, "'If You're Light You're Alright': Light Skin Color as Social Capital for Women of Color," *Gender and Society* 16, no. 2 (2002): 175–193.

15. Margaret Hunter, *Race, Gender, and the Politics of Skin Tone* (New York: Routledge, 2005), 70.

16. Berger and Luckmann, *The Social Construction of Reality,* 23.

17. Signithia Fordham and John Ogbu, "Black Students' School Success: Coping with the Burden of 'Acting White.'" *Urban Review* 18 (1986): 176–206.

18. Patricia Hill Collins, *Black Feminist Thought* (New York: Routledge, 2000).

19. Audrey Elisa Kerr, *The Paper Bag Principle: Class, Colorism, and Rumor in the Case of Black Washington, D.C.* (Knoxville: University of Tennessee Press, 2006), 14.

20. Krystal Brent Zook, "Light-Skinned-ded Naps," in *Making Face, Making Soul: Haciendo Caras,* ed. Gloria Anzaldúa (San Francisco: Aunt Lute, 1990), 94.

21. Obiagele Lake, *Blue Veins and Kinky Hair: Naming and Color Consciousness in African America* (Westport, CT: Praeger, 2003).

22. Golden, *Don't Play in the Sun,* 43.

23. Kerr, *The Paper Bag Priniciple*, 9.

24. Joe Feagin, "The Continuing Significance of Race: Anti-Black Discrimination in Public Places," *American Sociological Review* 56, no. 1 (1991): 101–116.

CHAPTER 4

1. M. Okazawa-Rey, T. Robinson, and J. Ward, "Black Women and the Politics of Skin Color and Hair," *Women and Therapy* 6 (1987): 89–102.

2. A portion of this chapter was previously published: JeffriAnne Wilder and Colleen Cain, "Teaching and Learning Consciousness in Black Families: Exploring Family Processes and Women's Experiences with Colorism," *Journal of Family Issues* 32, no. 5 (2011): 577–604.

3. Peter L. Berger and Thomas Luckmann, *The Social Construction of Reality: A Treatise in the Sociology of Knowledge* (New York: Anchor Books, 1966), 130.

4. Patricia Hill Collins, *Black Feminist Thought* (New York: Routledge, 2000).

5. bell hooks, *Sisters of the Yam: Black Women and Self-Recovery* (Boston: South End Press, 1999): 63.

6. Nancy Boyd-Franklin, *Black Families in Therapy: Understanding the African-American Experience* (New York: Guilford Press, 2003), 79.

7. Lawrence Otis Graham, *Our Kind of People: Inside America's Black Upper Class* (New York: HarperCollins, 1999), 2.

8. Boyd-Franklin, *Black Families in Therapy*, 79.

9. Toni Morrison, *The Bluest Eye* (New York: Plume Books, 1970), 62–63.

10. Margaret Hunter, "The Persistent Problem of Colorism: Skin Tone, Status, and Inequality," *Sociology Compass* 1, no. 1 (2007): 243.

11. Charles Parrish, "Color Names and Color Notions," *Journal of Negro Education* 15, no. 1 (1946): 17.

12. Margaret Hunter, *Race, Gender, and the Politics of Skin Tone* (New York: Routledge, 2005), 73.

13. This a direct reference to the ABC television sitcom (airing from 2006 to 2010) *Ugly Betty*, which featured a relatively plain-looking, slightly overweight woman of color as the title character.

14. Hunter, *Race, Gender, and the Politics of Skin Tone*.

15. Mark Hill, "Skin Color and the Perception of Attractiveness among African Americans: Does Gender Make a Difference?" *Social Psychology Quarterly* 65, no. 1 (2002): 77–91.

16. Rana Emerson, "African-American Teenage Girls and the Construction of Black Womanhood in Mass Media and Popular Culture," *Perspectives* (n.d.): 87.

17. bell hooks, *Cultural Criticism & Transformation* (Media Education Foundation, 1997), video.

CHAPTER 5

1. Henry Louis Gates, "Thirteen Ways of Looking at a Black Man," *New Yorker*, October 23, 1995.

2. Martin McQuillan, *The Narrative Reader* (New York: Routledge, 2000).

3. The Great Migration refers to a period of time in American history, dating from 1910 to 1970, in which a significant number of African Americans migrated from Southern states to Northern U.S. cities including Cleveland, Detroit, Chicago, and New York.

4. "Down South" refers to the current reverse migration of African Americans from cities in the North and Midwest regions of the United States back to the Southern states in the United States.

5. Monique W. Morris, *Black Stats: African-Americans by the Numbers in the 21st Century* (New York and London: New Press, 2014).

6. Greg Toppo and Paul Overberg, "After Nearly 100 Years, Great Migration Begins Reversal," *USA Today*, February 2, 2015, http://www.usatoday.com/story /news/nation/2015/02/02/census-great-migration-reversal/21818127/.

7. For the purpose of confidentiality, a pseudonym for the city the respondent was describing was replaced with the actual one she refers to.

8. See, for example, Audrey Elisa Kerr, *The Paper Bag Principle: Class, Colorism, and Rumor in the Case of Black Washington, D.C.* (Knoxville: University of Tennessee Press, 2006).

9. There are no census or demographic data available to support these participants' claims.

10. The Mason-Dixon line is a symbolic marker denoting the Northern and Southern regions of the United States during the Civil War. The geographic territory included the line around the four border states of Maryland, Virginia, West Virginia, and Delaware.

11. In October 2007 twenty-seven-year-old Ulysses Barnes, a Detroit party promoter, was reproached by the black community and antiracism advocates for throwing a "Light-skin Bash," an event guaranteeing all light-skinned women free entry. Word of the party spread rapidly (thanks to the advent of the Internet), and black women across the country demanded the party be cancelled.

12. Due to patterns of increased migration, the number of Africans and Afro-Caribbeans living in the United States has grown considerably in the 21st century. The majority of these "other" African Americans reside along the East Coast. For more information, refer to Yoku Shaw Taylor and Steven A. Tuch, *The Other African-Americans: Contemporary African and Caribbean Families in the United States* (Lanham, MD: Rowman and Littlefield Press, 2007).

13. Henry Louis Gates, "Dominicans in Denial," *The Root*, August 5, 2011.

14. Frances Robles, "Black Denial," *Miami Herald*, June 13, 2007.

15. John Lobb, "Caste and Class in Haiti," *American Journal of Sociology* 46, no. 1 (1940): 23.

16. Christopher A. D. Charles, "Skin Bleaching, Self-Hate, and Black Identity in Jamaica," *Journal of Black Studies* 33, no. 6 (2003): 711–728.

17. Obiagele Lake, *Blue Veins and Kinky Hair: Naming and Color Consciousness in African America* (Westport, CT: Praeger, 2003), 76.

18. Domonique Appollon, "Don't Call Them Post-Racial: Millennials' Attitudes on Race, Racism, and Key Systems in Our Society," *Applied Research Center* (2011).

19. Edward H. Ransford, "Skin Color, Life Chances, and Anti-White Attitude," *Social Problems* 18 (1970): 168.

CONCLUSION

1. Alice Walker, *In Search of Our Mothers' Gardens* (San Diego: Harcourt Brace Jovanovich, 1983), 311.

2. Ibid.

3. John M. Goering, "Changing Perceptions and Evaluations of Physical Characteristics among Blacks: 1950–1970," *Phylon* 33, no. 3 (1971): 241.

4. Pierre Bourdieu, *Distinction* (Cambridge: Harvard University Press, 1984).

5. Eduardo Bonilla-Silva, *Racism Without Racists: Color-Blind Racism and the Persistence of Racial Inequality in the United States* (Lanham, MD: Rowman and Littlefield, 2006).

6. bell hooks, *Talking Back: Thinking Feminist, Thinking Black* (Boston: South End Press, 1989), 20.

7. For more information on the survey and methodology, please refer to https://www.unf.edu/uploadedFiles/aa/coas/porl/FL%20Statewide%20Poll%20Oct%202013%20Press%20Release%20I(1).pdf.

8. Corey Williams, "NAACP Symbolically Buries N-Word," *Washington Post,* July 9, 2007.

9. Eduardo Bonilla-Silva, "From Bi-Racial to Tri-Racial: Towards a New System of Racial Stratification in the USA," *Ethnic and Racial Studies* 27, no. 6 (2004): 931–950.

10. Barbara Smith, *Home Girls: A Black Feminist Anthology* (New Brunswick, NJ: Rutgers University Press, 1983), xlvii.

11. Sheila Radford-Hill, *Further to Fly: Black Women and the Politics of Empowerment* (Minneapolis: University of Minnesota Press, 2000).

12. Katrina Bell McDonald, *Embracing Sisterhood: Class, Identity, and Contemporary Black Women* (Lanham, MD: Rowman & Littlefield, 2007).

13. hooks, *Talking Back,* 8.

14. In order to protect the identity of the people in this story, fictitious names will be used.

15. hooks, *Talking Back,* 182.

16. Lance Hannon, "White Colorism," *Social Currents* 2, no. 1 (2015): 13–21.

Index

activism, 35, 74
African Diaspora, 143
Africentricity, 114–116
Alexander, Marissa, 167
Allegheny College, 3, 34, 40
Allen, Irving, 68
Alpha Kappa Alpha, 71, 79, 123
Applied Research Center, 151
Arie, India, 9–10

Bahamian, 104
Balan-Gaubert, Tania, 30–31
Banks, Tyra, 78, 134
Beale, Francis, vii
Berger, Peter, 64, 72, 100
Berry, Halle, 78, 134
Bertrand, Tamara, 33
Bethune, Mary McLeod, 34
Black Bourgeoisie, 51, 159
black community; gender politics, 14;
    intersection of race, gender and
    color in, 13–15; sexual politics, 14
Black Elite, 8
black feminists/feminism, 2, 14–15,
    18–20, 26, 35, 53, 165;
    accountability and, 24;

epistemology, 16; public
    intellectualism and, 33–34;
    thought, 26
Black Girls Rock!, 15
black hate, 43–44
Black is Beautiful movement, 87, 151,
    159
Black Metropolis, 51, 69, 159
Black Power movement, 151
black pride, 43–44, 119
Black Stats, 138
Black Twitter movement, 35–36, 39, 167
Black Women's Alliance, vii
Black Women in the United States, 2014,
    13–14
Black Women's Roundtable, 13–14
black women; negative stereotypes
    of, 25–26, 38–39, 76–77; public
    presence of, 29–33; sexualizing of,
    68, 76–77, 119
The Blacker the Berry, 40
Blay, Yaba, 167
bleaching, 86, 88–89, 106, 146–147
Blitzer, Wolf, 12
blogs, 22, 31, 32, 43–44, 167
Blue Vein Societies, 9

About the Author

JeffriAnne Wilder, PhD, is Associate Professor of Sociology and Founding Director of the Institute for the Study of Race and Ethnic Relations at the University of North Florida, Jacksonville, FL. Wilder holds a doctorate in sociology from the University of Florida.